CW00648402

Picton's Division at Waterloo

Picton's Division
at Waterloo

Philip J. Haythornthwaite

Pen & Sword
MILITARY

First published in Great Britain in 2016 by
Pen & Sword Military
an imprint of
Pen & Sword Books Ltd
47 Church Street
Barnsley
South Yorkshire
S70 2AS

Copyright © Philip J. Haythornthwaite 2016

ISBN 978 1 78159 102 4

The right of Philip J. Haythornthwaite to be identified as the Author of
this Work has been asserted by him in accordance with the Copyright,
Designs and Patents Act 1988.

A CIP catalogue record for this book is available from the British
Library

All rights reserved. No part of this book may be reproduced or
transmitted in any form or by any means, electronic or mechanical
including photocopying, recording or by any information storage and
retrieval system, without permission from the Publisher in writing.

Typeset in Ehrhardt by
Mac Style Ltd, Bridlington, East Yorkshire
Printed and bound in the UK by CPI Group (UK) Ltd,
Croydon, CR0 4YY

Pen & Sword Books Ltd incorporates the imprints of Pen & Sword
Archaeology, Atlas, Aviation, Battleground, Discovery, Family
History, History, Maritime, Military, Naval, Politics, Railways, Select,
Transport, True Crime, and Fiction, Frontline Books, Leo Cooper,
Praetorian Press, Seaforth Publishing and Wharncliffe.

For a complete list of Pen & Sword titles please contact
PEN & SWORD BOOKS LIMITED
47 Church Street, Barnsley, South Yorkshire, S70 2AS, England
E-mail: enquiries@pen-and-sword.co.uk
Website: www.pen-and-sword.co.uk

Contents

Author's Note and Acknowledgements

In general it has been found practical to use footnotes largely to identify the sources of quotations; further references appear in the bibliography.

The author extends especial thanks to: Derek Green, Dr John A. Hall, Alan Harrison, and Dennis Sully.

The 1815 Campaign

To the members of the Duke of Wellington's army stationed in and around the Belgian city of Brussels, Thursday, 15 June 1815 began as an unexceptional day. Since the return of Napoleon to France some fourteen weeks earlier, there had been the expectation of a renewal of the war that had ended with his abdication in the previous year, but it was not imagined that hostilities were imminent. The Thursday was thus a very ordinary day: for the troops some drills, some exercise, but time for both officers and soldiers to spend relaxing hours amid a friendly population in a handsome city. Probably the greatest sense of anticipation was on the part of the most

Charlotte, Duchess of Richmond, who hosted the ball on the eve of the campaign – Byron's 'sound of revelry by night' – and whose connection to the 5th Division lay with her family association with the 92nd Highlanders: she was the daughter of the 4th Duke of Gordon, whose name was carried by the regiment, and her brother had been its colonel until 1806.

The Duke of Wellington portrayed
shortly after the Waterloo campaign.
(*Engraving after Sir Thomas Lawrence*)

Sir William Howe De Lancey,
Wellington's deputy quartermaster
general in the Waterloo campaign and his
chief of staff. De Lancey played a crucial
role in the administration of the army and
in the issuing of orders; he was mortally
wounded at Wellington's side at Waterloo.

prominent members of society, both military and many of the civilian tourists
enjoying a holiday in Brussels, who looked forward to the grand ball to be given
that night by a leading society hostess, the Duchess of Richmond.

Among those invited to the ball was Wellington's chief of staff, Sir William
De Lancey, with his young bride of ten weeks, Magdalene, and so relaxed was
the atmosphere that he spent the day regaling her with stories of his career until,
somewhat unwillingly, he left her to keep a dinner engagement with Wellington's
friend, the Spanish general Miguel Alava. In the late afternoon the peace was
shattered by the arrival of an aide-de-camp who asked urgently for De Lancey;
Magdalene directed him to Alava's quarters and moments later saw her husband
pelting up the street on the ADC's horse to Wellington's lodgings. Leaving the
horse in the street he ran inside with dire news: unexpectedly, Napoleon was
advancing at speed. Against all expectations the campaign had begun, with the
early advantage entirely in Napoleon's favour.

In the spring of 1815 Europe's leading statesmen were assembled in Vienna for the congress that was intended to resolve the problems of the Continent following the defeat of Napoleon in the previous year. The ex-emperor of the French had been consigned to the tiny Mediterranean island of Elba, but smarting at his fate he had resolved to risk all in an attempt to regain his previous throne. His return to France was greeted with enthusiasm by a population disillusioned with the restored Bourbon monarchy that had replaced him, and once again he posed an acute military threat to the nations that had collaborated in his overthrow in 1814. These allied states were in no mood for compromise and resolved to defeat him again, but the only troops immediately to hand were those stationed in the Netherlands, the presence of which determined Napoleon's strategy: rather than await an invasion of France by overwhelming numbers of enemy forces, he planned to take the offensive himself, achieve a brisk victory over the allied troops in the Netherlands and then negotiate from a position of strength. His plan precipitated the last, climactic campaign of the Napoleonic Wars.

Two allied armies were present in the Netherlands: a Prussian force under the aged but irrepressible Gebhard Leberecht von Blücher, Prince of Wahlstädt, and a very mixed army of contingents supplied by Britain, the Netherlands, Hanover, Brunswick and Nassau. Its command was entrusted to the greatest British general of the age, Arthur Wellesley, 1st Duke of Wellington, whose victory in the Peninsular War had helped undermine Napoleon in the years leading to his abdication. Wellington had been at Vienna, but arrived in Belgium to lead an army of varied quality and experience; his well-known comment was that 'I have got an infamous army, very weak and ill-equipped, and a very inexperienced staff'.[2] Under such circumstances, the presence of hardened troops and experienced commanders would be of vital significance. In no formation were these qualities to be more relevant than in what was to become the 5th Division of his army: Picton's Division.

'The Most Complete Machine'
(Wellington's description of his Peninsular army)

The Divisional System

The organization adopted by the Duke of Wellington for the 1815 campaign was a system that had become fairly universal, his version of which had been perfected during the Peninsular War. Its primary component element was the division.

Although the principal element for manoeuvre was the infantry battalion or cavalry regiment, it had long been recognized that orders and supplies could be delivered more effectively when two or more such units were associated under a unified command. This was the origin of the brigade, in which two or more battalions or regiments were associated on an often permanent basis, marching, living and fighting together under the leadership of a general officer, most commonly a major general or one who acted temporarily in his stead. In British service the brigade had remained the primary organizational structure in the early stages of the French Revolutionary and Napoleonic wars, partly because the forces employed were originally not sufficiently numerous to require anything more sophisticated. Two or more brigades might act together, usually led by the senior of the brigade commanders, sometimes styled 'columns', but these were employed mostly for specific operations without any permanence in the organization. This had been the case in the Netherlands campaigns of 1793–94 and 1799, and in Egypt in 1801, and in the latter case there was a theoretical arrangement into 'lines' of two or three brigades each. This system worked well enough when armies were sufficiently small for the general in overall command to direct movements and oversee affairs in person; but as the numbers and scope of operations increased, a different organization became essential.

The solution was to adapt a system that had been used, albeit sparingly, by the French and other European armies towards the end of the Seven Years' War: the division. In this formation, two or more brigades were linked permanently, under a single commander, a system that possessed tactical, strategic and logistical advantages. In the strategic sense, the division permitted formations to move and act independently, outside the personal supervision of the army's commanding general, a significant factor as armies grew in size. With divisions normally commanded by a lieutenant general, the transmission of orders from headquarters was facilitated in that brigades no longer had to be contacted individually by headquarters staff, their directions coming from the divisional commander, who received his orders direct from the commanding general. Divisions were sufficiently large for staff officers to be attached to them permanently, rather than on an ad hoc basis, changing with every operation; and similarly, the Commissariat could maintain a permanent presence at divisional level, in theory facilitating the delivery of supplies.

Divisions usually had artillery batteries attached permanently (two for each Anglo–Hanoverian division in the Waterloo campaign), so that the division had its own integral fire support, with additional artillery attached from the central reserve as required. (It should be noted that at the time the term 'battery' more usually referred to an artillery position, the units themselves being styled as companies of foot artillery and troops of horse artillery.) The presence of such artillery units permitted a division to fight unaided, without requiring immediate support for it to be fully operational, and the self-contained nature of the formation allowed it to be sent by individual routes, free of the need of support, thus providing the commanding general with an enhanced scope of movement.

Although the divisional system became essential as armies grew in size, it was not common as late as the beginning of the Peninsular War. The first true exposition of the organization at this period was in the expedition to Denmark in 1807, but the brigade remained the basic organizational element at the commencement of the Peninsular War. Sir John Moore began the Corunna campaign with his army organized only in brigades, but instituted a radical revision midway through the campaign, in which the structure of a number of brigades was changed and a nominal divisional system introduced. In this there were three numbered divisions, two of three brigades each and one of two brigades, plus a reserve division of two brigades and two individual flank brigades, with artillery attached at divisional level, plus a reserve; but this system had little time to settle down before the end of the campaign. In Wellesley's first campaign in the Peninsula he employed eight infantry brigades, with no divisional organization, but the strength of the army was such (just over 16,000 infantry) that a higher tier of command was unnecessary. On his return to the Peninsula, with the size of the army increasing, a divisional structure was soon implemented.

By a General Order issued at Abrantes on 18 June 1809 – curiously six years to the very day before the Battle of Waterloo – Wellesley noted that 'As the weather will now admit of the troops hutting, and they can therefore move together in large bodies, brigades are to be formed into divisions as follows', after which the disposition of brigades is listed: four divisions, numbered 1st to 4th, the first of three brigades and the remainder of two each. The preliminary remarks indicate that this change was driven by organizational motives as much as tactical and command, for the statement regarding 'hutting' (i.e. the building of huts or camping in decent weather rather than having to be billeted in existing buildings) shows that this was a paramount feature, so that the location of troops' camps was no longer reliant upon the availability of billets.

From the outset it is clear that the organization included a set command structure, with a lieutenant general in command of each division: 'Lieutenant General Sherbrooke will take command of the 1st division; the senior General Officers of brigades will respectively take command of the division in which their brigades are placed, till the other Lieutenant Generals will join the army.' An embryo staff organization was also included in the order: 'An Assistant Adjutant General will be attached to the Officer commanding the division; an Assistant Provost will also be attached to each division.'

The staff organization, much smaller than the large number of officers employed to administer some foreign armies, was centred on two departments, those of the adjutant general and of the quartermaster general. Their responsibilities overlapped: officially the department of the adjutant general was concerned with equipment and discipline and that of the quartermaster general with quarters, conveyance of troops and marches, but the tasks undertaken by the officers of these departments generally depended upon the circumstances prevailing in any particular operation. In the Peninsular War the department of the quartermaster general came to predominate simply because its head, Sir George Murray, was more efficient than William Stewart, his equivalent in the department of the adjutant general.

Unlike the staffs of some foreign armies, the officers employed in these departments were mostly members of infantry or cavalry regiments; the only truly full-time staff officers, apart from general officers and the commandants of garrisons, were the ten permanent assistants of the Quartermaster General's Department, three of whom were present at Waterloo. Next in seniority were the assistant adjutants general and assistant quartermasters general (commonly abbreviated to 'AAGs' and 'AQMGs'), and below them deputy assistant adjutants and quartermasters general ('DAAGs' and 'DAQMGs'). The assistants were usually field officers (although in the Waterloo campaign two were captains) and the deputy assistants either captains or, more rarely, lieutenants. The appointment of these officers to divisions was not always so permanent as to be announced in General Orders, and they could be replaced or transferred if they were unable to establish an efficient working relationship with the divisional general. (An example from the Peninsular War that involved Picton's Division concerned Captain Thomas Anderdon of the 7th Fuzileers, who had a high reputation and had been trained in staff duties at the Military College; but when appointed to the 4th Division its commander, Galbraith Lowry Cole, found him somewhat haughty and he was appointed to Picton instead. Perhaps Cole had a point, for after his requests for leave were refused Anderdon went home without permission, left the army and embarked upon a career in the law. This affair provoked much anger at Horse Guards and presumably caused some anguish to his father, who, an important city merchant, was a notably patriotic individual much involved in the volunteer movement in London.)

While the members of the Adjutant and Quartermaster General's departments were deployed at divisional level, each brigade usually also had a staff officer as part of the brigade commander's entourage, although unlike his aides-de-camp they remained with the brigade, even when the commander changed. These officers were styled brigade majors or 'majors of brigade'; their duties were described as being equivalent within the brigade to the tasks of the adjutant general's officers for the division. They transmitted the orders received from divisional level and conveyed a daily report of the units in the brigade to the adjutant general. Every day the brigade major attended on the divisional adjutant general to receive orders, which he then transmitted to his brigade commander and to the regiments in the brigade. In the reverse direction, he provided the adjutant general with a return of the men present with the brigade and of any on detached duty, so that headquarters always had precise details of every unit. One explanation of the duties of a brigade major hinted that it could provide a route for advancement: 'As all orders pass through the hands of the majors of brigade they have many opportunities of displaying their talents and proving their exactness.'[1]

The role of brigade major could involve additional duties, if the officer were especially capable or experienced. Harry Smith recounted an unusual incident in the Peninsula when newly appointed to the brigade commanded by Colonel George Drummond. He arrived to take up his post during a heavy skirmish, and as it ended:

> I said to my Brigadier, 'Have you any orders for the picquets, sir?' He was an old Guardsman, the kindest though oddest fellow possible. 'Pray, Mr. Smith, are you my Brigade Major?' 'I believe so, sir.' 'Then let me tell you, it is your duty to post the picquets, and mine to have a d—d good dinner for you every day.' We soon understood each other. He cooked the dinner often himself, and I *commanded* the Brigade.[2]

The relationship between the brigade major and the brigade commander was rarely as close as that of the aide-de-camp. Every general officer (and brigade commanders of field rank) had at least one ADC, whose duties included carrying messages, writing letters and assisting the general in every way, from attending him in battle to administering his household. ADCs were usually young officers appointed because of some personal connection with the general, either a relative or the offspring of a friend or colleague, or upon a personal recommendation. Every general officer had one ADC, and lieutenant generals two, paid by the general, for which he was reimbursed by the Treasury at a rate of 9*s.* 6*d.* per diem; the general also provided the ADC's food. At the discretion of the force commander the general might appoint an 'extra ADC' above the official establishment, who might be paid by the general but for whom he received no official allowance (such an ADC might serve without pay, just to gain experience). The official establishment might be exceeded: in the Waterloo campaign, for example, Sir Thomas Picton had three ADCs, one an 'extra', plus briefly another young officer who attached himself to the general's 'household' just to see action.

A not uncommon, if rather unjust, perception of ADCs might be exemplified by Harry Smith's remark concerning his own appointment as an ADC, when he was prevented by a wound in the ankle from performing regimental duty. His colonel declared, 'You are a mad fool of a boy, coming here with a ball in your leg. Can you dance?' "'No," says I; "I can hardly walk but with my toe turned out." "Can you be my A.D.C.?" "Yes; I can ride and eat," I said, at which he laughed.'[3]

Captain Hugh Harrison of the 32nd, one of a number of Irish officers in the regiment. Commissioned in 1805, he had served in the 1st Battalion in the Peninsula, including at Salamanca, and was severely wounded at Waterloo. He went on half-pay in 1822 and was still drawing it in 1865. (*Courtesy of Alan Harrison*)

A number of other services might be incorporated in the small divisional staff. Cavalry regiments never formed an integral part of an ordinary (infantry) division, but detachments might be allocated on an ad hoc basis. Conversely, artillery units were usually assigned to particular divisions, and if more than one company or battery were involved, a senior artillery officer would be appointed as the divisional artillery chief. Similarly, an engineer officer might be attached, although this was far from being a universal practice.

Probably the most unpopular member of the divisional staff was the provost marshal, responsible for the enforcement of discipline in the field. The assistant provost marshals attached to divisions were experienced NCOs appointed on a fairly temporary basis, and they wielded enormous power. In addition to their authority to apprehend stragglers and plunderers, they were permitted to carry out any prescribed punishment on the spot, without recourse to higher authority, if the perpetrator were caught in the act – even capital punishment. The army's General Regulations, for example, decreed that 'If any Soldier is base enough to attempt to desert to the Enemy, on being apprehended he will suffer immediate Death.'[4]

Unsurprisingly, the provost marshals were regarded with suspicion by the soldiers, as described by a Peninsular veteran, Joseph Donaldson of the 94th: 'We were often inclined to think that the provost marshals were possessed of more power than they ought to have had, particularly as they were generally men of a description who abused it, and were guided more by caprice and personal pique than any regard to justice. In fact, they seemed to be above all control, doing what they pleased, without being brought to any account, and were often greater robbers than the men they punished.'[5] Thomas Morris of the 73rd remarked that provost marshals were regarded by the army in the same way as the hangman Jack Ketch, and such was the opprobrium they attracted that when they returned to ordinary duty they were usually transferred to another regiment, where their provost appointment might not be known.

One of the most vital parts of the army was the Commissariat. The army's official transport service, the Royal Waggon Train, was small and quite insufficient to convey the required quantities of supplies; indeed, in the Peninsular War the Waggon Train was split up into divisional units in 1812 and its duties restricted to the conveyance of the wounded. Instead, supplies were generally transported by civilian vehicles and drivers hired in theatre specifically for the task, a very imperfect system as the personnel were not subject to military discipline and might well run off on the approach of the enemy. They were supervised and commanded by members of the Commissary General's Department, a uniformed though officially civilian organization under the administration of the Treasury. Personnel were assigned to divisions as required, typically an assistant commissary general at divisional level, usually assisted by a clerk, with a more junior assistant commissary general attached to each brigade.

Under the prevailing circumstances, supplying the rations to a division posed a very considerable logistical problem. With an official ration that included 1½lbs of bread and either 1lb of beef or ½lb of pork per man per day, for the two British brigades of Picton's Division in the Waterloo campaign, at a very rough estimate the daily requirement was about 3½ tons of bread and almost

2⅓ tons of beef or 1⅕ tons of pork, with other foodstuffs in smaller amounts. Rations were often issued in three days' supply at a time, so that every third day the divisional commissary had to provide about 10½ tons of bread and either almost 7 tons of beef or 3½ tons of pork. The Hanoverian commissary Augustus Schaumann, who served with Wellington's army in the Peninsula, implied that the recipients of such rations were not much help, for 'it is hard to be an English war commissary; for the men, together with their officers, are like young ravens – they only know how to open their mouths to be fed.'[6]

The problem of transportation was compounded by the quantity of munitions required. Delivery was the responsibility of the Field Train Department of the Ordnance, with much the same method of conveyance. If each musket-armed soldier in the two British brigades of the 5th Division initially carried sixty cartridges, the weight of ammunition required would be roughly just in excess of 12 tons. For resupply, when cartridges were packed in barrels, the weight of munitions and packaging combined for a similar quantity of cartridges would be approximately 16¾ tons. When the Hanoverian brigade or brigades are included, the logistical problem of supplying so large a weight of materiel was truly formidable.

A most significant part of a division's 'support' element was the medical service, although it was very inadequate in the case of a major action. There was virtually no medical corps as such, and no organized means of casualty evacuation. A small body of surgeons, with some semi- or virtually unqualified assistants, existed for the makeshift hospitals that were established after a battle, but the treatment of casualties on the field was dependent almost entirely upon the surgeons belonging to each battalion. In theory every battalion should have had one surgeon and two assistant surgeons, all properly qualified, but this was not always the case: at Waterloo, for example, the 28th Foot had just one assistant surgeon as its regimental medical officer. For the two British brigades of the 5th Division in the campaign there were only seven surgeons and fourteen assistants.

It is likely that the medical training of some regimental surgeons was patchy. Until 1796 the regimental surgeon was assisted only by 'mates', who unlike the surgeons were not commissioned officers but ranked more akin to senior NCOs. In that year they were renamed as assistant surgeons, commissioned and ranking as subalterns, although the appointment of 'hospital mate', not part of individual regiments, continued. The mates required no qualification apart from an apprenticeship to a surgeon in general practice and attendance at medical lectures at a recognized teaching facility. Initially a regimental surgeon had only one assistant, but in 1803 a second assistant was allowed for units of 500 men or more, although no further increase occurred until 1826 when units serving in the East Indies were permitted a third, on account of the sickness prevalent in that climate.

Of the medical officers in Picton's Division, apparently only three held the degree of MD (Medicinæ Doctor) prior to Waterloo, although others qualified later, and John Collins of the 44th Foot had gained a BA from Trinity College, Dublin, at age 17 (he also had the somewhat unusual experience for a surgeon of having been taken prisoner in the Peninsula in 1814). Twelve of the division's surgeons had been appointed from the position of hospital mate (although James Robson of the 1/95th was appointed after only three weeks as a mate), but all had years of experience in their role. The surgeon with the longest military service was Swinton McLeod of the 42nd, and even the least experienced had served since 1812 (Hugh M'Clintock of the 32nd and Robert Hett of the 1/95th).

When an action was imminent, the regimental surgeon and his assistants would establish a regimental aid post (not so named at the time) in the rear of the battalion's position, and there await casualties. There were no nominated orderlies or stretcher bearers, so the 'walking wounded' were expected to make their own way to the rear, with more serious casualties (and certainly officers) being carried there by the battalion drummers or musicians; generally it was forbidden for any combatant soldier to leave the ranks to assist a comrade lest it be used as an excuse to be absent from the firing line. Battlefield treatment was fairly rudimentary, for whilst amputations might be performed on the field, often the treatment would be directed to the preservation of life long enough for the casualty to reach hospital alive. With virtually no systematic casualty evacuation, many doubtless bled to death whose lives could have been saved with more immediate treatment; but for those who did reach hospital, the outcomes were often surprisingly good.

In addition to treating the casualties of his own battalion, a regimental surgeon might also have to attend to those of adjoining units, and at the conclusion of a battle the enemy's wounded as well, so that often they were simply overwhelmed to the degree that casualties might have to wait many hours or even days to receive treatment, if they survived so long.

Within a battalion but not part of the medical establishment there might be a few individuals with knowledge of first aid. In the 1/95th at Waterloo, for example, Lieutenant George Simmons had trained as a surgeon before taking up his combatant role, and after the fighting had ended he could have assisted the 'official' medical personnel had he not himself been grievously wounded. A further incident involved Corporal John Olday of the 1st Royals, who had been shot in the knee at Vittoria, leaving him with a limp. On the passage from Ireland, en route for the Netherlands, the wound had broken out again, but the surgeon declined to operate. An old hospital assistant named Fraser who had been attached to the battalion was prepared to attempt what the surgeon would not; he dug into the wound, finally extracted the ball and sucked the injury clean with his mouth. It enabled Olday to stand with his battalion at Waterloo, but there he was shot again just below his old injury.

If medical facilities were inadequate, spiritual support was almost non-existent. Regimental chaplains – never an efficient system – had been abolished in 1796, and replaced on campaign by a small number of Church of England clergymen attached to headquarters or to divisions. Many of these were not especially efficient, but in the Waterloo campaign Picton's Division was particularly fortunate in having attached the Reverend Charles Frith, a remarkable individual known as 'the Fighting Parson'. Unlike many of his colleagues he was always in action besides his flock and on a number of occasions rescued casualties from the line of battle and carried them on his back to the aid post, then returned for more. Justifiably he was admired and respected by the entire division.

The divisional system was perfected during the Peninsular War and proved its worth as the army grew in numbers until there were eight infantry divisions (numbered 1st–7th plus the Light Division). One aspect of the Peninsular organization also extended to the Waterloo campaign, and was a particular feature of Wellington's administration. In both campaigns Wellington led an army composed of more than one nationality, a factor that could have produced great problems had it not been for Wellington's organizational skill. In the Peninsula, while the Spanish troops under Wellington's command served in their own formations, the Portuguese army was integrated to a considerable degree into Wellington's British formations. The Portuguese army was re-formed under British command, with British officers integrated at command and regimental level to provide a leavening of experienced leadership. This integration was almost entirely at divisional level: except for a few battalions serving in the Light Division as part of British brigades, the Portuguese regiments were assembled into their own brigades, one brigade being attached to each British division (excluding the 1st Division). Thus a 'British' division commonly comprised two brigades of British infantry and one of Portuguese, so that the experienced and reliable British element would bolster the morale and effectiveness of the sometimes newly constituted Portuguese, rather than permit the Portuguese to operate without experienced support. (There was, though, one entirely Portuguese division outside the numbered sequence of British divisions.) This was an important factor in the earlier stages of the Peninsular War, when the Portuguese units were finding their feet; latterly they were often reckoned to be the equal of the British (although some diehard Britons disagreed!). This organization, instituted by Wellington, had the effect of raising the standard of the whole to approach that of the best, producing what Wellington himself termed probably 'the most complete machine' for its size then existing in Europe. Although this remark was descriptive of the excellence of the army he commanded in the Peninsula, it terms of efficiency of operation, it could have applied equally to the divisional system in general.

In 1815 Wellington was confronted by a similar organizational problem, in that his army was composed of troops from a number of states, notably the Netherlands and Hanover, in addition to his British. Initially he was unimpressed by some of the foreign contingents, especially when compared with his victorious Peninsular army. Wellington's well-known comment on his 'infamous army' (written at an early stage, 8 May 1815) demonstrated his concern about the quality of the allied troops that he was expecting to be involved – 'the Saxon troops ... are in such a state at present that no dependence can be placed upon them; and they will be of no use to any body ... the troops of the Hanse Towns and of Oldenburg exist by name rather than in reality'; and also about the support he was receiving from his own government: 'they are doing nothing in England. They have not raised a man ... [and] are unable to send any thing.'[7] Under such circumstances, an efficient organization was essential.

It was impossible for political reasons to integrate the forces of the King of the Netherlands into the British divisions, so that the Netherlands troops served in the campaign in their own divisions; the fact that many officers, other ranks and even generals had only recently been fighting for Napoleon was another reason for disquiet. The Hanoverians were a different matter; owing allegiance to King George III (as elector of Hanover), they could be integrated into the British divisions just as the Portuguese in the Peninsula. They were, however, largely inexperienced; until 1813 Hanover had been under French occupation and a new Hanoverian army had only been created in that year so that while there were some experienced troops there were also large numbers of relatively newly formed Landwehr (militia). To maximize their combat potential, Wellington adopted a practice similar to that employed in the Peninsula, by the integration of experienced officers and NCOs into the Hanoverian formations.

The British Army had had its own originally Hanoverian element in the King's German Legion, formed in 1803 from the king's Hanoverian subjects who had fled their homeland after Napoleon's invasion to continue the fight in British service; subsequently other nationalities had been accepted into the Legion and throughout the Peninsular War it had proved to be among the very best of the British Army. After the end of the Peninsular War the non-Hanoverians had been discharged, so that in 1815 the KGL battalions operated on a weaker establishment of six companies per battalion rather than the usual ten. It was proposed that the new Hanoverian troops be drafted into the existing KGL battalions to bring them up to strength, so that the new men would benefit from serving shoulder to shoulder with reliable veterans; but this proposition was declined by the Hanoverian government. The reduction in the size of the KGL battalions, however, had left a surplus of officers and NCOs, so a number of these experienced men were transferred temporarily to the Hanoverian units to guide and inspire them.

As in the Peninsular army, each of Wellington's divisions in 1815 comprised two brigades of British infantry and one of Hanoverians (except the 1st Division, entirely British, and the 6th, one British brigade and one Hanoverian). In this way it was intended that the raw Hanoverians would be inspired by their more experienced comrades, and in general this did occur. (In the 2nd and 4th divisions, one of the British brigades was from the King's German Legion, so in one sense these formations were two-thirds Hanoverian, although the KGL was always regarded as much British as those who came from Great Britain.) The level of integration within the British forces is indicated by the fact that the artillery commander of Picton's 5th Division was himself a Hanoverian, Major Lewis Heise.[8]

Wellington organized his army into two corps, plus a reserve, with the cavalry organized separately in eleven brigades (seven British, three Netherlandish, one Hanoverian, plus the two regiments of the Brunswick Corps). I Corps, led by the young Prince of Orange, comprised the 1st and 3rd British and 2nd and 3rd Dutch–Belgian divisions. II Corps was commanded by Wellington's trusted deputy, Rowland, Lord Hill, and was composed of the 2nd and 4th British and 1st Dutch–Belgian divisions, plus the Netherlands Indian Brigade. The Reserve, under Wellington's personal control, comprised principally the 5th and 6th British divisions, although as the latter consisted of only two brigades, of which the British brigade was comparatively late in arriving, the primary element of the Reserve was the 5th Division. As one of its officers remarked shortly before the campaign began, it was 'composed entirely of veteran regiments, and commanded by a veteran officer, who, with the two Major Generals in command of brigades, served, with great distinction, in Portugal, Spain, and France, under our present illustrious leader. From these hints, I dare say, you will be expecting great things from us on the day of trial. When that day comes, I hope we will do our duty.'[9]

When it was realized that a campaign in or launched from the Netherlands was imminent, a number of senior officers were instructed to hold themselves in readiness, but despite his position Wellington was not given a free hand in selecting his subordinates. In May, before the composition of his army was finalized, he complained that 'I might have expected that the Generals and Staff formed by me in the last war would have been allowed to come to me again; but instead of that, I am overloaded with people I have never seen before; and it appears to be purposely intended to keep those out of my way whom I wished to have.'[10]

For his divisional commanders, however – the most important command echelon and who could imprint their personality on their divisions – Wellington was largely allowed some of his Peninsular War subordinates. Of the commanders of the eight infantry divisions present at the end of the Peninsular War, five were appointed to divisional commands in 1815, including Sir Henry Clinton (commander of the 2nd Division in 1815), Sir Charles Alten (3rd Division), Sir Charles Colville (4th Division) and Sir Galbraith Lowry Cole (6th Division, although having been recently married he did not arrive in time for the campaign). Only one of Wellington's British divisions in the Waterloo campaign was led by an officer who had not held a similar command at the conclusion of the Peninsular War – Major General George Cooke, 1st Division – and he had for a considerable period commanded the British troops at Cadiz. There was a further divisional appointment, in the vital Reserve: the 5th Division received as its leader Lieutenant General Sir Thomas Picton, arguably the most famous of them all.

Sir Thomas Picton

Sir Thomas Picton had been one of the most renowned divisional commanders of the Peninsular War, and was one of the toughest and most able of Wellington's subordinates, although clearly not the easiest of associates.

Picton was born at Pyston in Pembrokeshire in August 1758; his father was a country squire and Thomas remained very much a Welsh country gentleman all his life. As one of several sons and thus in need of employment, a military career was regarded as a respectable occupation for him, and he had a distinguished relative: his uncle, William Picton, rose to the rank of general and commanded the 12th Foot at the siege of Gibraltar. William was described as a 'most upright and respectable personage' who had 'made his way to public distinction by the force of his private character: he had no powerful friends; he had no Parliamentary interest; and, although in his manners one of the most finished gentlemen of his day, he was no courtier.'[2] That he owed his advancement to his own merits would seem to be exemplified by his appointment as colonel of the 12th: when he attended court to have it confirmed the king remarked that he owed it all to his conduct as captain of the regiment's grenadiers in the Seven Years' War. Clearly young Thomas enjoyed his support, for he was first commissioned in the 12th while his uncle was its commanding officer; and when William became colonel of the 75th (Prince of Wales's) Regiment, a corps recruited in Wales, Thomas followed him to it, and thus missed serving with the 12th at Gibraltar when William led it after his appointment as colonel in

1779. Such was his uncle's attachment that Thomas was his sole executor and residuary legatee upon William's death in 1811.

The 75th was disbanded in 1783[3] and Thomas entered a long period of unemployment during which he resumed the life of a country gentleman, but the outbreak of war in 1793 provided an opportunity. Hearing that an acquaintance and neighbour, Sir John Vaughan, had been appointed to a command in the West Indies, Picton set off on his own account. The Welsh connection must have been a factor – Vaughan was the second son of the 3rd Viscount Lisburne and a member of a very historic Welsh family – and he welcomed Picton to his staff, and secured for him a full-pay captaincy and promotion. Vaughan's death in 1795 left Picton temporarily unemployed, but the arrival in the region of a new commander, Sir Ralph Abercromby, brought him another staff appointment (they had never met previously but Abercromby had been a great friend of Picton's uncle, William). Picton must have impressed for in 1797, as a colonel, he was appointed as governor of the newly acquired island of Trinidad, a duty that was to have long-lasting repercussions.

Although born a 'gentleman', Picton seems not to have been unduly concerned with social mores, and his plain-speaking, gruff manner may have encouraged opposition and the circulation of stories of perhaps dubious veracity; it was suggested, for example, that he kept a young mistress who used her association with him to profit financially and to exert her will over the island. Complaints were made about him – he built up considerable wealth, acquired plantations and slaves – and the civil commissioner appointed to the island (himself a man of dubious honesty) raked up complaints of Picton's harshness. Picton's temper boiled over; he resigned and left Trinidad in June 1803, but his reputation followed him to England and in December 1803 he was arrested. He was accused of a number of misdemeanours, but most famously that among his cruelties he had permitted the torture by 'picketing' of one Luise Calderon, a young mulatto girl, to obtain information regarding a theft from her employer. ('Picketing' involved the suspension of the victim from the wrists, with their weight taken upon one foot resting upon a 'picket' or wooden stake; it was permitted by the Spanish law still pertaining in Trinidad and until relatively recently had been practised in the British Army.) Amid a fever of publicity Picton was tried in 1806 – the great lawyer William Garrow prosecuted – and he was convicted; but a second trial was ordered in 1808 with less hysteria about it, and although no judgment was ever given, it was accepted that the 'torture' had been legal and that no malice on Picton's part was suggested, but not until 1812 was the matter finally concluded.

Free of the legal threat, though with damaged reputation, Picton returned to his military career in command of a brigade in the disastrous expedition to Walcheren in 1809, where there was little fighting but where the army was wrecked by illness. Picton himself was stricken with 'Walcheren fever', malaria which recurred subsequently, and his career seemed to be in decline.

It was resurrected by a request from Wellington, then commanding in the early stage of the Peninsular War. Given that Picton had hardly ever served in action or commanded large bodies of troops in the field, he was not the most obvious choice; but he owed his association with Wellington to the latter's encounter with the Spanish-American revolutionary Francisco Miranda, who had known Picton in Trinidad. Wellington recalled that:

> Miranda said that he knew an extremely clever man called Picton, a man to be much employed – but don't trust him! for he has so much vanity that if you sent him out to the Caraccas [*sic*] or the West India Islands, he would attempt to become the prince of them. I said to Miranda, of course, that such an idea of an English officer was quite absurd. When we were afterwards in Spain we wanted major generals; they sent me out one man after another who could do nothing, and I remembered what Miranda had said to me, and I wrote to the Government to ask them to send me Picton. Well, he came; I found him a rough foul-mouthed devil as ever lived, but he always behaved extremely well; no man could do better in different services I assigned to him, and I saw nothing to confirm what Miranda had said of his ambition.[4]

Picton arrived in the Peninsula in February 1810 and was appointed to command the 3rd Division. He led it with a distinction that may be inferred from its nickname, 'The Fighting Division', although he was not with it throughout. He was wounded at Badajoz when struck in the groin by a ball that failed to penetrate when it hit a bundle of papers in his pocket, and later in the year, before the decisive Battle of Salamanca, his health broke down and he returned home. He rejoined the 3rd Division in May 1813, before returning home again between September and December of that year. In the intervening period he had taken his seat in the House of Commons, having been elected unopposed to the pocket borough of Pembroke County. He received some rewards: a knighthood of the Order of the Bath on 1 February 1813 (advanced to a GCB on 2 January 1815), the colonelcy of the 77th Foot from October 1811, and the Army Gold Cross for eight battles.

Wellington's comment that Picton performed well in the 'different services I assigned to him' is probably indicative of Picton's military talents: that he could execute a specific task but had no great innate skill in the handling of troops – perhaps not surprising given his relative lack of command experience earlier in his career. Certainly some in the Peninsular army had doubts about his generalship; Harry Smith, for example, remarked of Toulouse that 'Sir Thomas Picton, as usual, attacked when he ought not, and lost men.'[5] (In this action Picton disobeyed

Sir Thomas Picton: a classic portrait showing the uniform of a lieutenant general, including the aiguillette on the right shoulder that replaced the previous epaulettes in 1811. The grades of general officer were designated by the arrangement of lace on the coat: buttons and loops in groups of three represented the rank of lieutenant general. The castle of Badajoz is shown in the background. (*Print after Sir Martin Archer Shee*)

direct orders and most unwisely attacked a fortified position in an operation characterized by Sir Charles Oman as displaying 'criminal disobedience').[6] Certainly, when Picton was required to use his initiative in a situation akin to independent command, as in the Pyrenees, he was notably undistinguished.

It was possible, however, for a divisional commander to stamp his personality upon his command, and in this regard Picton was undoubtedly prominent, and seems to have enjoyed the trust of the ordinary soldiers, who were inspired by his demeanour. Writing of the escalade at Badajoz, William Grattan described how Picton 'called out to his men – told them they had never been defeated, and that now was the moment to conquer or die. Picton, although not loved by his soldiers, was respected by them; and his appeal, as well as his unshaken front, did wonders in changing the desperate state of the division.'[7] Other glimpses of Picton in action were recorded by John Kincaid of the 95th, who recalled attempts to prevent confusion during the storm of Ciudad Rodrigo, where 'the voice of Sir Thomas Picton, with the power of twenty trumpets, began to proclaim damnation to everybody,' and at Vittoria, where 'Old Picton rode at the head of the third division, dressed in a blue coat and round hat, and swore as roundly all the way as if he had been wearing two cocked ones.'[8]

The latter highlights two of Picton's eccentricities: his language and his dress. He seems to have disliked wearing uniform, and customarily wore civilian clothes, usually with a round hat (although he wore his nightcap at Busaco). This sense of dress was evidently emulated by his aides, from which, and from Picton's physical presence, led to them being nicknamed 'the Bear and ragged staff'.

John Bainbrigge of the 20th Foot observed him in the Pyrenees, in characteristic appearance – he was wearing his round hat – and behaviour, in an encounter that exemplifies the attitude of the private soldiers:

> Sir Thomas Picton met us. One of our men who knew Sir Thomas recognized the gallant General at a distance, and exclaimed, 'Here comes old Tommy; now, boys, make up your minds to fight.' Sir Thomas held a folded umbrella in his hand; he rode up to Major Westcott, and in his usual blunt manner asked, 'Where the devil are you going?' 'The division is retreating, sir, by Sir Lowry's orders,' was the reply. 'Then he's a d—d fool.'[9]

Picton's uncouth speech and blunt manner, to the point of rudeness, did not endear him to some of his officers, although his martial character came to be appreciated. William Grattan of the 88th recalled his arrival to command the 3rd Division, with the Calderon affair casting a long shadow:

> It would be impossible to deny that a very strong dislike towards the General was prevalent. His conduct at the island of Trinidad … had impressed all ranks with an unfavourable opinion of the man. Besides this, the strong appeal made by Mr. Garrow, the Attorney General, to the

jury by whom he was tried and found guilty, was known to all, and a very general, and I do believe a very unjust clamour was raised against him … and as we of his division had never seen him, his first appearance before his troops was looked for with no little anxiety … as first impressions are generally very strong and very lasting, his demeanour and appearance were closely observed. He looked to be a man between fifty and sixty, and I never saw a more perfect specimen of a splendid-looking soldier. In vain did those who had set him down in their own minds as a cruel tyrant, seek to find out such a delineation in his countenance. No such marks were distinguishable; on the contrary, there was a manly open frankness in his appearance that gave a flat contradiction to the slander, and in truth Picton was *not* a tyrant, nor did he ever act as such during the many years that he commanded the 3rd Division. But if his countenance did not depict him as cruel, there was a caustic severity to it, and a certain curl of the lip that marked him as one who rather despised than courted applause. 'The stern countenance, robust frame, caustic speech, and austere demeanour' told in legible characters that he was not one likely to say a thing and not do as he said. In a word, his appearance denoted him as a man of strong mind and strong frame.[10]

Picton then undermined whatever good impression he had created by having two men flogged in front of the division for stealing a goat, and exacerbated the situation by addressing the brigade 'in language not of that bearing which an officer of his rank should use, for turning to the 88th he said, "You are not known in the army by the name of Connaught Rangers, but by the name of Connaught *footpads*!" He also made some remarks on their country and their religion.'[11]

Unsurprisingly, given that the 88th was one of the toughest and most reliable regiments in the army, if admittedly somewhat light-fingered, his remarks infuriated the regiment. Its commanding officer demanded an interview with Picton, which apparently was 'very animated', and at its conclusion Picton recanted his remarks. Perhaps a prolonged association with this colourful regiment mellowed his opinion, for on one occasion he was recorded as exchanging good-natured banter with a Ranger who was making off with a goat. Such was the soldier's wit that Picton let him proceed with his plunder, remarking to his ADC Tyler, who was in fits of laughter, that if the soldier were apprehended with the stolen animal he would probably make Picton the scapegoat, a pun that must have given him so much pleasure that he would tell the story as one of the funniest things he had ever encountered. Much as he valued the fighting spirit of the 88th, however, Grattan claimed that Picton never recommended one of its officers for promotion, and when at the end of the Peninsular War the officers of his division subscribed £1,600 to purchase him a set of plate, not one of the 88th's officers contributed a penny.

British soldiers were notoriously unreceptive to the kind of heroic peroration to which the troops of some other nations responded; Thomas Brotherton of the 14th Light Dragoons stated that if a general had addressed British troops in the theatrical manner that Napoleon spoke to his, the Britons would just have called out 'Fudge!', and that the less said to them the better.[12] Consequently, when Picton spoke to his men it was in the terms expressed by another officer as 'short and sweet, like the gallop of a jackass'.[13] William Grattan gave a typical example, and the reaction it elicited, when Picton spoke to the 88th before the storm of Ciudad Rodrigo, which

> was so characteristic of the General, and so applicable to the men he spoke to, that I shall give it word for word; it was this:
>
> 'Rangers of Connaught! it is not my intention to expend any powder this evening. We'll do the business with the could [*sic*] iron' … the man who would be silent after such an address, made in such a way, and in such a place, had better have stayed at home. It may be asked what did they do? Why, what would they do, or would any one do, but give the loudest hurrah he was able.[14]

After the capture of the place some Rangers encountered Picton and called to him, '"Well, General, we gave you a cheer last night; it's your turn now!" The General, smiling, took off his hat, and said, "Here, then, you drunken set of brave rascals, hurrah! we'll soon be at Badajoz!" A shout of confidence followed; we slung our firelocks, the bands played, and we commenced our march … in the highest spirits.'[15] This exemplified Grattan's assessment that although Picton was not loved by his men, he was respected, so that when at Badajoz he called to them to conquer or die, 'his appeal, as well as his unshaken front, did wonders in changing the desperate state of the division.'[16]

An interesting perspective on Picton's character and abilities as a general was provided by William Napier in the context of an incident that did not reflect well upon him, concerning the action on the river Coa in July 1810. The forward position was held by the Light Division under its stern and mercurial commander Robert 'Black Bob' Craufurd, with his immediate support provided by Picton's 3rd Division. Some three weeks earlier Picton had effectively pledged that support, requesting that Craufurd station a dragoon to relay any communications that Picton might make, 'and I have also to request as early information as possible of your movements, that I may be enabled to co-operate with them, in obedience to his Excellency the Commander of the Forces' [Wellington's] instructions.'[17]

On 24 July the belligerent Craufurd was attacked in force by the French, having refused to withdraw over the river a couple of days earlier when advised so to do by Wellington. As a desperate fight developed, the firing was heard by Picton at Pinhel, some distance to the rear, and he rode up to the Coa to confer with Craufurd. James Shaw, an officer on Craufurd's staff, recalled an ill-tempered meeting:

> They were primed and ready for ... an altercation, as angry communications had passed between them previously regarding the disposal of some sick of the light division. I have heard Craufurd mention in joke his and Picton's testiness with each other, and I considered that he alluded both to the quarrel as to the sick; and to that which occurred when they met during the action.[18]

William Campbell, also on Craufurd's staff, stated that:

> on notice being given of general Picton's approach, general Craufurd turned and moved to meet him. Slight was the converse, short the interview, for upon Craufurd's asking enquiringly, whether General Picton did not consider it advisable to move out something from Pinhel in demonstration of support, or to cover the light division, in terms not bland, the general made it understood that 'he should do no such thing'. This as you suppose put an end to the meeting, further than some violent rejoinder on the part of my much-loved friend [Craufurd] and fiery looks returned!

William Napier, perhaps suggesting that Picton's posthumous reputation as a general was overstated, compared the two:

> Picton and Craufurd were ... not formed by nature to act cordially together. The stern countenance, robust frame, saturnine complexion, caustic speech, and austere demeanour of the first promised little sympathy with the short thick figure, dark flashing eyes, quick movements, and fiery temper of the second; nor, indeed, did they often meet without a quarrel. Nevertheless they had many points of resemblance in their characters and fortunes. Both were inclined to harshness, and rigid in command, both prone to disobedience, yet exacting entire submission from inferiors, and they were alike ambitious and craving of glory. They both possessed decided military talents, were enterprising and intrepid, yet neither were remarkable for skill in handling troops under fire. They, also, had in common, that both, after distinguished services, perished in arms, fighting gallantly, and being celebrated as generals of division while living, have, since their death, been injudiciously spoken of, as rivalling their great leader in war. That they were officers of mark and pretension is unquestionable, and Craufurd more so than Picton, because the latter never had a separate command, and his opportunities were necessarily more circumscribed; but to compare either to the Duke of Wellington displays ignorance of the men and of the art they professed. If they had even comprehended the profound military and political combinations he was conducting; the one would have carefully avoided fighting on the Coa; and the other, far from refusing, would have eagerly proffered his support.[19]

Picton seems to have been notably unpopular with the officers of the Light Division, perhaps arising from the Coa incident. Writing of April 1811, for example, Harry Smith recalled that 'we had a long march, but did not see a vestige of the enemy, nor of our commissariat either. We were literally starving. That old rogue Picton had seized the supplies of the Light Division for his 3rd. If he be now in the Purgatory that we condemned him to, he is to be pitied.' Smith described how at Orthez, the Light Division was 'moving on the right of the 3rd Division, Sir Thomas Picton, who was ever ready to find fault with the Light, rode up to Colonel Barnard. "Who the devil are you?" knowing

Barnard intimately. "We are the Light Division." "If you are the Light, sir, I wish you would move a little quicker," [he] said in his most bitter and sarcastic tone. Barnard says very cool, "Alten commands ... Wherever the 3rd Division are, Sir Thomas, we will be in our place, depend on it."[20] The officer who answered back, the supremely capable Sir Andrew Barnard of the 95th, was one of Picton's battalion commanders in the Waterloo campaign; after such unnecessarily sharp words, what the two thought of this later association must be a matter of conjecture.

Picton clearly believed that his merits had not been recognized, although his complaints to Wellington received a frosty reply:

'I received last night your letters ... and I acknowledge that I wish ... you had omitted to send me either ... I have never interfered directly to procure for any officer serving under my command those marks of His Majesty's favor [*sic*] by which many have been honoured: nor do I believe that any have ever applied for them ... They have been conferred ... spontaneously, in the only mode, in my opinion, in which favor can be acceptable, or honor [*sic*] and distinction can be received with satisfaction ... and I am happy to state, that no General in this army has more frequently than yourself deserved and obtained [a] favorable report of your services and conduct ... What I would recommend to you is, to express neither disappointment nor wishes upon the subject, even to an intimate friend, much less to the Government ... The comparison between myself ... and you, will not be deemed quite correct ... Notwithstanding the numerous favors I have received from the Crown, I have never solicited one ... I recommend to you the same conduct, and patience; and above all, resignation, if, after all, you should not succeed in acquiring what you wish; and I beg you to recall your letters, which you may be certain will be of no use to you.[21]

When later in the same year Picton took his seat in the House of Commons (in the Tory interest) he seems to have been genuinely affected by the thanks of Parliament he received for his services in Spain; but the peerage he believed he deserved remained out of reach: probably Trinidad still cast a shadow.

Picton's outspoken nature and the vehemence of his language led to a number of anecdotes of dubious veracity. The most notable described him threatening to hang a commissary if his division's rations were late; the commissary then complained to Wellington, who simply advised him to supply the rations or Picton would surely carry out his threat. The story was also told of Craufurd, and while it might reflect upon the determination of both generals, William Napier dismissed it and noted that Picton's biographer (Robinson) should not have attributed to Picton 'all the standard jokes and smart sayings, for the scaring of those gentry [commissaries], which have been current ever since the American war, and which have probably come down to us from the Greeks'. He stated that instead Robinson should have 'set forth some of the general's generous actions towards the widows of officers who fell under his command … they … would do more honour to his memory than a thousand blustering anecdotes'.[22]

A notable incident that demonstrated Picton's generosity – or simple fairness – involved Lieutenant James Macpherson of the 45th who at Badajoz tore down a French flag and hoisted his red coat in its place to show that the position had been taken. He offered the captured flag to Picton, who refused it, sending him to present it to Wellington to ensure that he received his due reward; but when in 1814 he discovered that Macpherson had not been promoted, Picton personally took up his case and got him his captaincy.

Wellington commented on Picton's intemperate language, thinking that:

> It was of little importance, however, and sometimes mere good-humoured jest. Thus when Sir Lowry Cole was announcing to the Duke his intended marriage … Sir Lowry explained his views by saying that he did not think he was going to do a very imprudent thing, for that the lady was not very young … Sir Thomas, who was present, and between whom and Sir Lowry there had always been a little rivalry, suddenly broke in with, 'Well, when I marry I shall do a d— imprudent thing, for I mean to marry the youngest tit I can find!' The Duke hastened to add, however, as his observation, that there was no harm in this – nothing wrong either meant or done.[23]

Despite Picton's temper, Major Harry Ross-Lewin, who served with the 32nd at Waterloo, had no doubts about his value:

> brave, energetic, and enterprising. Unsurpassed in spirit, zeal and devotion, his example infused additional life and vigour into the troops who had

the good fortune to be placed under his command; what Ney was to the French, he was to the army that beat them … wherever danger assumed its most terrific form, there he was to confront it. A noble specimen of the true soldier; the compass by which he steered through life had honour for its pole, and knew no variation.[24]

At the conclusion of the Peninsular War it appeared that Picton's active military career was over; he returned home resenting that he had not received a peerage like some other senior commanders, even though he had not held independent command as had some: it was said that he remarked that if a peer's coronet had lain atop a breach to be stormed, then he would have had as good a claim as any. Perhaps he felt unsettled, even depressed, without a close family and affected by the death of his brother, who had just returned home after retiring as a major general in the service of the Honourable East India Company. Wellington recounted how 'In France Picton came to me and said: My Lord, I must give up. I am grown so nervous, that when there is any service to be done it works upon my mind so, that it is impossible for me to sleep at nights. I cannot possibly stand it, and I shall be forced to retire.'[25]

This glimpse into Picton's apparently, and unexpectedly, fragile state of mind was written down from Wellington's account by Earl Stanhope in 1835, and he stated that Wellington believed this had occurred only days before Picton's death, but either Stanhope or the duke must surely have been mistaken, for the incident must have occurred towards the very end of the Peninsular War. Some suggestion was made that Picton may have had a premonition of death in 1815, for a story was told of how, when walking with friends, he had spied a newly dug grave in a cemetery and had laid down in it, trying it out for size; it alarmed the ladies of the party but may have been nothing more than a mischievous if macabre joke.

DIVISIONAL STAFF

Within the 5th Division in the Waterloo campaign, Picton's personal staff consisted of his aides-de-camp (ADCs), of whom the senior was Captain Algernon Langton of the 61st Foot, a member of a Lincolnshire family and son of the dowager Countess of Rothes, who had been the second wife of Lieutenant General John, 10th Earl of Rothes. Langton had served in the Peninsula and had experience of staff duties, having been a deputy assistant quartermaster general.

Junior to Langton in terms of seniority, but much closer to the general, was Captain John Tyler of the 93rd Foot, arguably, because of his association with Picton, one of the most important officers in the division. Although not yet 24 years of age he was an experienced campaigner, having entered the 45th Foot at age 16 and almost immediately had been thrown into the Peninsular War, in which he served almost throughout. He was severely wounded by a shot through the shoulder at Busaco and after convalescence had been appointed as extra ADC to Picton in May 1811. A Welshman like Picton, he came from a Glamorganshire family, his father being Admiral Sir Charles Tyler. Family and (evidently in Picton's case) national connections exerted a strong influence over a general's selection of ADCs, and one of Picton's in the Peninsula, Captain Robert Cuthbert of the 7th Fuzileers, was probably a member of a family Picton had met in the West Indies. When Cuthbert was killed at Badajoz, Tyler was appointed as senior ADC and served with Picton for the remainder of the war. Perhaps Tyler exemplified Harry Smith's quip regarding the abilities required of an ADC: he could ride, and certainly eat; in later life, when serving in the West Indies, he was regarded as a gourmet and in the Peninsula his figure was the reason for his Portuguese nickname, 'Adjunto Gordo', the fat ADC. He was also referred to as a 'very popular Amphitryon',[26] an allusion arising less from Greek mythology, perhaps (the husband of Alcmene), than from the Molière character who gives a great dinner. A portrait, however, seemingly by John Kay (an artist not known to flatter his subjects), shows a sturdy but certainly not obese individual.[27] Conceivably his reputation as a gourmet arose subsequent to his association with Picton, for his superintendence of Picton's household led Wellington to remark that in the Peninsula Lowry Cole gave the best dinners, Hill the next best, Wellington's own were passable, but that Beresford's and Picton's were very bad! Perhaps Tyler's reputation as a raconteur compensated for the quality of his general's dinners.

Picton's third ADC was another with high connections: Captain Newton Chambers of the 1st Foot Guards was a grandson of Admiral Lord Rodney. He had been taken on by Picton on the recommendation of the Attorney General William Garrow, in late 1813; that he accepted this recommendation is perhaps evidence of Picton's generosity, in as much as Garrow had been his prosecutor in the Calderon affair. Two further officers with Welsh connections completed the general's personal staff. Captain Barrington Price had served in the Peninsula with the 43rd and was currently on the half-pay list of the 50th; the other was a purely unofficial attachment that came about through friendship with Newton Chambers.

Rees Howell Gronow, later renowned as a man about town and recorder of anecdotes of high society, was a 21-year-old ensign in the 1st Foot Guards, son of a deputy lieutenant of Glamorganshire, friend of Shelley at Eton and an officer from the age of 18 who had fought in the later stage of the Peninsular War. Shortly before Picton's departure for the campaign, Gronow was introduced to him at a dinner at which Tyler and Chambers were present. Gronow belonged to the 1st Battalion of his regiment, but it was the 2nd and 3rd battalions that had been selected for the campaign, and Gronow lamented that he would thus miss the showdown with Napoleon. Tyler and Chambers informed Picton of his desire to see service, whereupon the general said, 'Is the lad really anxious to go out?', adding that if Tyler got himself killed he would need someone else, and as Gronow was a fellow Welshman declared that he could come along if he could get leave from his battalion. Gronow seized the opportunity and did not bother to apply for leave lest it were refused; and to finance his campaign kit he borrowed £200 from the agents Cox and Greenwood and used it as a stake in a gaming club, where he won a further £600. Purchasing two good horses, he set off hotfoot to follow Picton to get a passage to Belgium.

Personnel often overlooked were the officers' 'soldier-servants', generally a reliable man taken from the ranks to perform the duty of valet-cum-butler or what subsequently became known as a batman. For the men themselves this was a prized appointment, for they were usually excused drill and were paid an extra shilling a week, but the regulations specified that they were to be fully trained; 'No Soldier is to be employed as an Officer's Servant, who is not perfect in the Drill, and who has not acquired a complete knowledge of his Duty as a Soldier.'[28] Picton's servant was Sergeant Alexander Campbell of the 77th Foot; Picton had been appointed colonel of the 77th in October 1811 and the regiment had been in his division from that July, so presumably he selected a steady NCO to be his personal orderly. (Alexander Campbell was the only member of his regiment to be awarded the Waterloo Medal – at the time of the battle the 77th was in Ireland – and he received not only the 77th's regimental medal, instituted in 1818 for Peninsular veterans, but survived to claim the Military General Service Medal, with clasps for Ciudad Rodrigo and Badajoz, in 1848.)

The division was especially fortunate, perhaps, in having as its assistant quartermaster general, in effect the senior staff officer, Lieutenant Colonel Sir William Maynard Gomm of the 2nd Foot Guards, aged 31 and from January 1815 a KCB (Knight Commander of the Order of the Bath) – recognition of a very distinguished record in the Peninsular War. He had received training as a staff officer at the Royal Military College and had served in the Quartermaster General's Department from September 1810. He had

Sir William Maynard Gomm, Assistant Quartermaster General, in the uniform of a lieutenant colonel in the Coldstream Guards; the decoration is the Army Gold Cross, which he received for five actions, from Badajoz to Nive.

been commissioned as ensign at the age of 10, in recognition of the gallantry of his father, Lieutenant Colonel William Gomm, killed at Guadeloupe in 1794, and had himself carried the colours of the 9th Foot in the Netherlands in 1799.

The British Infantry

The formation that Picton was to lead was composed largely of the one element upon which Wellington could place total reliance: his British infantry. Throughout the Peninsular War it had never let him down in combat – unruly in the aftermath of victory and prone to misbehaviour – but in battle it was the ultimate professional force, lacking the elan of some French units but stolid, determined and brave. Wellington admitted as much shortly before the beginning of the Waterloo campaign, when discussing the approaching conflict with Thomas Creevey. Spying a British infantryman who was sauntering about, taking in the sights, the duke pointed at him and said, 'There, it all depends upon that article whether we do the business or not. Give me enough of it, and I am sure.'[1]

The infantry was organized in regiments, which the ordinary soldier regarded as claiming his principal allegiance. In general, if the average redcoat were asked to describe himself in a military sense, in as far as he understood the nature of the question, he would state that he was a member of the 28th (or whatever) Regiment, not of the British Army in general. His regiment, with all its traditions and foibles, he would claim to be superior to all others, a belief that was no hollow remark but could play a vital role in the maelstrom of battle, when unusual loyalties were required to inspire men to stand by their comrades and perform their duty in the face of unimaginable terrors. This was exemplified by a writer who interviewed many Waterloo veterans, many of whom stated that so terrible had been the battle that they expected to be beaten and that other regiments would give way, but 'certainly not my own corps':

> Such was the universal answer; and this is the true English feeling: this indignancy of being supposed likely to be the first to give way before an enemy is the true harbinger of success … Our regiments, accustomed to act and live alone, are not taught to dread the failures of adjoining corps in combined operations; they cannot readily yield to the belief that a corps in their neighbourhood can licence themselves to flee; penetrate an English line, you have gained nothing but a point; cut into a continental line, even a French one, and the *morale* of everything in view, and vicinity, is gone. The English regiment will not give way, because the English regiment of the same brigade has done so, but will mock the fugitives, and in all likelihood redouble its own exertions to restore the fight – a true bulldog courage against all odds – if well led.[2]

Aside from its traditions and identity, the regiment was largely an administrative body. The tactical entity was the battalion, of which a regiment might possess two or more, the original intention being that in a two-battalion regiment, one would go on campaign and the other remain at home to provide drafts for the 1st battalion; but due to the pressures of war, many 2nd battalions were also sent on campaign. Of the 27 line infantry battalions in Wellington's army in the Waterloo campaign, 17 were 1st battalions or single-battalion regiments, seven were 2nd battalions and three were 3rd battalions. Each battalion comprised ten companies, eight 'battalion' or 'centre' companies – the latter name taken from their position when the battalion was drawn up in line – and two 'flank' companies, named for the same reason, one of grenadiers (in theory the largest and most stalwart men) and one of light infantry, specially trained in skirmishing. Each company had a notional complement of 100 men, but the resulting battalion strength of 1,000 was rarely achieved, and most had very many fewer.

Light infantry tactics had proved especially significant in the Peninsular War, in providing a screen between the enemy and the army's main body, as well as preceding an advance or covering a retreat, to the extent that the light companies of the component battalions of a division could act in concert. By

The infantry uniform of the British Army, including the 1812-pattern shako worn by the line regiments, with the distinctions of 'battalion' or 'centre' companies: tufted shoulder straps and a white-over-red plume. This was the uniform worn by three regiments of the 5th Division, the 32nd with white facings, the 2/44th yellow and 3/1st dark blue.

a General Order dated Brussels, 9 May 1815, it was decreed that the light companies of a brigade were to 'act together as a battalion of light infantry, under the command of a Field Officer or Captain, to be selected for the occasion by the General Officer commanding the brigade, upon all occasions on which the brigade may be formed in line or column, whether for a march or to oppose the enemy', but on all other occasions the light companies were to remain part of their own battalions, as indeed many did at Waterloo.

All regiments were recruited by voluntary enlistment; unlike most European armies, there was no conscription. In 1782 most regiments had been assigned a county affiliation in addition to their number; it was intended to aid recruiting by associating the regiment with a specific area, but in practice regional identities were very limited outside the Scottish regiments. The composition of regiments had changed considerably when, to facilitate recruiting, militiamen were permitted to enlist in the regular army. This often mass transfer of men from county militia regiments had a very positive effect, for the enrolment of militiamen brought into regular service soldiers who were already trained in the use of arms and inured to military discipline, so that although the experience of campaigning might still have come as a shock to them, they were at least halfway to becoming experienced soldiers before they even joined their regular battalion. As county militiamen rarely transferred into their own county's regular regiment, the system could alter fundamentally the identity of a battalion; in the Waterloo campaign, for example, even that most Welsh of regiments, the 23rd Royal Welsh Fuzileers, contained less than 29 per cent Welshmen, but 11.5 per cent Lancastrians and 8.75 per cent Norfolkians, more than one-fifth of the men having joined directly from the militia.[3]

Ireland had proved a most fertile recruiting ground for the entire army, not just for the relatively few regiments that had an official Irish identity, and thus many regiments contained a strong Irish contingent; the 23rd, for example, had more than 9 per cent Irishmen and, most significantly, almost one-third of the senior NCOs. The difference between the official territorial identity of a battalion and its actual composition is demonstrated perhaps most markedly in the case of the 3rd Battalion of the 1st (Royal) Regiment, nominally and famously a Scottish regiment – the Royal Scots – although less than 19 per cent of its 'other ranks' were Scottish (but almost two-thirds of its officers).

A most important element in 'command and control' were the officers of the battalion. At least in theory, each company was commanded by a captain, with two or more subalterns as his assistants. The battalion commander was supposedly a lieutenant colonel, assisted by one or more majors, who comprised the 'field' (rather than 'regimental') ranks; but the system of ranking was sometimes somewhat more complex. There were two principal forms of rank: regimental and 'Army', the 'Army' rank being that held by the individual irrespective of the rank in his own regiment. The 'Army' rank was used to accommodate brevets, promotions instituted as a form of reward but not applying primarily to the individual's role in his own battalion. Thus it was fairly common for a regimental captain to hold the 'Army' rank of major, with officers being addressed by their higher rank, and the system could give rise to anomalies.

The ranking of officers in terms of seniority was an important factor in case of casualties in battle. If an officer were killed or wounded, his place was taken automatically by the individual most senior of those below him, irrespective of experience or aptitude: thus it was possible for a wounded battalion commander to be replaced as head of his unit by an officer of no campaign experience instead of by a veteran, simply because of the date of their respective commissions. (While not necessarily paramount, experience of service in the field was very significant; of the ability 'to speak as familiarly of roaring cannon as maids of fifteen do of puppy-dogs', as Sir Walter Scott expressed it in his account of his tour to Waterloo shortly after the battle.)[4] Cases might be cited from the 5th Division in the Waterloo campaign: in the 32nd Foot, the second in command, Major Felix

Calvert, had been with the regiment barely a month and had little command experience, whereas the three senior captains all held brevet majorities predating his. In the 42nd the senior captain in terms of date of commission was Archibald Menzies, although the next two captains in terms of chronological seniority both held brevet majorities. Such factors assumed significance if casualties mounted in a major action, when a battalion might have several changes in command within a short period, as occurred within the division during the campaign.

This emphasized the importance of an established method of operation that could survive despite frequent changes in personnel. Also key to this was the proficiency of the non-commissioned officers, most crucially the sergeants, who might have to take command of their company if all the officers went down, as actually happened within the 5th Division at Waterloo.

In considering how the 5th Division assembled for the campaign, it is appropriate to note, given the very Welsh identity of its commander, that to a considerable extent the division was Celtic in composition, in both the notional territorial affiliations of its battalions and in their actual constitution.

Prior to the renewal of the war upon Napoleon's return from Elba, some fifteen battalions of British infantry were already in the Netherlands, having been part of the expedition to that region under Sir Thomas Graham in the previous year. They had remained there under the overall command of the Prince of Orange, according to an agreement among the allied powers to secure the provisions of the Treaty of Paris prior to the final settlement of European affairs at the Congress of Vienna. When renewed hostilities became obvious they were reinforced by battalions from home, although some of the most reliable of Wellington's old Peninsular regiments were not available immediately, having been sent to serve in the war in America that had been concluded so recently.

Eight battalions of British infantry were to come under Picton's command: the 3/1st, 1/28th, 32nd, 1/42nd, 2/44th, 79th, 92nd and 1/95th (the notation 1/-, 2/-, etc., indicated the 1st Battalion, 2nd Battalion of the regiment). Only one of these was already 'in theatre', the 2/44th, which for almost a year had been in garrison in Ostend; all the others were sent to the Netherlands from their postings in Britain.

The 1/95th had landed at Portsmouth from the Peninsula in 1814, and was currently stationed at Dover. Six companies were detailed for service in the Netherlands, with some junior officers being disappointed as the senior men claimed the right to go on campaign, leaving four companies at home. Having been stationed in Dover, the battalion had become popular and when on 25 April they embarked on the transport *Wensleydale* the local people gathered in numbers to cheer and wave them off. They landed at Ostend on 27 April after what must have been a rough crossing; Lieutenant George Simmons, still suffering from a wound sustained in the previous year, recalled that his throat was so sore from vomiting that he could scarcely speak for a week. From Ostend they travelled by barge to Ghent, moving from there to Brussels on 10–12 May.

The other six battalions all sailed from Ireland, where they had been posted following the end of the war. The 3/1st had been quartered at Fermoy, and their men received news of Napoleon's return to France from a placard bearing the news affixed to the boot of a stagecoach. They set off to Cork to the strains of the old leaving quarters tune *The Girl I Left Behind Me*; they, too, arrived at Ostend, and from there travelled to Ghent and Brussels.

Bad weather permitted other battalions to serve in the Waterloo campaign: some had embarked for service in North America (the 28th for Bermuda) but sailing had been delayed by contrary winds, so their orders were changed when Napoleon's return was confirmed. The 79th had twice sailed for America and twice been driven back by the weather, so went instead to Northern Ireland, marching from Belfast to Dublin and sailing from there to Ostend, also making the canal trip to Ghent before moving to Brussels. The 32nd also had its orders for America countermanded, and made the same trip. The 92nd moved from Cork on 1 May, embarking on three transports, and encountered weather that in their case was too mild, twice being becalmed before they finally reached Ostend on 9 May ('our voyage was very pleasant, having scarcely been troubled with what seamen call a stiff breeze').[5] They also took the canal to Ghent.

The 42nd had been stationed in the region of Kilkenny, intended to ensure the tranquillity of the country, before being sent to Cork to embark for Ostend. They lost one man before they even reached the coast: when his affections were not reciprocated by a local barmaid, the soldier, recently a prisoner of war, shot himself. The case of the 42nd highlights a universal practice of regiments on campaign: all were accompanied by a number of soldiers' wives and their children, the women receiving rations (half that provided for a soldier) in return for services such as washing or help in encamping. It was usual to permit four wives per company to march with a battalion, but at Ostend it was ordered that only two per company would be allowed. The remainder, amid much weeping, were left at Ostend for conveyance back to Britain; but when the 42nd was at Ghent they all turned up. The women were sent back to Ostend, but within a short time reappeared, and the authorities gave up trying to enforce the order and all were permitted to remain with their husbands.

The eight battalions were organized into the 8th and 9th brigades within the 5th Division which, and the brigade commanders, are covered below within their brigade organization rather than strictly in terms of regimental seniority.

THE 8TH BRIGADE

The 8th Brigade was led by a tough and experienced soldier, Major General Sir James Kempt. Born in Edinburgh in 1764, the son of Gavin Kempt of Batley Hall, Hampshire, he was commissioned in the 101st Foot in 1783 but was consigned to half-pay upon the reduction of the regiment in the following year. During this suspension of his military career he became a clerk with the army agent Greenwood, perhaps an appropriate occupation as his father was himself an army agent with offices in Whitehall. It was said that James attracted the notice of the Duke of York, through whose influence he obtained a captaincy in the 113th Royal Birmingham Volunteers, one of the regiments of which his father was agent, in May 1794. From 1796 he occupied a number of staff positions, including as ADC to Sir Ralph Abercromby in the Netherlands campaign and in Egypt, and held the same position to Abercromby's successor, John Hely Hutchinson. In 1805 Kempt returned to regimental duty with the 81st Foot in the Mediterranean, and commanded the light brigade at Maida. From 1807 to 1811 he was quartermaster general to the forces in North America, and as a major general joined Wellington's army in the Peninsula. Following the death of Major General Henry Mackinnon at Ciudad Rodrigo, Kempt was appointed to lead his brigade in the 3rd Division, thus beginning his association with its commander, Sir Thomas Picton; but both were wounded at Badajoz and upon his recovery Kempt was assigned to command a brigade of the Light Division, which he led for the remainder of the war, at Vittoria, Nivelle, Nive and Toulouse. He was awarded a KCB in January 1815.

Kempt's two closest assistants were both very experienced officers. His ADC came from a more elevated background than the general himself: Captain Hon.

Charles Stephen Gore was the sixth son of Arthur, 2nd Earl of Arran and his third wife. Born in 1793, Gore entered the army as a cornet in the 16th Light Dragoons, and as a lieutenant in the 43rd Light Infantry from January 1810, he joined that regiment in the Peninsula in 1811 and was among the storming party that captured the San Francisco fort at Ciudad Rodrigo. He began his career in the staff as ADC to Sir Andrew Barnard at Salamanca, and from 1813 held the same position with Kempt, joining him again in 1815. Officially he transferred to the 85th Light Infantry three days before the Battle of Waterloo.

Sir James Kempt in the later uniform of a lieutenant general. Commander of the 8th Brigade and Picton's senior subordinate, his decorations illustrated include the GCB (awarded 22 June 1815), Waterloo Medal and the Army Gold Cross for seven actions.

Kempt's brigade major was Captain Charles Eeles, who like his brother William was a well-known member of the 95th Rifles. He had seen much service during the Peninsular War and had been mentioned by name, although only a lieutenant, in one of Wellington's despatches for an action in April 1811, having only recently recovered from a severe wound having been shot through the body in the previous October. He had also lost a thumb.

1ST BATTALION, THE 28TH (NORTH GLOUCESTERSHIRE) REGIMENT OF FOOT

The 28th Foot was one of the most distinguished regiments in the army. Raised at Portsmouth in 1694 – its first colonel was lieutenant governor of that city – the regiment had received the county title of 'North Gloucestershire' in 1782. It had had a very distinguished career in the Peninsula, both its battalions seeing service there, including under Moore and on the north-east coast of

Spain as well as in Wellington's army. The regiment appears to have carried the nickname 'The Slashers', although the origin of this sobriquet is debated; it might date from 1794 but the reason is uncertain.

The nature of the 28th as a reliable and experienced battalion is exemplified by the experience of the rank and file: whereas some units had considerable numbers of relatively new soldiers in their ranks, of the survivors of the Waterloo campaign some 76 per cent of the privates and corporals had enlisted before 1810, so that most would have been battle-hardened veterans of the Peninsula.

The same applied to many of the officers. Their commanding officer was Colonel Sir Charles Philip Belson (who appears to have preferred 'Philip' as his forename). Aged 42 in 1815, he had served in the West Indies and in the Netherlands (in the latter as a cavalry officer), had been with the 28th since 1804 and had led them in the Peninsula. He seems to have had a dry wit, for at Barrosa (where he had succeeded to command the brigade in which the 28th served) he exhorted his men to maximize the effect of their musketry by not firing too high, declaring, 'be sure to fire at their legs and spoil their dancing'.[6] His deputy, the Irish-born Lieutenant Colonel Robert Nixon, was relatively old for his rank, at 54. Although an officer of the 28th of long standing, his command experience had come in the Peninsula when attached to the Portuguese army, whose 2nd *Caçadores* he had commanded at Busaco and Fuentes de Oñoro.

The next officers in terms of seniority were Captains William Prescott Meacham and William Irving, whose dates of their brevet majorities were identical. Meacham's second forename was well known in the 28th for General Robert Prescott had been associated with it for more than fifty years, having commanded it, and from 1789 he had been its colonel. He became godfather to a number of the sons of his old comrades in arms, and William's father had been the regimental paymaster. In the Peninsula Meacham had been chosen to command the Tarifa Volunteers, a local Spanish corps in that city, because he was 'a gallant and experienced officer'[7] and for his knowledge of the Spanish language, acquired when stationed in Minorca. (Not even he could make this corps efficient, leading to their nickname 'Meacham's Blind Nuts'.) He was a rare example of an officer who was known to carry a musket. Irving had been in the regiment for twenty years, had seen much active service and had been wounded in both arms in the West Indies and the Peninsula, to the degree that after another shot in the arm at Quatre Bras he became considerably disabled.

In appearance the 28th was one of the most recognizable regiments in the army by virtue of their headdress. Unlike the remainder of the ordinary line infantry regiments, the 28th apparently never adopted the distinctive, false-fronted 1812-pattern shako (although plates for it are recorded), but instead retained a version of the previous 'stovepipe' cap, not dissimilar to that worn by light infantry regiments. It was especially distinguished by the presence of a badge at the rear of the cap, depicting the regimental number and a sphinx upon a tablet inscribed 'Egypt', the device awarded as a battle honour to those regiments that had served in Egypt in 1801. The 28th received this singular distinction in consequence of an incident at Alexandria when, arrayed in line, they were attacked by French cavalry in the rear, whereupon the rear rank faced about and drove them off with musketry. (The 44th was to perform a similar back-to-back manoeuvre at Quatre Bras in circumstances just as desperate, but without receiving the same acknowledgement.) It has been suggested that the 28th's unique cap was worn only by the grenadier company, but an eyewitness who saw them marching to Quatre Bras recalled how he recognized Picton's Division: 'First came a battalion of the 95th Rifles in their sombre green dress and black accoutrements. The old 28th followed, having their number both in front and rear of their low caps – a memorial of Egypt.'[8] This so-called 'back number' was sanctioned officially in 1830 and has been worn by the regiment and its successors ever after, even to the modern era. Otherwise, the appearance of the 28th was fairly standard, the uniform having yellow facings with silver lace for officers, although at least the grenadier company carried French hide knapsacks captured in Egypt.

THE 32ND (CORNWALL) REGIMENT OF FOOT

The next in seniority in Kempt's Brigade was the 32nd Regiment, which had been formed in 1702 as a regiment of marines, recruited in the south and southeast, in Sussex, Surrey and Hampshire; it had been re-formed as a regiment of infantry in 1715. When county affiliations were allocated in 1782 the regiment expressed a preference for Warwickshire, but as more senior regiments had requested the same, it became the 32nd (Cornwall) Regiment. It had had a long and distinguished career in the Napoleonic Wars; it had been virtually destroyed by disease in San Domingo in 1796–98, and when recruited up to strength had served with Moore and Wellington in the Peninsula and at Walcheren. In 1815 it was a single-battalion regiment; its 2nd Battalion, formed at Launceston in 1804, had been disbanded in October 1814, never having served abroad.

The commanding officer of the 32nd was Lieutenant Colonel John Hicks, who had spent his entire military career in the regiment, which he had joined in 1786. He had seen much active service, in the West Indies and in the Peninsula from 1811, where he had commanded the regiment. Conversely his deputy, Major Felix Calvert, a relatively young officer, had been with the 32nd barely a month, joining from a period on half-pay. He had served in the Peninsula, at Walcheren and in North America, but had relatively little command experience, as from 1810 he had been ADC to Sir Thomas Graham. He came from a family of some note: his mother Frances was the daughter of Viscount Pery and his father, Nicholson Calvert of Hunsdon House, Hertfordshire, was a member of Parliament (and from 1798 had commanded the Stanstead Abbot and Hunsdon Volunteers).

Despite the 32nd's Cornish connection – exemplified by the Launceston association mentioned above – it had a strong Irish element, at least among its company commanders. The most famous of these was Captain Harry Ross-Lewin of Ross-hill, County Clare, who in 1815 was an experienced campaigner. Born in 1778, he had served in the Caribbean and notably in the Peninsula, and was to write a notable account of his military service. His younger brother Thomas was a lieutenant in the 32nd in the campaign.

Also of Irish origin were three captains who were great friends and who had met under the most unusual of circumstances: Jacques Boyse, Thomas Cassan and Edward Whitty. Boyse, a Franco-Irishman, was serving aboard a French privateer that captured the transport vessel in which one of his future friends was sailing, and was himself subsequently captured by the 74-gunner HMS *Russell*, aboard which the third Irishman was serving as a midshipman. Both the seafarers subsequently joined the British Army, and all three served in the 28th, where they messed together as a Milesian club; and, even more bizarrely, all three received their death wound at Quatre Bras.

Statistics concerning the 32nd present an interesting snapshot of the experience within a 'veteran' battalion. Of corporals and privates, some 14 per cent had served for fourteen years or more, some 30 per cent between seven and fourteen years, and of the remainder most had only two or three years' service, including those transferred from the 2nd Battalion. Two men had enlisted as long before as 1793, one in the 32nd and one originally in the 4th Dragoons, and thirty-three had joined the regiment in 1799. Of all the regiments in the brigade, the 32nd was the least remarkable in terms of its appearance, wearing the standard infantry uniform with white facings and gold lace for officers.

THE 79TH REGIMENT OF FOOT
(CAMERON HIGHLANDERS)

The third regiment of the brigade was perhaps its most unusual, in that from its origin it retained a vestige of the ancient Highland clan system. The 79th had been raised in 1793 by Sir Alan Cameron of Erracht (Inverness-shire) and although recruited in the normal manner, the Cameron family influence was strong, with many of the original recruits drawn from Sir Alan's own district. The regiment retained its national character: between 1800 and 1815, of those men whose nationality is recorded, less than 12 per cent were English, less than 8 per cent Irish, and less than half of one per cent were foreigners (the Scottish percentage was probably even higher due to the number of those whose nationality is unrecorded but who bore Scottish names). It is perhaps evidence of a paternalistic attitude that Alan Cameron was known as 'Old Cia Mar tha', from his habit of addressing his men with the Gaelic greeting '*Cia Mar tha thu?*' (How are you?). They seem to have reciprocated his sentiments, for when his son, Philips Cameron, was killed at Fuentes de Onoro when commanding the 79th, they raised a cry of '*Thuit an Camshronach!*' ('Cameron has fallen!'), which drove them to fall upon the enemy with particular fury. In the 1815 campaign, including the quartermaster and one volunteer, nine of the officers bore the name of Cameron, and including a nephew of Sir Alan – in the regiment as a whole there were twelve officers named Cameron, not including the volunteer – but only twelve other ranks of that name (whereas there were, for example, twenty-five McKays, twenty-three Macdonalds and twenty-two Campbells). Alan Cameron paid a heavy personal price for the formation of his regiment: in addition to the loss of his son Philips, his youngest son Ewan died of illness while serving as Alan's ADC in the Peninsula, and the family losses continued to the end of the war: two of his nephews serving as officers in the 79th were killed at Toulouse.

The 79th was an experienced regiment, its 1st Battalion having served widely in the previous decade, including much hard service in the Peninsula. During

The Highland uniform, depicted in a portrait of Sergeant William Duff of the 42nd, wearing his Waterloo Medal. Born into the regiment in which his father served, he was enlisted at the age of 14 and according to James Paterson, author of the commentaries to *A Series of Original Portraits and Character Engravings … by John Kay* (Edinburgh, 1838) he was 'a gallant soldier – loved his country … was humane in disposition – of a free, affable manner – and much esteemed by his fellow-soldiers'. He survived a wound at Waterloo and was commissioned as adjutant in 1825. (*Print after John Kay, 1816*)

An officer of a Highland regiment, evidently intended to represent the 92nd, from a contemporary French print. Highland officers wore trousers on campaign: in the Peninsula those of the 92nd had worn blue web pantaloons, which were remarked upon as being so different from the kilts of their men that French sharpshooters could target them deliberately. Wearing the lapels open was probably a regimental custom, as a Regimental Order of 26 April 1810 noted that on parade officers should appear 'in full Highland dress, with the breasts of their jackets open, and without gorgets'. (*Print by Jacquemin*) the deadly expedition to Walcheren in 1809, where disease destroyed regiments to a degree almost unprecedented for a European campaign, the 79th lost only two individuals out of more than a thousand, and although an outbreak of what was probably malaria afflicted them after their return to England, only ten men died, a quite extraordinary resilience that may be evidence of the care and supervision exercised by the officers.

The 79th had formed a 2nd Battalion in April 1804 but it remained at home until its disbandment in December 1814. In the usual way, upon its disbandment some 261 rank and file were transferred to the 1st, and then the only battalion, under Captain John Sinclair. For officers this would have been welcomed as a way of continuing their military career, but for Sinclair and others it proved a very dubious blessing: he died of wounds received at Quatre Bras and other 2nd Battalion officers also suffered: Lieutenant Ewan Kennedy was killed at Waterloo and Lieutenant John Powling was wounded at Quatre Bras and succumbed in October 1815.

The commanding officer was the 32-year-old Lieutenant Colonel Neil Douglas, the fifth son of a Glasgow banker and a kinsman of the Earls of Angus. He had joined the 79th in 1804 and had seen extensive service, sustaining a severe wound when shot through the left shoulder at Busaco. He had commanded the 1st Battalion in the Peninsula from February 1813, and also had experience of staff duty, having served as a brigade major at Cadiz. His deputy, conversely, had been relatively old when commencing his military career: the Edinburgh-born Lieutenant Colonel Andrew Brown had joined the 79th almost from its origin, at the age of 29 in 1795. He had served in Egypt and throughout the Peninsular War and had suffered three injuries in battle.

In appearance the regiment wore the Highland version of the infantry uniform, including feather bonnets and kilts of the distinctive regimental tartan, 'Cameron of Erracht', basically the Macdonald sett minus three red lines and with a yellow overstripe. The regimental facing colour was dark green and the officers' lace gold.

1ST BATTALION THE 95TH REGIMENT OF FOOT (RIFLES)

The fourth of Kempt's battalions was one of three of its regiment that served in the campaign (the 2nd Battalion, and two companies of the 3rd, were in Adam's

An officer of the 95th Rifles in the uniform worn by the 1st Battalion in Picton's Division, a style clearly copied from hussar uniform but in the dark ('rifle') green of the rifle corps. (*Print by Goddard & Booth, 1812*)

A private of the 95th Rifles depicted in a French print by Genty in 1815. The dark uniform, green with black facings and white piping, led to the contemporary nickname 'The Sweeps', to differentiate them from the ordinary redcoats. The artist appears to have depicted a Continental-style 'French' bugle on the shako, instead of the bugle horn with cords commonly used in British uniform.

Brigade of Sir Henry Clinton's 2nd Division). The 95th Rifles was among the elite of the army – it certainly regarded itself as the elite – although one of the youngest in the Army List, having been formed in 1800 as an experimental corps of light infantry armed with rifled muskets capable of immeasurably greater feats of marksmanship than the remainder of the infantry's smoothbores. The 95th's feats were legendary, and their skill as scouts and skirmishers was unmatched, confirmed by a stellar reputation won in the Peninsula in which, as they boasted, they were always the first into action and the last out. Unlike the rifle-armed light infantry of some European armies, the 95th was equally capable of acting in a conventional manner in line like ordinary infantry, making them a most valuable asset. The regiment's appearance was as remarkable as its skill and training: their uniform was very dark ('rifle') green with black facings, with blackened leather equipment; their weapon the formidable Baker rifle with a stirrup-hilted sword bayonet.

It was appropriate that such a remarkable battalion should have an outstanding officer as its head. Colonel Sir Andrew Barnard was born in County Donegal in 1773 and had seen extensive service in a number of infantry regiments and the 1st Foot Guards before joining the 95th, relatively late in his career, as lieutenant colonel in March 1810. He was acknowledged as a skilled soldier and was universally popular with those under his command. Jonathan Leach, his senior captain in the Waterloo campaign, recorded a remarkable tribute:

> If a thorough knowledge of their profession, calm, cool courage, great presence of mind in action, frank and gentlemanly manners, and the total absence of what may be termed teazing [*sic*] those under their command, I do say … that both Baron Alten and Colonel Barnard merited the high estimation in which they were held.[9]

The regard of his men was demonstrated after Barnard was shot through the body at Nivelle, a desperate wound but one that led him, with characteristic nerve, to declare, 'If any man can recover, I know I shall.'[10] He was as good as his word: when he rejoined his men only a month later he was greeted with prolonged and spontaneous cheering. He was also experienced in command, having commanded a brigade of the Light Division in the Peninsula, and indeed the whole division for a period after the death of Craufurd at Ciudad Rodrigo. Any brigade commander would have counted himself fortunate to have Barnard as his deputy, but the convention of seniority meant that in the Waterloo campaign he was junior to Philip Belson of the 28th, whose brevet colonelcy predated Barnard's by exactly a year (and his regimental lieutenant colonelcy by some five and a half years). Apparently the only criticism ever raised about Barnard concerned the choking smoke produced by his cigars.

Barnard's deputy was another resolute officer, Lieutenant Colonel Alexander Cameron of Inverailort in Argyllshire. He had joined the 95th in 1800 and had collected wounds in Egypt and a serious one in the thigh at Vittoria. John Kincaid of the 95th wrote:

Of him I can truly say, that as a *friend*, his heart was in the right place, and, as a *soldier*, his right place was at the head of a regiment in the face of an enemy. I never saw an officer feel more at home in such a situation, nor do I know any one who could fill it better.[11]

Sir Denis Pack, commander of the 9th Brigade. The decorations shown include the Army Gold Cross with an amazing seven clasps, representing service in eleven battles (only Wellington himself had more clasps), Waterloo Medal, KCB (bestowed on 2 January 1815), the Portuguese Order of the Tower and Sword, the Austrian Order of Maria Theresa, and the Russian Order of St Vladimir. (*Engraving by C. Turner after John Sanders*)

Among other personalities in the battalion were three of the 95th's later memorialists: the senior captain, Jonathan Leach, who was to succeed to command of the battalion after Barnard and Cameron were wounded; Lieutenant John Kincaid, the adjutant, arguably the most quoted writer of all British veterans of the Napoleonic Wars, another Scot with a wry sense of humour; and George Simmons, a lieutenant at Waterloo who had been a surgeon before embarking on a military career. The battalion's most junior captain was William Johnstone, yet another Scot, who had had a most distinguished career in the Peninsula and of whom Kincaid remarked, 'I had never set my eyes upon a nobler picture of a soldier.' At Badajoz Johnstone had been severely wounded in the arm, but continued to serve despite having a stiff elbow; which his friends said deprived him of the ability to annoy them by playing Scottish reels on his violin. Among the lower-ranking officers was

Lieutenant John Stilwell, known as 'Scamp' for his mischievous nature, who was believed to be a natural son of the Duke of York.

THE 9TH BRIGADE

The 9th Brigade, nominally three-quarters Scottish in composition, had at its head the tough and formidable Major General Sir Denis Pack. Born in 1772, he was the son of the Very Reverend Thomas Pack, Dean of Ossory, and obtained his first commission in 1791. The extraordinary nature of his career was summarized in 1820:

> Sir Denis Pack has received eight wounds, six of them rather severe ones: he has been frequently struck by shot, and had several horses killed and wounded under him. He purchased all his commissions; never was on half-pay, or absent from a service on active duty that he could possibly have been employed on.[12]

He served as a cavalryman in the Netherlands in 1794, in 1800 became lieutenant colonel in the 71st Highlanders and led them at the Cape and in South America, where he served under Marshal William Beresford (whose half-sister he married subsequently), and was captured at the capitulation of Buenos Ayres. With the fever from Walcheren afflicting both Pack and his regiment, its despatch to the Peninsula was delayed; but Pack preceded it on his own to offer his services and was given command of a Portuguese brigade. He tried to rejoin the 71st when it did arrive, but was retained as a brigade commander, latterly with a British brigade in the 6th Division (which he also led temporarily), in which were two of the battalions that were to serve in the 5th Division in 1815, the 42nd and 79th.

Pack was clearly a formidable man, and it was said that his regiment was particularly impressed when at Walcheren he decapitated a Frenchman with one blow of his sword. He was also known for an irascible nature and a fierce temper, to the extent that when he escaped from captivity in South America lines were composed to the effect that

> *The devil break the gaoler's back*
> *That set thee loose, sweet Denis Pack.*

Nevertheless, his merits were recognized; as one private remarked, he was 'a very forward and bold officer; one of those who says, "*Come*, my lads, and do this", and who goes *before* you to put his hand to the work'.[13]

Pack remained fiercely devoted to the 71st, and when in January 1817 his wife presented them with new colours, he 'bellowed like a bull, proclaiming the glories of the regiment.'[14] When the same colours were retired they were hung over Pack's tomb in Kilkenny Cathedral (where his father had become dean), a gesture that he might well have appreciated even more than the five votes of thanks he had been accorded in Parliament.

As was often the case when generals selected their ADCs, Pack appointed an officer from his old regiment. Major Edmund L'Estrange had served as his ADC in the Peninsula, achieving a brevet majority at the relatively early age of 26. He was the eldest son of Captain Anthony L'Estrange of the 88th, of the Irish branch of the Hunstanton family of which the most famous member had been Roger L'Estrange, the seventeenth-century literary personality and pamphleteer in the Royalist cause during the Civil War. At 29, Pack's brigade major was two years older than L'Estrange, but an officer who had also served with distinction in the Peninsula: Major Charles Smyth of the 95th. He was the fourth son of the Right Hon. John Smyth of Heath Hall, near Wakefield, and his wife Lady Georgiana Fitzroy, daughter of the 3rd Duke of Grafton; he had been wounded severely at Nivelle in November 1813 but had recovered to serve in the Waterloo campaign. Pack's determination was clearly shared by those he chose for his staff: at Orthez his brigade major, Lieutenant John Innes of the 42nd, 'might have retired after delivering the orders, without throwing a blot on his good name, but his heart was with the regiment, and he advanced to the charge in person,'[15] and was killed on the spot by a shot through the head. In this respect, Pack was unlucky with his brigade majors: Charles Smyth was mortally wounded at Quatre Bras.

3RD BATTALION, THE 1ST (ROYAL SCOTS) REGIMENT OF FOOT

The 1st or Royal Regiment of Foot (Royal Scots) was, as the number implied, the most senior infantry regiment in the British Army, with a proud and very ancient tradition. Its seniority dated officially from 1661, but its origins went back at least to 1633, when members of previous Scottish regiments, some previously in the service of Gustavus Adolphus of Sweden, were united to form a regiment in French service; and a more tenuous connection to Scots in French service pushed the regiment's possible lineage back to 1590. In 1815 the 1st Foot was one of the largest in the army, numbering four battalions. In some regiments the senior battalions were those that had experienced most active service; but the 3/1st, which had been raised at Hamilton in 1804, had had a more active career than any of the other three battalions, with much hard service in the Peninsula. Despite its title, the battalion was not predominantly Scottish; for the period of its existence (1804–17) it comprised 43 per cent Irish, 37 per cent English, 18 per cent Scots and 2 per cent foreigners, and when inspected in January 1817 it comprised about 46 per cent English, 34 per cent Irish, 19.5 per cent Scots and the remainder foreigners. On this occasion it received a glowing report: that the officers understood their duty, were 'intelligent and extremely zealous', the other ranks 'good, healthy, cheerful and zealous in duties, conduct in the field and quarters exemplary and soldier-like'; and that unanimity prevailed in the battalion. The regiment wore ordinary infantry uniform with the blue facings that distinguished 'royal' regiments, and gold lace for officers.

The battalion was commanded by Lieutenant Colonel Colin Campbell, who had led his command at Salamanca and Vittoria, having joined the Royal Scots in 1810. The 1813 Inspection Return described him as 'an intelligent and steady officer'.

His deputy was Major Lawrence Arguimbau,[16] who had joined the Royals as a 17-year-old ensign in 1801 as a protégé of the Duke of Kent, who was the regimental colonel from 1801 to 1820. Arguimbau had lost his left arm in the first, unsuccessful assault of San Sebastian in July 1813, but continued to serve. Next in seniority was Major Robert Macdonald, who had interesting family connections: his brother was to become Sir John Macdonald, the army's adjutant general 1830–50, and his cousin was Jacques-Étienne-Joseph-Alexandre Macdonald, Marshal of France, who had remained loyal to Napoleon until the end of the 1814 campaign, but then had accepted the Bourbon restoration and had not returned to his old master in 1815. Especially distinguished at San Sebastian, Robert Macdonald was to be one of four commanding officers of his battalion in the campaign, until he too was wounded at Waterloo. Another of the battalion's officers had noted command experience: Captain William

Gordon, although only sixth in seniority in the battalion, had led the 24th Portuguese Regiment in the Peninsula, and it was fortunate that he had gained that experience for he was the battalion's senior unwounded officer at the end of the Battle of Waterloo.

THE 42ND (ROYAL HIGHLAND) REGIMENT OF FOOT

The 42nd Regiment was the oldest Highland corps in the army, raised as independent Highland companies from 1725 and regimented as the 43rd, later 42nd, Foot in 1739. From 1758 the corps became the Royal Highland Regiment, but although the name did not officially become part of the regimental title until 1861, it was known colloquially as the Black Watch. The derivation of the name is disputed: 'Watch' from the original security duties of 'watching' the Highlands, but the 'Black' is said to have referred to the dark tartan of their kilts: *Am Freiceadan Dubh* in Gaelic, to distinguish them from the *Saighdearan Dearg*, or 'red soldiers', the regular troops. That, at least, was the story accepted by David Stewart of Garth, one of the regiment's most distinguished officers and an early historian of the Highlands.[17]

The regiment had garnered eight battle honours during long and hard service in the Peninsula, with both 1st and 2nd battalions serving there; but the 2nd Battalion had been disbanded in 1814. The battalion that fought at Waterloo was predominantly Scottish in composition: between 1814 and 1816 it recruited about 10 per cent Irish, 3 per cent English, and a single foreigner. Stewart of Garth, admittedly not an unbiased commentator, held that the true Highland recruit was a superior being to the ordinary rank-and-file soldier, infinitely more educated and religious, and quoted statistics to support the assertion. From the period from 1740 to the end of 1815, only six privates were executed, only two during the Napoleonic Wars (one for murder in 1797, the other for shooting his officer in 1812), and 'In the course of seventy-nine years' service, no individual has ever been brought to a General Court-Martial for theft, or any crime showing moral turpitude or depravity.' Such rectitude of conduct was very obvious during the regiment's sojourn in Brussels prior to Waterloo, and perhaps confirmed Garth's belief that to exemplify bravery and honour it was only necessary to say, 'he belongs to the Black Watch'.[18]

Nevertheless, the battalion was not composed entirely of veterans, as Sergeant James Anton reflected:

> We had the name of a crack corps, but certainly it was not then in that state of discipline which it could justly boast of a few years afterwards. Yet notwithstanding this disadvantage, none could be animated with a fitter feeling for the work before us … One half of us had never been on a campaign before [but] our young hands … were anxious to be led to face the enemy.[19]

Commander of the battalion at Waterloo was Colonel Sir Robert Macara, son of the Reverend Macara of Fortingal, Perthshire. He had joined the regiment in 1803 and was an experienced officer who had commanded the unit in action from the Pyrenees onwards, receiving the Army Gold Cross for leading it in five battles, and in January 1815 the KCB. It is likely that the wearing of these decorations would prove fatal at Quatre Bras. His deputy was Lieutenant Colonel Robert Henry Dick, who had joined the regiment in 1808 and had commanded his battalion at Busaco, Fuentes de Oñoro and Salamanca.

Another noted personality was Major John Campbell, the only one of the battalion's fourteen most senior officers to come through the campaign unscathed. He had joined the 42nd as a lieutenant in 1804 and had some command experience (he had the Gold Medal for Orthes and Toulouse), and his background exemplifies the tradition of military service that ran through some families. His great-grandfather was Sir William Johnson, 1st Baronet, who had had a most famous military career in North America, while John Campbell's father was Lieutenant General Colin Campbell, and his elder brother Sir Guy Campbell, who had been awarded a baronetcy for service in the Peninsula with the 6th Foot and who was present at Waterloo as an assistant adjutant general.

The 42nd wore the Highland version of the infantry uniform, with dark blue facings and gold lace for officers, the feather bonnet with the regiment's traditional red hackle (the origin of which is uncertain), and kilts of the dark 'Government' tartan, now known more familiarly as 'Black Watch'.

2ND BATTALION THE 44TH (EAST ESSEX) REGIMENT

The sole English regiment in the brigade was the 44th Foot, which from 1782 had borne the county designation of East Essex, apparently because its then colonel, Major General Charles Rainsford, had personal connections with that county (he was MP for Maldon 1772–74, for example). The regiment had been raised as the 55th Foot in 1741 and was renumbered as the 44th in 1748. The 1st Battalion served in the Mediterranean during the Napoleonic Wars, so it was the 2nd Battalion that had served in the Peninsula, where at Salamanca it had captured the Eagle of the French 62me Ligne, a depiction of which was used as a badge by the regiments that developed from the 44th, even to the present day. The battalion had joined Sir Thomas Graham's force in the Netherlands in 1813, and was still there when the Waterloo campaign erupted. For almost a year, until April 1815, it had been in garrison at Ostend, where it 'acquired the good-will of the inhabitants, who, for years after spoke of the officers and men in very gratifying terms.'[20] Its facing colour was yellow, and the officers' lace silver.

Both the senior officers of the battalion had Irish connections. The commanding officer, John Millett Hamerton, had joined the 44th at the age of 15 in 1792 and led the regiment's 1st Battalion in the later Peninsular War period. His deputy, Major George O'Malley, had had an unusual start to his military career. During the 1798 rebellion in Ireland he attached himself to the Castlebar Yeomanry as a volunteer, and there being no officer present was begged to command it by the NCOs and men. He performed so well at the Battle of Castlebar that he was commissioned, then removed to the North Mayo Militia with the intention of joining the regulars at the first opportunity, which he did in 1800. After service in Egypt, North America and Jamaica he returned home, desperate to participate in the Peninsular War, but found no employment until a further entreaty in 1815 resulted in a transfer to the 2/44th, which he joined only on 12 June.

For the Waterloo campaign, the battalion lost a number of officers for administrative reasons: three were detained at Ostend as the town's commandant, engineer and adjutant, and two captains, two lieutenants and Major Fountain Elwin were also detained at the same place as members of a general court martial. Among the battalion's experienced campaigners was a dog belonging to Lieutenant Robert Grier, which had been born in the Peninsula and was a great favourite in the battalion; like its master it was wounded at Quatre Bras and they recuperated together.

THE 92ND (HIGHLAND) REGIMENT
(GORDON HIGHLANDERS)

The fourth battalion of Pack's Brigade was another, very distinguished, Highland corps. The 92nd Foot had been raised in 1794 as the 100th Foot, renumbered as the 92nd in 1799, by George, Marquess of Huntly, son of the 4th Duke of Gordon and at that time serving in the 3rd Foot Guards. The recruits were overwhelmingly Scottish, about three-quarters Highlanders and almost a third of the total from Inverness-shire. The subsidiary title of Gordon Highlanders was derived from the family involved in its creation; not only Huntly but also his sisters and mother, who wore its uniform and helped raise recruits. Huntly's mother, the Duchess of Gordon, was said to have been especially effective in persuading men to join; one of the great beauties of the age, known colloquially as 'Bonnie Jean', she was said to have used an unusual stratagem in putting the proverbial 'king's shilling' between her lips and presenting it to the recruit in the form of a kiss.

The original pattern of recruiting seems to have continued: of men who joined the 1st Battalion between 1811 and 1825 more than 81 per cent were Scots, less than 13 per cent Irish and less than 6 per cent English. In 1815 the battalion included at least one German, Frederick Zieger, a musician, whose career in the regiment was short: he was enlisted in 1815 and was killed at Waterloo. (Only the 1st Battalion went on service; the 2nd Battalion existed from 1803 to 1814 and remained at home.) Statistics for the time of Waterloo emphasize the experienced nature of the battalion: only about 23 per cent of the men had served for four years or less, the remainder including many hardened campaigners, of whom more than 40 per cent had served for four years or more. More than half were aged over 25, and 34 per cent or more were 30 years or over; the average height was 5 feet 6 inches, with less than 2 per cent being 6 feet tall. The regiment had served with distinction in Egypt and the Peninsula, from where it garnered eight battle honours and where many of these men would have fought.

The Gordon family connection at Waterloo was slight, only three of its officers bearing that name, but its famous commander was yet another Cameron. (It is indicative of the martial nature of some Scottish families that in the Army List prior to Waterloo there were some seventy officers named Cameron, but

Lieutenant Colonel John Cameron of Fassiefern, commanding officer of the 92nd, in an engraving from a portrait apparently executed in 1814. The decorations include the Army Gold Medal (for Vittoria, with clasps for Nive and Orthez), the Ottoman Order of the Crescent (awarded for service in Egypt), and the Portuguese Order of the Tower and Sword. The Waterloo Medal is also shown, which must have been added posthumously.

even this was not the most prevalent name: there were 155 named Stewart or Stuart, and no less than 244 Campbells.)

Colonel John Cameron of Fassiefern was arguably one of the most famous battalion commanders in the army. Born in 1771 at Inverscadale, his family moved to their ancestral home at Fassiefern (or 'Fassfern') on the shores of Loch Eil in Inverness-shire, from where his branch of the family took its name. John Cameron acquired his first commission in 1793 and in the following year joined the newly formed Gordons as a captain. He served with them in Egypt and the Peninsula, attaining a regimental lieutenant colonelcy in June 1808 and brevet colonelcy in June 1814, and led them with great distinction. William Napier described him as 'by nature a soldier', and Sir Walter Scott wrote of his 'spirit that knew no fear and shunned no danger',[21] and it was said his only fault was reckless bravery. He was, however, a strict disciplinarian and was reserved and cool towards his officers. According to Captain William Fyfe of the 92nd, his men 'considered him their best and never-failing friend, and reposed the most implicit and unbounded confidence in him as a commander,' but recognized his temper and keen sense of discipline; as one remarked, he was a 'fine, brave, splendid man when duty was well done, but the very devil when anything went wrong'. His reputation was such that the lament by Ailean Dail ('Blind Allan'), the bard of Glengarry, compared him to the shepherd of the flock and described him as:

The man who never turned his back
When the matter to the tug-of-war came.[22]

He was, though, apparently seething that he had not been awarded the knighthood he thought he deserved – a dissatisfaction not unlike that felt by Picton. Even when it was explained that the criterion for the award of a KCB was the Gold Cross or Medal for five actions (he had only three) he badgered those in authority for what he thought was his due, even writing to Wellington with the claim that the 92nd 'feel, as a reproach to themselves, the contempt and neglect shown to their commander.'[23] It did no good, but by way of compensation he received an augmentation to his arms: appropriately, the figure of a 92nd Highlander.

Regiments with a definite Highland character preserved some old traditions; many of the genuine Highlanders, for example, spoke English, if at all, as a second language and usually communicated in Gaelic. Another tradition involved Cameron being accompanied on campaign by his foster-brother, son of John Cameron's nurse and of one of his father's old retainers: Ewen Macmillan served as a private in the 92nd and acted as a faithful follower. He was evidently as dauntless a man as his master, as exemplified by an incident in the Netherlands campaign in 1799. An expert deerstalker, Macmillan left his sentry post and crept up on a Frenchman he had spied at some distance; but before he could shoot, the Frenchman fired his own musket and clipped off part of Macmillan's ear. Ewen returned the fire, shot the Frenchman and finished him off with his bayonet. On his return to his post, minus part of his ear, he exclaimed to Fassiefern, 'The devil's son; do you see what he did to me?' Cameron replied that it was Macmillan's own fault for leaving his post, which brought forth the dark rejoinder, 'He'll not do it again!'[24]

The battalion was fortunate in having as Cameron's immediate subordinates two very tough and experienced field officers. Lieutenant Colonel James Mitchell of Auchindaul, Lochaber was, like Cameron himself, one of the regiment's original officers. He had served throughout the Peninsula and at Orthes had commanded the combined light companies of the regiment's brigade. Next in line was Major Donald Macdonald of Dalchosnie, Perthshire; he had joined the 92nd as a lieutenant in 1799 and had been wounded at least five times.

Like the other Highland regiments, the 92nd wore Highland uniform with yellow facings, silver lace for officers, and kilts of Gordon tartan, the 'Government' sett with a yellow overstripe.

THE HANOVERIANS

Due to sharing a sovereign with Britain from 1714, the Hanoverian army had often operated alongside the British in the eighteenth century, but it was disbanded in 1803 when Napoleon overran the state. It was resurrected during the 'War of Liberation' in 1813, and its infantry in 1815 comprised both regular battalions (Feld-Bataillone) and militia (Landwehr). From February 1815 each 'field battalion' was linked to three Landwehr battalions in a regimental structure, but for actual service each battalion was an independent entity. Organization was largely on British lines, although the Landwehr battalions each had only four companies; battalions were combined in brigades just like their British counterparts, the brigades allocated to divisions in Wellington's army. The integration of British and Hanoverian forces was such that Wellington reported Hanoverian losses in the same way as the British, and casualties were published together in *The London Gazette* just as Portuguese and British losses had been recorded during the Peninsular War, when they had also operated as part of a joint army. Nevertheless, some thought that they were not treated as equals by their British counterparts, or even by German officers in the King's German Legion. As noted already, to help remedy the lack of experience among the often untried Hanoverian troops, officers and NCOs from the King's German Legion were attached to the Hanoverian battalions to provide an experienced cadre of leadership.

Hanoverian Landwehr (right) and Brunswick Leib-Bataillon (left). In numbers the Landwehr formed a significant part of the 5th Division, but were inexperienced: John Kincaid of the 95th recalled how at Quatre Bras Sir Andrew Barnard 'repeatedly pointed out to them which was the French and which our side [but] they stood fast, and began blazing away, chiefly at our skirmishers too.' (*Print after Richard Knötel*)

The Hanoverian infantry wore a British-style uniform in red (dark green for the light battalions), and although they wore the same black cockade as the British, officers' sashes were yellow in place of the British crimson.

Picton's 5th Division was supposed to comprise three brigades: Kempt's, Pack's, and the 5th Hanoverian Brigade of Colonel E. von Vincke, composed of four Landwehr battalions: Battalions Hameln (Lieutenant Colonel Klencke), Hildesheim (Major Rheden), Gifhorn (Major Hammerstein) and Peine (Major Westphalen). Each received six or seven officers from the King's German Legion. Due to its initial position, however, the brigade was not with the 5th Division at the start of the campaign, only reaching it after the end of the Battle of Quatre Bras.

Instead, Picton had under his command an extra brigade, the 4th Hanoverian, Led by Lieutenant Colonel Charles Best of the 8th Line Battalion of the King's German Legion. This had been intended to act as part of the 6th Division; but that formation otherwise consisted only of Sir John Lambert's British 10th Brigade, which only joined the main army on the day of Waterloo, having marched thence from Ghent, and even then left one of its battalions as the garrison of Brussels. Best's 4th Hanoverian Brigade had instead been attached to Picton's Division, and fought with it at Quatre Bras. It comprised four Landwehr battalions: Lüneburg (Lieutenant Colonel de Ramdohr), Münden (Major de Schmidt), Osteröde (Major Baron Reden) and Verden (Major Decken); all had KGL officers attached. The brigade commander, Charles Best, had joined the Legion in 1803 and had seen service in the Peninsula 1808–09, in the Walcheren expedition, in North Germany and in the Netherlands in 1814.

THE ARTILLERY

Like others in the army, the 5th Division had two artillery batteries permanently assigned to it, under a divisional artillery commander. Those allocated to Picton were a British company of the Royal Foot Artillery, armed with 9-pounder guns, under Major Thomas Rogers, and a Hanoverian foot battery under Captain William Braun of the King's German Legion. Rogers had been a member of the Royal Artillery since 1795, and just a fortnight before Waterloo had been appointed a Companion of the Order of the Bath. Braun was an experienced officer who had served in the Peninsula from 1808 to 1812, in 1810–12 in Portuguese service; he held the Gold Medal for Albuera. However, his company was not actually with the 5th Division in the campaign; it had just been re-

A contemporary depiction of an important unit sometimes overlooked: a member of the Corps of Drivers, Royal Artillery, in a uniform combining elements of the dress of horse and foot artillery: like the horse troops but with a jacket similar to that of the foot companies. (*Engraving after Carle Vernet*)

equipped with 9-pounder guns from the arsenal at Ghent, and was still there when on the morning of 16 June Braun was ordered to join Lambert's Brigade, cantoned nearby, for the campaign.

Instead, the 5th Division received another Hanoverian battery, that commanded by Captain Charles von Rettburg, who had served throughout the Peninsular War with the King's German Legion. Its men included some personnel from the Hanoverian Landwehr and even a few veterans from the old Westphalian army that had fought alongside Napoleon. Equipped with 9-pounders, the company had been quartered near Brussels and had been assigned to Sir Charles Colville's 4th Division, until in the early morning of 16 June it was ordered to join Picton's Division.

Another German officer was the divisional artillery commander Major Henry Lewis Heise, who had served with the King's German Legion artillery in the Peninsula from 1808 to 1810.

In Brussels

The reception given to the British troops upon their arrival in the Netherlands was cordial; indeed, some expressed surprise at just how well they were received, especially as all the troops were billeted upon the local people who had little say in the matter. In Ghent Harry Ross-Lewin of the 32nd lodged in the mansion of an old gentleman who gave him breakfast and two dinners a day, told him to use the house as his own, and regaled him with a guided tour of his collection of old masters. At Brussels Ross-Lewin was billeted upon a German merchant who was a wine connoisseur, who plied him with copious rare draughts: 'A residence under the roof of such an entertainer, while campaigning, made some amends for privations endured in the Peninsula,'[1] as Ross-Lewin remarked. George Simmons of the 95th was placed with a merchant named Overman, who gave him the use of his summerhouse in which to entertain his friends; and after a desperate wound at Waterloo, Overman virtually saved Simmons's life, the family tending him as if he had been one of their own.

The rank and file were equally popular with the local population, partially because of the British practice, strictly enforced, of paying for what they needed instead of merely helping themselves; even if, as Scott observed some weeks later of Highlanders in France, when shopping they held their coin between finger and thumb 'with the gripe [sic] of a smith's vice'.[2] This contrasted markedly with the rapacity of the Prussians, who robbed and treated the civilians as harshly as if they had been French, repaying Napoleon's exactions upon Prussia after his victory over them in 1806, which was hardly surprising given that Belgium had been part of France at that time.

Numerous accounts singled out the Highlanders of the 5th Division for especial praise, as mentioned already in reference to the 42nd, and this seems not to have been entirely national bias on the part of the writers. For example, Major William Frye, an officer of the 3rd Ceylon Regiment, who was on holiday in Brussels at the time, reported that:

> The city is filled with British and Hanoverian troops. Their conduct is exemplary, nor is any complaint made against them. The Highland regiments however are the favourites of the Bruxellois, and the inhabitants give them the preference as lodgers. They are extremely well behaved (they say, when speaking of the Highlanders) and they cheerfully assist the different families on whom they are quartered in their household labour … Their superior morality to those of the same class either in England or Ireland must strike every observer.[3]

Frye attributed this superior morality to a greater degree of liberal education in Scotland.

He wrote of a woman who had Highlanders billeted upon her; she remarked to him that they were such good men, as gentle as lambs. Frye replied that nevertheless they were lions on the day of battle (and he must have been speaking from experience, for he had served in Egypt with the 2nd Queen's Royals and must have seen the 42nd and 92nd in action).

Sir Walter Scott, in Brussels shortly after the battle, wrote of the two latter regiments, whose 'good behaviour had attracted the affection of the inhabitants in an unusual degree. Even while I was there, *Les petits Ecossais*, as they called them, were still the theme of affectionate praise among the Flemings. They were so domesticated in the houses where they were quartered, that it was no uncommon thing to see the Highland soldier taking care of the children, or keeping the shop, of the host.'[4]

An element of reality was injected by a writer who recorded one Highlander observing ruefully that the Prussians took what they liked, but the British were held to their discipline: 'Aye, we're *praised* enuch [*sic*]. Ilka body *praises* us, but very few *gie* us ony thing.'[5]

Although remarkably little bad behaviour affected the locals, the army was not entirely free from crime. At Ghent the 42nd put their greatcoats in store and received instead remarkably fine blankets that could be adapted for use as tents. (It was thought that carrying both a blanket and greatcoat imposed too great a burden on the soldier, these together being 'more than [a man] can carry. The Duke of Wellington tried it in the year that his army entered France, but it distressed the troops greatly.'[6]) So fine were the new blankets that the soldiers found they could sell them at a high price – almost a pound in British money – so some were disposed of to the locals. So that the sale might not be noticed, gangs of three men would sell one blanket and cut up the other two, stitching the pieces together so that each man still had a blanket, albeit missing a third of its size. When this was discovered the entire battalion was assembled and their equipment inspected, those with altered blankets being punished. According to Sergeant James Anton, the severity was justified, for otherwise their commander 'might have led a half-naked regiment out of Brussels.'[7]

Although military operations were clearly in the offing, there seems to have been no sense of urgency or apprehension. Brussels was thronged with British tourists and Frye described how the inhabitants seemed entirely at ease, as 'Female minstrels with guitars stroll about the streets singing French romances and collecting contributions from this cheerful, laughter-loving people.' There was, perhaps, a deliberate attempt to encourage an air of normality, extending to the very highest level. Frye noted, somewhat waspishly, that the commander of the forces was not always immersed in military planning:

> The dark walk, as it is called, near the park is a favourite walk of the upper classes in the evening. There his Grace of Wellington is sometimes to be seen with a fair lady under his arm. He generally dresses in plain clothes, to the astonishment of all the foreign officers. He is said to be as successful in the fields of Idalia as in those of Bellona, and the ladies whom he honours with his attentions suffer not a little in their reputations.[8] [Idalia was a city in Cyprus, sacred to the goddess of love, Venus; Bellona was the Roman goddess of war.]

For the ordinary soldiers there were inspections and drill. After a day of firing practice the landlord of Lieutenant James Hope of the 92nd remarked that he thought they should instead conserve their ammunition, 'in case we should soon have occasion to fire it at real Frenchmen, and not at their painted figures!'[9]

Until shortly before the commencement of the campaign, the 5th Division was under the command of Sir James Kempt, its nominated head not having arrived. Sir Thomas Picton had received news that he was needed towards the end of May, had put his affairs in order and moved to London, instructing his ADCs – principally Tyler – to procure sufficient horses. Picton set off with Tyler for Ramsgate, dining at Canterbury, and on 12 June embarked with all his staff and servants in a vessel chartered for the purpose, arriving at Ostend on the afternoon of the same day. They stayed at the hotel there for the night, where his unofficial aide Gronow was surprised to hear the general flirting, in excellent French, with a pretty waitress. Such a diversion did not delay Picton long, however, for he set off with Tyler next day to Ghent, and from there travelled to Brussels. Gronow followed, taking a boat to Ghent where, without stopping, he hired a coach and reached Brussels before Picton, booking rooms for him at the Hotel d'Angleterre, rue Madeleine, to await his arrival.

Serving with Picton for the first time, Gronow described him as a strongly built man of medium height, resembling the Cossack hetman Matvei Platov, who had become a hero in Britain for his conduct in the recent campaigns against Napoleon; although Gronow stated that Picton had a stern look about him. He described his customary dress as a blue frock coat fastened to the neck, with a large black silk neckcloth that hid his shirt collar, dark trousers, boots and a round hat. That this was his dress at Quatre Bras, Gronow noted, because he claimed that Picton's uniform had not arrived; yet those who knew him better would have realized that this was the general's usual costume on campaign.

Sir Thomas Picton as a major general, wearing the old–style uniform for general officers, with epaulettes, c. 1811. He was awarded the KB in February 1813, with the star presumably added subsequently to the original portrait. (*Print after Sir Martin Archer Shee*)

At breakfast on the following morning Wellington's ADC, Charles Fox Canning, arrived to say that the duke wished to see Picton immediately. Leaving the table without delay he made his way to the park, where Wellington was strolling with Fitzroy Somerset, his military secretary, and with his friend the Duke of Richmond. Gronow claimed that Picton's manner was more familiar than Wellington liked, and here he spoke to the duke in a manner more appropriate to a friend than as a subordinate. Seemingly, Wellington was irritated by this; he bowed formally, and said, 'I am glad you are come, Sir Thomas; the sooner you get on horseback the better: no time is to be lost. You will take command of the troops in advance.' Equally, Picton disliked the duke's reserved manner, for when he had bowed and left, according to Gronow, he went away muttering in a way that convinced those with him that he was not pleased with his reception.

Picton also encountered some officers of the 28th, wandering in the park; he went up to Sir Philip Belson and asked to be introduced to the others, saying he was happy to have the 28th in his division.

The nature of Picton's meeting with Wellington, and the instructions he was said to have received, may not have been remembered quite correctly, for there is some doubt about the time at which Wellington first received news that Napoleon was approaching.

As early as the morning of 15 June there was little sense of urgency within the army. Two days before Wellington had written to his old subordinate Sir Thomas Graham, Baron Lynedoch, in a manner that suggested that action was not perceived to be imminent: 'There is nothing new here. We have reports of Buonaparte's joining the army and attacking us; but I have accounts from Paris of the 10th on which day he was still there; and I judge from his speech to the Legislature that his departure was not likely to be immediate. I think we are now too strong for him here.'[10] He was very soon undeceived.

Napoleon initiated the campaign by crossing the frontier into the Netherlands in the early hours of 15 June, and his troops were probably well under way by the time Picton's breakfast was interrupted. The Prussian chief of staff, August von Gneisenau, may have realized that something was afoot on the previous day, for he issued orders for Prussian concentration; but intelligence was confused, the troops widely dispersed, and the direction of Napoleon's advance was unclear. In Brussels at that moment there was perhaps an air of complacency, and the city's society, especially the British tourists thronging there, were probably more concerned by the entertainments available, notably a grand ball arranged for the evening of the 15th by the Duchess of Richmond, whose husband the duke, Wellington's great friend, was actually the second most senior British general in the region, although he was there in an entirely private capacity.

It is not certain precisely when definite news was received in Brussels of Napoleon's initial attack on the Prussian sector of the allied front, but it seems to have been in the late afternoon of 15 June, although some intimation may well have arrived earlier. De Lancey's rush to Wellington's headquarters, as already recounted, was probably the first positive news of Napoleon's advance; Wellington's military secretary Fitzroy Somerset stated that it was about 5.00 pm, and on 19 June Wellington himself wrote that 'I did not hear of these events till the evening of the 15th.'[11] There was, however, dispute about the timing of the receipt of the news, with Prussian sources claiming it to have been in the morning; indeed, William Siborne, the earliest outstanding British historian of the campaign, altered his text between his first and third editions to reflect this view. (In the original edition he stated that 'It was between three and four o'clock

Wellington's headquarters, signified by the sign hanging from the bracket over the door: 'Le Grand Quartier du Duc de Wellington'. (*Engraving by and after J. Rouse, published 1816*)

in the afternoon of the 15th that the Duke of Wellington received information of the advance of the French army'; in the 3rd edition, '[the] report to the Duke of Wellington arrived in Brussels at 9 o'clock in the morning,'[12] and in both cases he excused Wellington's apparent delay in getting his army in motion by suggesting that the report was so vague that the duke waited until the direction of Napoleon's main attack was verified.)

Despite the reception of the news that Napoleon was approaching, the Richmond ball was allowed to go ahead, probably partly to allay the fears of the many British visitors to Brussels, and as a way of ensuring that many of the most significant officers would be gathered in one place should orders need to be issued in haste. As usual Wellington was the centre of attention at the ball, but as Lady Jane Hamilton Dalrymple recalled:

> Although the Duke affected great gaiety and cheerfulness, it struck me that I had never seen him have so much an expression of care and anxiety on his countenance. I sat next to him on a sopha [*sic*] a long time, but his mind seemed quite pre-occupied; and although he spoke to me in the kindest manner possible, yet frequently in the middle of a sentence he stopped abruptly and called to some officer, giving him directions.[13]

While attendance at the ball would have ensured that some of the most important officers were close to Wellington's hand to receive orders, this factor did not extend to the lower command echelon of the 5th Division. Sir Thomas Picton probably attended, although his presence is not certain, and as he only arrived in Brussels on the previous day his invitation may have been issued at the last minute. Certainly none of his ADCs received invitations. Both brigade commanders of the 5th Division, Kempt and Pack, were invited officially but only Kempt's ADC was invited, the Honorable Charles Gore, although Pack took with him his brigade major, Charles Smyth.

Very few regimental officers were invited, but these included two battalion commanders, Sir Andrew Barnard of the 95th and John Cameron of Fassiefern of the 92nd. The latter might have been expected not only because of his own prominence, but because of a family connection: the Duchess of Richmond was the daughter of the 4th Duke of Gordon, who gave the 92nd his family name, and the duchess's brother had raised it. There exists a jacket said to have been worn at the ball by Lieutenant Claude Alexander of the 92nd, who had not received an invitation, but it is likely he accompanied Fassiefern as he was the battalion's adjutant. Other members of the 92nd were also present: Pipe Major Alexander Cameron and four sergeants, who had been asked to perform some Scottish dancing to entertain the guests. The duchess's daughter Louisa recalled that her mother 'thought it would interest the foreigners to see them … There was quite a crowd to look at the Scotch dancers'[14]; some, she thought, were to be killed in the next few days.

Only two other officers of the 5th Division appear to have attended the ball: Lieutenant Colonel Robert Dick of the 42nd was his battalion's second in command but may have been a friend of the Richmonds (he was sufficiently well regarded to be appointed an ADC to the king in 1825); and Lieutenant James Robinson of the 32nd. For an officer of such low rank to be invited, he must have been a friend or distant kinsman of some member of the Richmond family.

As further messages were relayed to Wellington it became obvious that an attack on the army's southernmost outposts was imminent – in the vicinity of Quatre Bras, where Netherlands troops would experience the first attack – and the ball broke up as officers were ordered to return to their regiments in readiness for an immediate concentration at Quatre Bras.

It was supposedly at this time that Wellington consulted Richmond's map of the area, explained that he was ordering the army to Quatre Bras, but pointed to the map (or marked it with his thumbnail) at the position he expected to fight, between Quatre Bras and Brussels (where the Battle of Waterloo actually took place) and supposedly remarked, 'Napoleon has humbugged me, by God!' Doubt has been cast over the authenticity of the story, but in effect it was true: he had been caught off-balance by the rapidity of Napoleon's advance.

The precise time of the receipt of the first definitive news of Napoleon's advance is not much clarified by those members of the division who recorded their memories. Some claimed to have been warned of impending action relatively early in the day. Lieutenant John Molloy of the 95th stated that he was told by 'Major Smith of the Rifles, who was aide-de-camp to Picton', 'that matters had not gone very well in front, and that they would move on that night'[15] as early as 2.00 pm on 15 June. Whether this was Molloy's own description or that of the writer of his memoirs is unclear, for 'Major Smith' was of course not

Picton's ADC. The officer in question was clearly not Harry Smith, Sir John Lambert's brigade major in the 6th Division, who at that moment was marching with that formation from Ghent to Brussels, so it must have been Pack's brigade major, Major Charles Smyth.

Harry Ross-Lewin of the 32nd was dining with Sir James Kempt, clearly before the latter was due to attend the Richmond ball, when:

> Coffee and a young aide-de-camp from the Duke of Wellington came in together. This officer was the bearer of a note from the Duke, and while Sir James was reading it, said: 'Old Blücher has been hard at it; a Prussian officer has just come to the Beau [Wellington], all covered with sweat and dirt, and says they have had much fighting.' Our host then rose, and, addressing the regimental officers at the table, said, 'Gentlemen, you will proceed without delay to your respective regiments, and get them under arms immediately.' … On my way I found several of our officers sitting at a coffee-house door, and told them Sir James Kempt's orders. They seemed at first to think that I was jesting, being hardly able to credit the tidings of being so near and so unexpected an approach of the French; but they soon perceived that I spoke seriously, and dispersed each to his own quarters.[16]

He then implied that the regiments stood to their arms immediately, but actually it was evidently some hours before they were ready, as it would not have been prudent to rush out of Brussels in the blackness of the night. Another officer noted that the same regiment received its orders to be ready to march at a moment's notice at 9.00 pm, but they thought it was just a ruse by Picton to keep them alert.

Lieutenant James Hope of the 92nd wrote that:

> About four o'clock in the afternoon of the 15th, it was first whispered, in Brussels, that the French army was in motion; but it was merely a report to which very few gave credit. Two or three of us having proceeded to the Park, after dinner, to take our usual walk, found that the rumour had been considerably strengthened by subsequent reports from the front. A little after seven o'clock, an officer of our acquaintance, who possessed the means of knowing what credit was due to the floating rumours of the day,

candidly told us that the Prussian hero had been attacked that morning – the advices to that effect had been received by the Duke of Wellington, during dinner, and that his Grace (without communicating the contents of the dispatch to any one), on the cloth being removed, desired those at table to fill a bumper to 'Prince Marshal Blücher and his gallant army'. He advised us to pack our baggage and prepare for a sudden movement, as it was extremely probable that we would leave Brussels during the night. Between nine and ten the order of readiness was issued; and, about half past eleven, the bugles were heard in every corner of Brussels, calling on the warriors, of the four nations, to prepare for battle.[17]

However, some were appraised of the situation somewhat later. George Simmons of the 95th, for example, had retired to bed and was roused by his servant at 11.00 pm with the news that the assembly was sounding.

'Hark, now the drums beat up again'
(*Over the Hills and Far Away*)

The Assembly

Throughout the British cantonments the alarm sounded and regiments began to assemble. Although the troops were scattered throughout the city, the assembly was remarkably efficient thanks to a system established in the previous days. Every company was billeted in the same or adjacent streets and the orderly sergeants had a written record of the location of their men, including street name and house number; each detachment had a designated alarm post where they mustered, before concentrating into their battalions.

The regiments were called to arms in varied manner. A number of eyewitnesses recalled bugle calls, as appropriate for light infantry and rifle corps, although one officer of the 32nd remembered them as well, and it might be expected that some regiments would have been roused by drums beating the 'assembly'. Given that they prided themselves on being the first into action and the last out, the 1/95th Rifles fell in before most of the others, were issued with two days' rations and were ready to march before midnight. Having nothing to do until the other parts of the army came into the same state of readiness, they removed their knapsacks and using them as pillows, those who could fell asleep; the officers slumbering in doorways were in some cases awakened by guests returning from the Richmond ball.

The Highland regiments were mustered by their traditional pipe music. Sir Walter Scott described how the 79th roused to a tune whose fearful declaration must have sent a chill through the many who knew the lyrics of 'the *Camerons*'

Gathering, a well-known pibroch, the corresponding words of which are, "Come to me and I will give you flesh", an invitation to the wolf and the raven for which the next day did, in fact, spread an ample banquet at the expence [*sic*] of our brave countrymen as well as of their enemies.'[1] Pipe Major Alexander Cameron rallied his 92nd to the tune – appropriate given the hour – of *Hey Johnny Cope, are ye waukin' yet?*, a song relating to the Jacobite era and to the surprise of the English army at Prestonpans in 1745, and which was to be used for many generations as a reveille for Highland regiments.

Rations were issued as the battalions mustered; some recalled that food for two or three days was provided, but James Hope, of the 92nd, stated that his battalion received six days' rations, but as part of this was in the form of soft bread rather than biscuit, it was too bulky to fit into the men's haversacks so much of it was left in the streets. Edward Costello of the 95th recalled that 'Being orderly non-commissioned officer of the company at the time, I received orders to draw three days' rations for my company, the chief part of which was left behind, as none but old soldiers felt inclined to carry them; some of the men, however, cursed their hard fate for not taking a portion with them.'[2]

A few men failed to assemble on time, if they were temporarily absent from their billets when the alarm sounded; officers were left behind in Brussels to collect the stragglers and march them off to join the others some hours later.

The hurried assembly, so late at night, was a cause of considerable consternation to the civilian population, not least to the many British tourists. As Hope was waiting, baggage packed, for the order to march, the gentleman in whose house he had been billeted came to chat in a fairly gloomy manner, saying that the Prussian army included many untried militiamen, the Hanoverians were mostly 'mere children', many of the Dutch and Belgians had recently fought *for* Napoleon, and then 'he took me by the hand, and with considerable emotion, said: "Farewell – remember that our sole dependence is upon the British troops, and their unconquered leader."'[3]

One of the British tourists, Charlotte Waldie, stood at her window watching the assembly and departure of the army, and being Scottish took especial interest in the Highlanders of the 5th Division:

> Unconcerned in the midst of the din of war, many a soldier laid himself down on a truss of straw, and soundly slept, with his hands still grasping his firelock; others were sitting contentedly on the pavement ... Numbers

were taking leave of their wives and children, perhaps for the last time, and many a veteran's rough cheek was wet with the tears of sorrow. One poor fellow, immediately under our windows, turned back again and again, to bid his wife farewell, and take his baby once more in his arms; and I saw him hastily brush away a tear with the sleeve of his coat, as he gave her back the child for the last time, wrung her hand, and ran off to join his company, which was drawn up on the other side of the Place Royale. Many of the soldiers' wives marched out with their husbands to the field, and I saw one young English lady mounted on horseback, slowly riding out of town with an officer, who, no doubt, was her husband.[4]

Some of the battalions stepped off to the accompaniment of their bands; that of the 28th, for example, played the jaunty tune to Thomas Moore's *The Young May Moon*, rather appropriate for the nocturnal assembly and the early hour of marching:

> *The best of all ways*
> *To lengthen our days*
> *Is to steal a few hours from the night, my dear.*

(This may have been quite a gentle musical accompaniment, for when the regiment was inspected the following year the inspector thought the band played too quietly!)

Soft music would not have featured as the Highland battalions marched, for their pipers struck up with full power. Jane Hamilton Dalrymple told how, at 4.00 am, 'I went to the window (it was the finest morning possible)'[5] and recognized the tune *Hielan Laddie* as the Highlanders marched past. Charlotte Waldie found the sight and sound of her countrymen most affecting, as

the 42nd and 92nd Highland regiments marched through the Place Royale and the Pare, with their bagpipes playing before them, while the bright beams of the rising sun shone full on their polished muskets, and on the dark waving plumes of their tartan bonnets. We admired their fine athletic forms, their firm erect military demeanour and undaunted mien.

We felt proud that they were our countrymen: in their gallant bearing we recognized the true hardy sons of Caledon, men who would conquer or die; and we could not restrain a tear at the reflection, how few of that warlike band who now marched out so proudly to battle might never live to return ... We saw our gallant army leave Brussels with emotions which may be better imagined than described ... our brave countrymen were followed by our tears, our warmest wishes, and our most fervent prayers for their safety and, success.[6]

Pack's Brigade, however, had been late in starting; three of its battalions were ready and under arms for some time before the 42nd arrived, 'stood in column, Sir Denis Pack at its head, waiting impatiently for the 42d [*sic*], the commanding officer of which was chidden severely by Sir Denis for being so dilatory.'[7]

Despite the hour, many inhabitants of Brussels turned out to watch the army leave, the Highlanders attracting particular attention from their popularity with the local population. One of them 'was most affected with, and loved to recount the steady, serious, and business-like march of the Highland regiments ... "God protect the brave Scotch", "God cover the heads of our gallant friends" were exclamations often repeated as they passed along, and many a flower was thrown by many a fair hand into their ranks.'[8]

Magdalene De Lancey stood with her husband at the window of their house as the troops marched past: 'It was a clear refreshing morning, and the scene was very solemn and melancholy. The fifes played alone, and the regiments one after another marched past ... and melted away in the mist of the morning.'[9]

The senior officers followed the regiments out of Brussels, as Charlotte Waldie observed: 'Sir Thomas Picton ... rode through the streets in true soldier-like style, with his reconnoitring glass slung across his shoulders, reining in his charger as he passed, to exchange salutations with his friends.' Having got their men on the road, some officers tarried a while: as Charlotte and her friends were breakfasting they were surprised by the appearance of Major Richard Llewellyn of the 28th, who had ridden some way with his regiment but had ridden back to Brussels for breakfast, and he was accompanied by Sir Philip Belson, who had his own business. Llewellyn chatted with his friends until Belson returned, and Charlotte recorded the poignancy of the moment:

At last the moment of parting arrived; Sir Philip Belson called for Major Llewellyn, and, after sitting a few moments, they got up to go away, and we bade farewell to one who from childhood had been our friend and companion, and whom we loved as another brother. We could not but feel how probable it was that we might never see him more; and, under this impression, some minutes after he had left us, which he had spent in bidding farewell to my brother below, we ran to the window, saw Sir Philip Belson and him mount their horses and ride away, and caught the last glimpse of them as they passed under the gateway of the Place Royale.[10] [Although Llewellyn would be wounded, both he and Belson were to survive.]

Llewellyn's battalion, which had received the alarm between 9.00 and 10.00 pm, had sat with their arms in parkland until they marched at 4.00 am, like the rest of the division halted in the Forêt de Soignes for breakfast without much sense of urgency. Edward Costello of the 95th recalled that 'Our men were as merry as crickets, laughing and joking with each other, and at times pondering in their minds what all this fuss, as they called it, could be about; for even the old soldiers could not believe the enemy was so near.'[11]

The 42nd had received four days' bread and three days' beef and a pint of spirits each, so were well provided when they halted in the forest to collect firewood and cook their breakfast:

We were flattering ourselves that we were to rest there until the next day; for whatever reports had reached the ears of our commanders, no alarm had yet rung on ours. Some were stretched under the shade to rest; others sat in groups draining the cup, and we always loved a large one, and it was now almost emptied of three days' allowance of spirits, a greater quantity than was usually served out at once to us on a campaign; others were busily occupied in bringing water and preparing the camp-kettles.[12]

Costello remarked on the tranquillity of the scene:

The recruits lay down to sleep, while the old experienced soldiers commenced cooking. I could not help noticing at the time while we remained here the birds in full chorus, straining their little throats as it were to arouse the spirits of the men to fresh vigour for the bloody conflict they were about to engage in … About nine o'clock, his Grace the Duke of Wellington, with his staff, came riding from Brussels and passed us to the front; shortly afterwards, orders were given for us to fall in, forming the advanced-guard of our division, and follow him.[13]

What hastened them on their way was the sound of distant gunfire, but this did not, apparently, dampen any spirits, but in some cases actually the reverse: Charles Cadell of the 28th recalled how they were called to arms just as they were finishing their breakfasts, and they set off in high spirits.

Quatre Bras

The desperate battle that occurred at Quatre Bras arose from Napoleon's plan of campaign. As previously in his career, when faced by two enemy armies he adopted the manoeuvre that has been called 'the strategy of the central position': by a rapid advance he would interpose himself between the two enemies, keep one occupied with the smaller portion of his own army, while assailing the other with the bulk of his force. Having thus achieved 'local superiority' in numbers he would hope to defeat the second enemy force, then detach part of his victorious army to pursue while switching the remainder to support his minor wing in their holding action against the first enemy, and then defeat that in turn. The organization of the French army into autonomous *corps d'armée*, each in effect

The enemy: Marshal Michel Ney, Picton's opponent at Quatre Bras and who was Napoleon's battlefield commander at Waterloo. His resolution in combat was exemplified by Napoleon's description of him as 'bravest of the brave', but as a tactician he was somewhat uninspired. (*Engraving by H.B. Hall after François Gérard*)

The Forêt de Soignes: the dense nature of the woodland is shown in this view of the main road from Brussels, down which the army marched en route to Quatre Bras, approaching Waterloo, with the Waterloo chapel in the distance. (*Engraving by and after J. Rouse, published 1816*)

a self-contained miniature army that could operate without support, provided the flexibility to accomplish this tactic, and in June 1815 it came near to success.

Napoleon's advance was so rapid that, for all the excuses advanced in subsequent years, the two allied armies, Wellington's and the Prussians, were caught severely off-balance and accordingly had to fight under inauspicious circumstances. Napoleon made his major effort against Blücher's Prussians, where he commanded in person; the holding action against Wellington he entrusted to Marshal Michel Ney with II Corps of his *Armée du Nord*. On the left of Napoleon's route of advance lay the strategic location of Quatre Bras, a small village named from the four arms of the crossroads upon which it stood: the north–south axis of the Charleroi to Brussels highway, and the transverse Nivelles–Namur road, the communication between Wellington, in the west of the allied position, and the Prussians in the east.

When the first news of Napoleon's advance filtered through to the allied high command, Wellington ordered his army to concentrate at Nivelles, but his troops were quite widely spread, mainly for logistic reasons. He could not be certain of the direction of Napoleon's advance, so a concentration at Nivelles to the west of Quatre Bras could have countered either a direct French drive on Brussels, or an outflanking movement to the far west. It did, however, have the disadvantage of moving the nucleus of Wellington's position further from his Prussian allies to the east.

It was not Wellington's initial intention to engage at Quatre Bras, but was the fortuitous consequence of disregard for his orders. The most advanced, Netherlandish, elements of Wellington's army had already pushed beyond Nivelles, and upon the appearance of the French the decision to hold the strategic crossroads was taken by the senior officer on the ground, the energetic and capable quartermaster general of the Dutch–Belgian army, Jean Constant de Rebecque, after consultation with Baron de Perponcher, commander of the 2nd Netherlands Division.

Early on the morning of 16 June the energetic but inexperienced Prince of Orange arrived to take command, and sent Constant de Rebecque to Nivelles to look for reinforcements, as the French pressure upon the Netherlands troops began to increase. The area where the battle was fought, largely to the south of the crossroads, was a mixture of woodland, some hamlets and farm buildings, and fields of standing crops, the height of which tended to obscure the view of the foot soldiers and led to some confusion. Marshal Ney had under his command a large number of excellent cavalrymen, whereas on the allied side it was largely an infantry battle: there was present a brigade of Dutch-Belgian horse, but no British cavalry was within marching distance to permit them to participate, and of the Anglo-Hanoverian artillery only two British and two King's German Legion were to come into action.

Until relatively late in the action the only support available to the stubborn Dutch–Belgian resistance to the French attacks was that provided by Wellington's reserve, marching from Brussels: Picton's 5th Division, together with the self-contained Brunswick Corps, and it was upon them that the whole security of Wellington's position was to depend.

The march from Brussels to Quatre Bras was long and tiring; it was remarked that the road through some of the woodland was so constricted that the sun filtered only fitfully through the trees, preventing the road from drying, and in several places the column had to move to the right or left to avoid the worst of the mud. Some refreshment was provided at Genappe, where the local people – perhaps at the instigation of staff officers from the army – had put out tubs of water for the weary marchers. At least one of the battalion commanders – Fassiefern of the 92nd – appreciated the nature of the coming trial and ordered his men to march in ranks as if on parade, and not to exceed 3 miles an hour to conserve their energy. As they drew nearer to the sounds of battle, the column encountered the dispiriting sight of walking wounded and local peasants fleeing from the fighting. The long march, under a hot sun, seems to have caused the first British casualty of the day: a rifleman of the 95th, leading the column, apparently went mad and died of heatstroke in a few minutes.

With Kempt's Brigade in the lead, the division reached Quatre Bras probably about or just after 2.00 pm. Instead of continuing down the Brussels–Charleroi highway, they turned left onto the Namur road, and took up a position along the road itself. The sound of firing immediately

Sir Thomas Picton in the uniform of a lieutenant general. His primary British decoration was the Order of the Bath, bestowed on 1 February 1813 and advanced to the level of Knight Grand Cross (GCB) on 2 January 1815. The decorations worn from the neck are the Army Gold Cross with four clasps, representing his participation in eight battles during the Peninsular War, from Busaco to Toulouse, and the Portuguese Order of the Tower and Sword. (*Engraving by W.L. Colls after Sir William Beechey*)

to the south, where the Dutch–Belgians still manfully contested the ground, would have been near, but the contending armies were hidden from view by crops so high that Cadell of the 28th stated that their only guide to deployment was that they could see where the mounted officers were, men on foot being entirely hidden. James Anton of the 42nd described how 'The stalks of the rye, like the reeds that grow on the margin of some swamp, opposed our advance; the tops were up to our bonnets, and we strode and groped our way through as fast as we could. By the time we reached a field of clover on the other side, we were

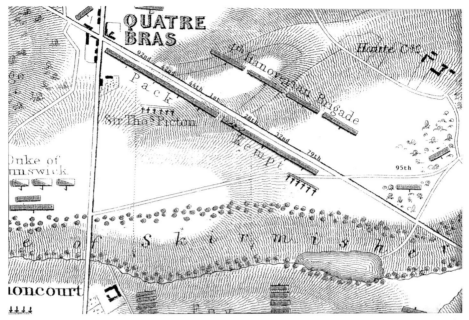

Battle of Quatre Bras: Picton's Division, with the positions of the eight battalions of Picton's Division.

very much straggled; however, we united in line as fast as time and our speedy advance would permit.'[1]

As the battalions drew up in line along the road many of the soldiers lay down to rest, some even intending to sleep; but the 42nd were disturbed by the irascible Pack, who for the second time that day had cause to berate the battalion commander Macara, this time for not having the men fix their bayonets. The order to 'fix' was given immediately, and must have brought home the imminence of combat; as Sergeant James Anton admitted, 'There is something animating to a soldier in the clash of the fixing bayonet.'[2] Following the two British brigades were Best's Hanoverians, who were ordered to take up a position immediately to the rear of Kempt and Pack, while the Brunswick Corps continued down the Brussels highway. The two artillery batteries deployed with Rogers's company on the left and Rettburg's on the right.

There is some doubt about the exact positioning of the eight British battalions along the Nivelles–Namur road, but Pack's Brigade was on the

Quatre Bras: Sir Philip Belson (mounted, left) directs the fire of his 28th against French cavalry. Clearly shown is the regiment's unique headdress, a 'stovepipe' shako bearing its singular regimental badges on front and back. (*Engraving by S. Mitan after Capt. George Jones, published 1817*)

right of the line, Kempt's on the left; the extreme right was held by the 92nd, the extreme left by the 79th, but for the 95th flung out beyond them, so that from right to left the order was almost certainly 92nd, 42nd, 44th, 1st, 28th, 32nd and 79th. In front of the position on the right was the large and dense Bossu Wood, and to the rear of the left flank the 'Cherry Wood', both of which could be used to secure the flanks. To the immediate front was a large farmstead, La Bergerie, on the Brussels highway, and further south two hamlets, Gemioncourt, just to the east of the highway, and Pireaumont, beyond the division's left flank. Further eastwards, down the Namur road, was a larger village, Thyle.

The 5th Division was a small enough force to oppose the numbers of French troops in their front, but they had one further asset: Wellington himself was present, and it was fortunate that he, rather than either the Prince of Orange or even Picton, was to conduct the action.

Wellington's initial task, when faced with an imminent major assault by the French, was to secure his position. On the right he ordered Prince Bernhard of Saxe-Weimar to clear the Bossu Wood with his Dutch–Belgians, and on the left he instructed the 95th – which having headed the British column was thus on the extreme left of the line they took up – to take Pireaumont and thus secure a position a short way south of the Namur road. Possession of Pireaumont was vital to facilitate communication with the Prussians. It was, however, already occupied by the French, and another party was seen to be making for the Cherry Wood, posing an immediate threat to Wellington's left wing.

The commander of the 95th's leading company, Jonathan Leach, had been temporarily detained in Brussels and had not at this stage caught up, so it was led in his absence by Lieutenant John Fitzmaurice. He was on the extreme left of the line when he saw Wellington ride up, looking pensive, and recognizing the dark green uniform of the 95th, the duke 'called out sharply, "Where is Barnard?" The word was passed for Sir Andrew and when he galloped up the duke said, "Barnard, those fellows are coming on; you must stop them by throwing yourself into that wood."'[3]

Barnard immediately told Fitzmaurice 'to take his company into the wood and "amuse" the enemy until he should bring up the rest of the Battalion'; and as he was moving off, Wellington called after him, telling him to go round a knoll that would shelter his men from incoming fire. Fitzmaurice got to the far edge of the Cherry Wood before the French came into view, and borrowing a rifle he loosed off the ball that he believed was the first British shot to be fired that day. (Shortly after this, Fitzmaurice's role in the battle ended when he was shot in the thigh, and although the ball was never extracted he lived for a further fifty-one years.) There was a sharp fight for possession of the wood until the 95th advanced and occupied some houses at Thyle, securing the flank.

Edward Costello gave an account of the 95th's fight:

The French, bringing up some artillery, commenced firing round-shot through the houses. At the time, feeling very thirsty, on entering the house and asking for a little water, while a young woman was in the act of handing me a jug, a shot passed through the house, knocking the dust about our ears; strange to say, she appeared less alarmed than myself … We were attacked by a number of light troops, and had to extend down a lane keeping up a hot fire. It is remarkable to see recruits in action generally more unfortunate than experienced soldiers; this I have often noticed. We had many fine recruits, who had only joined us of the eve of our leaving England, killed here. The reason of this is, that an old soldier will seek shelter from the enemy's fire if any near his post, while the inexperienced recruit appears, as it were, petrified to the spot by the whizzing balls.

We were now joined by a number of Belgians, and received orders to advance, which we did, driving the enemy through the skirts of a wood, passing a field of rye which obstructed our view of the enemy. A regiment of French infantry on our right, as we emerged from the wood, gave us a running fire; I was in the act of taking aim at some of our opposing skirmishers, when a ball struck my trigger-finger, tearing it off, at the same time turning the trigger on one side, while another ball passed through the mess-tin on my knapsack ... We wounded men made the best of our way to the rear, and, on my return to the house at the corner of the lane, I found the pretty girl still in possession, although there were not less than a dozen shot-holes through it. I requested her to leave, but she would not, as her father, she said, had desired her to take care of the house until he returned from Brussels.[4]

In the centre of the position, Wellington attempted to hold Gemioncourt with some Netherlandish troops, and as some battalions of the 5th Division were still arriving, ordered the 28th from the highway to assist. The Dutch temporarily took the village and formed on its southern side, but as French troops from the division of General Maximilien-Sébastien Foy came up to threaten their flank, the position clearly became untenable and they withdrew, the 28th counter-marching to resume their position along the Namur road.

In accordance with the usual practice, once the troops had drawn up in line their skirmishers were sent out to oppose their French counterparts who always preceded an attack. Kempt's Brigade sent out the light companies of the three battalions (the fourth, 1/95th, was still on the far left), supplemented by an extra company of the 79th, and some extra men that the battalion had trained as 'marksmen'. This movement was ordered by Wellington in person, and for about an hour they held their ground as the main position was bombarded by some forty-two French guns assembled between the Brussels road and Pireaumont, even though the troops in the line were largely hidden from the French by the standing crops.

The British light companies were supplemented by members of Best's Brigade, held at the rear of the British line. Except for their skirmishers, the Osteröde and Münden battalions were not engaged, although took some casualties from long-range fire (their only officer casualty was Lieutenant Janish, who was killed leading his battalion's skirmishers.[5] The Verden Battalion was also deployed in open order; they returned one officer killed, two wounded and two missing, the latter taken prisoner when they mistook some French skirmishers for Brunswickers, and the experienced Captain Siegmund Braune of the King's German Legion 8th Line Battalion, serving as major in the Verden, had a narrow escape when his horse was killed. The Lüneburg Battalion was deployed near the highway and covered Kühlmann's horse artillery troop of the King's German Legion, part of the 1st Division's artillery, when it came up; they lost two officers wounded and one missing.

The steadiness with which the Hanoverian skirmishers performed elicited admiration from the more experienced British witnesses; Harry Ross-Lewin remarked that despite suffering casualties, 'they continued the contest with undiminished gallantry. I afterwards heard German officers say, that it was hardly fair to send troops who were quite ignorant of this species of warfare, and had no idea of taking advantage of the ground to oppose the experienced French tirailleurs.'[6]

At this stage Wellington's only artillery available to support the 5th Division were its own two batteries, and thus they were greatly outmatched by the quantity of the French guns. Rettburg's company unlimbered near Quatre Bras village, on the right of the divisional line, with Rogers on the left. Rogers came under heavy fire and sustained casualties, but Rettburg demonstrated his experience by positioning his vehicles under cover, and manned his guns with the minimum of personnel to protect the rest, and consequently his casualties were very light. (Later in the day it appears that Rettburg was moved further left, so it is possible that Rogers had had to withdraw temporarily).

The skirmishing was followed by a concerted French attack along the entire line, the French possession of Gemioncourt in the centre of the position enabling Ney to deploy uninterruptedly. The assault involved Jérôme Bonaparte, Napoleon's brother, commanding the French 6th Division. He sent one brigade into Bossu Wood and led the other forward to the west of the Brussels highway, between it and the wood. To the immediate east of the highway, Foy led his 9th Division towards Quatre Bras village, while further east still General Gilbert Bachelu's 5th Division made for Wellington's left.

Wellington appears to have initiated his own attack before the main French force arrived; he ordered Picton to detach one battalion to support the skirmishers, and Kempt rode up to Lieutenant Colonel Neil Douglas of the 79th and ordered him to advance. As they drove back the French infantry the remainder of Kempt's battalions began to advance, rising from the cover of the high crops and sent musketry into the head of Bachelu's advancing column. Their sudden and perhaps unexpected appearance caused the head of the column to crumble. It broke before bayonets could be crossed and carried away with it the following units, which fled beyond Gemioncourt.

This reverse was witnessed by Foy in the centre of the French attack, and that most capable officer, while allowing three of his regiments to continue their advance, detached the 100me Ligne to a position south of Gemioncourt, which

Quatre Bras: Sir Thomas Picton orders Kempt's brigade to advance. Picton (centre, with sword upraised) is shown in the correct frock coat but with a regulation bicorn hat rather than his civilian 'round hat'. (*Engraving by S. Mitan after Capt. George Jones, published 1817*)

Before Quatre Bras: the Duke of Wellington (right) confers with the Duke of Brunswick, the latter wearing the black uniform and death's head shako badge of his Brunswick Corps. (*Print by S. Mitan after Capt. George Jones, published 1817*)

halted the advance of Kempt's men. The other two British battalions did not advance very far beyond the Namur road, but the 79th for some time exchanged musketry until their ammunition was expended, when, with No. 8 Company having rejoined from the skirmish line, and covered by the 32nd on their right, they retired to a position about 50 yards in front of their original line, and lay down under cover.

Elsewhere the French attack enjoyed more success; the Netherlanders were pushed back through the Bossu Wood, and Wellington directed some of the newly arrived Brunswick Corps to support them. All began to give way under French pressure; the Duke of Brunswick charged with his squadron of lancers to cover their withdrawal, but they were beaten off, and as, near La Bergerie, the duke attempted to rally one of his battalions he was shot through the body and borne from the battle, mortally wounded. At this critical moment the French attack was seconded by the light cavalry division of General Hippolyte Piré, who somewhat unusually for a French officer had emigrated at the time of the

Revolution and had served in British pay before returning to the country of his birth. His division formed the corps cavalry of II Corps, comprising the 1er and 6me Chasseurs à Cheval and the 5me and 6me Chevau-Légers-Lanciers, and their first participation in the battle almost led to the elimination of the enemy's commander.

When Kempt's Brigade advanced, part of Pack's did likewise, the 42nd and 44th moving further forward than the rest; the 92nd, being the last to take up their position, remained to secure the division's right flank. The battalion's own right flank rested upon the buildings of Quatre Bras village, with the regimental aid post being set up in the village itself. Wellington positioned himself, on foot and with his staff, on the left of the 92nd. One of their officers later suggested that so much fire was directed at them because the French had noted his presence, but despite the storm of shot the duke appeared as cool and detached as if he were observing a review. As the French charged, however, he realized that he was in mortal danger, had to mount hastily and even drew his sword as the French cavalry threatened to overrun his staff. He called to the 92nd to lie down and jumped the low bank behind which they were sheltering, men and all.

As the chasseurs came on, galloping up the Brussels highway, the 92nd fired, the company on their extreme right wheeling until they were parallel with the highway and so taking the chasseurs in the flank, and they also came under fire from Brunswickers in the edges of the Bossu Wood. The musketry brought down many and caused the remainder to veer away, and it seems that a second attempt was made, with similar result. A few horsemen managed to get up the road and into Quatre Bras village, where they cut down some stragglers, and attacked the 92nd's assistant surgeon John Stewart as he was helping a wounded man; he was stabbed in the side and had his bonnet cut in two, but survived. One French officer, not realizing that his men had fallen away, continued to charge on and galloped down the road into the rear of the battalion. Wellington observed his progress and called out, 'Damn it, 92nd, will you allow that fellow to escape?', whereupon some men faced about and brought him down. The French officer, whose name was Burgoine, was shot in both feet and must have been helped by the 92nd, for he became friends with Lieutenant Robert Winchester and they subsequently shared a billet in Brussels, presumably while both were convalescing. Burgoine and his family later entertained Winchester at their home in Paris.

Quatre Bras: a scene depicting an attack by French lancers (mid-ground, left centre), the British evidently intended to be the 5th Division from the presence of infantry in Highland dress. (*Print by T. Sutherland after William Heath*)

Piré's two lancer regiments appear to have charged rather later than the chasseurs, and to rather more effect. The 42nd and 44th, having advanced further than the others, were somewhat taken by surprise. There was clearly much confusion, caused partly by the tall crops, which also hindered the cavalry from seeing their target and thus from timing the pace of their charge so that they would engage at maximum speed. To mark the position of the infantry a singular tactic was employed, as described by Major Richard Llewellyn of the 28th: 'The rye in the field was so high, that to see anything beyond our own ranks was impossible. The Enemy, even, in attacking our Squares, were obliged to make a daring person desperately ride forward to plant a flag, as a mark, at the very point of our bayonets.'[7]

Each of the infantry battalions was left largely to its own devices, as stated by Lieutenant Alexander Forbes of the 79th: 'Every regiment, from the sudden and peculiar nature of the attack, seemed to act independently for its own immediate defence, a measure rendered still more necessary by the Enemy's superiority in Cavalry, and the Regiments being now posted, not at prescribed intervals of alignment, but conformably to the exigency of the moment, by which each of them was exposed to be separately assailed.'

The first of the battalions to be charged by the lancers was the 42nd, to the right of the 44th, both battalions in line. The 42nd saw them coming, but it appears they were mixed in with some fugitive Brunswickers, which may have caused confusion, and some of the lancers approached at a sedate pace – Sergeant Alexander McSween of the 42nd said as if they were reconnoitring – which must also have been the cause of hesitation. McSween had been a prisoner of war and knew what French cavalry looked like, and told his officer that they were French. The reply was, 'No, they belong to the Prince of Orange.' McSween was unconvinced and decided to see what the reaction would be if he shot at them; and some old soldiers of the battalion, and some of the 44th, recognizing the identity of the approaching horsemen, also began to fire. Sir Denis Pack himself ordered them to cease, thinking they were shooting at allies; but then the 42nd's skirmishers, who as usual had been thrown forward in front of the line,

The death of Sir Robert Macara at Quatre Bras, killed as he was being borne away, wounded, by French cavalry who supposedly recognized him as an officer of note by the decorations he was wearing. (*Engraving by S. Mitan after Capt. George Jones, published 1817*)

came running back shouting, 'Square! square! French cavalry!', and a German cavalryman, presumably a Brunswicker, rode up shouting, 'Franchee! Franchee!' The 42nd immediately began to form square, the universal protection against cavalry, but the lancers were upon them before the square could be closed, and there was hand-to-hand fighting as the Highlanders tried to complete the formation. The square did close, but some lancers were trapped within it, and were bayoneted by the two companies that were closing the square.

The 42nd saved itself by completing this manoeuvre, but suffered severely in the process. The battalion commander, Sir Robert Macara, was wounded and four of his men began to carry him away, presumably to an aid post near the village; but they were surrounded by French lancers who, it was said, recognized him as an officer of rank by virtue of the decorations he was wearing, and cut them all down. According to James Anton, Macara was killed by a lance thrust through his chin and into his brain. When this act became known to the men of the 42nd, its effect was profound for the rest of the campaign; when subsequently French troops begged for mercy they were answered

> by the appalling cry of 'no quarter' [and] 'where's Macara?' … until it was necessary for our officers, from a sense of humanity, to intervene in favour of the French, and they did all that was possible to restrain the fury of their men, often at the imminent peril of their own lives. An officer of the Highlanders … in relating to me these particulars, declared that he never saw our men so savage, and that for awhile it was impossible by any means to curb their fury.[8]

It was, as Sir Walter Scott observed, an example of the old Highland maxim, 'Today for revenge, tomorrow for mourning'.[9]

Upon Macara's fall, command of the battalion devolved upon Lieutenant Colonel Robert Dick, but he was wounded almost immediately. Major George Davidson then took command, but he, too, went down (he was conveyed to Brussels but died of his injury), so Major John Campbell took over, so that the battalion had four commanding officers within a few minutes.

As the square closed it is likely that some men were left outside it, including, apparently, Captain Archibald Menzies, who commanded the grenadier company. He was afoot, having left his horse in the charge of a drummer and, being a large, powerful swordsman ('hand to hand, more than a match for six ordinary men',[10] was reported to have downed a number of French cavalry before he collapsed with as many as sixteen wounds. One of the earliest published anecdotes of the battle claimed that the drummer left the horse to assist a severely wounded private, who lay nearby, Donald McIntosh; who exclaimed, as a French lancer made to seize the animal, 'ye manna tak that beast; it belangs to our captain here,' and then shot the lancer before himself falling back dead. The story continued with a French officer stooping over his mount to thrust at Menzies; but the captain 'resolutely seized him by the leg, and, after a short struggle, dragged him from the saddle.' Another lancer rode up and endeavoured to spear the Scot, but Menzies twisted the officer on top of himself and the lancer's blow ran through his own officer instead. Help was at hand, and a member of his own regiment dragged Menzies towards the square of the 92nd, into the safety of which he was deposited.[11] Despite extensive injuries Menzies survived – he had also been wounded severely at Burgos – and it was said in later life that he would entertain his guests with the story of his seventeen wounds, fourteen of which he claimed were mortal!

A curious story involving the 42nd, probably from this action, was told to a reporter from the *Newcastle Leader* in 1889 by an aged man, John Scott, who claimed to have been present as a musician, aged about 11, the son of a member of the Black Watch but not regularly enlisted. He claimed that his part in the battle was to play his triangle and shout 'Scotland for ever!' until he was hoarse. If his story were true – there were two Scotts in the regiment, Corporal Alexander and Private Duncan, one of whom may have been his father – then John Scott would have been one of the last survivors of the battle. (The longest-surviving British officer was Captain William Hewitt of the 14th Foot who died on 26 October 1891 – although Ensign Frederick Scharnhorst of the 5th KGL Line Battalion lived until 30 July 1893 – and the last British survivor of all is believed to have been Private Maurice Shea of the 73rd, who died in Canada on 4 February 1892.)[12]

On the left of the 42nd, the 44th was caught up in the same French charge. Some of the lancers wheeled and either passed behind the 42nd, or between the battalions, and came at the 44th from the rear.

Lieutenant Colonel Hamerton of the 44th realized that they were too near for the battalion to form square safely – indeed, the cavalry was only recognized as hostile when they began to cut down the men whose position was customarily at the rear of the line – so he decided on a remarkable manoeuvre. He ordered 'rear rank, about face', and when it stood back to back with the front rank, ordered them to deliver a volley at close range. It stopped the French charge in its tracks and threw them into confusion. Infantry in line were usually fatally vulnerable to a cavalry charge, and Hamerton's manoeuvre, for which no instruction existed in the drill manual, could only have been performed by troops of the highest calibre. William Siborne, whilst admitting that the troops' realization of the perilous nature of their position must have led them to take aim more deliberately than usual, put the incident into context:

> Never, perhaps, did British infantry display its characteristic coolness and steadiness more eminently than on this trying occasion. To have stood in a thin two-deep line, awaiting, and prepared to receive, the onset of hostile cavalry, would have been looked upon at least as a most hazardous experiment; but, with its rear so suddenly menaced, and its flanks unsupported, to have stood as if rooted to the ground, to have repulsed its assailants with so steady and well-directed fire that numbers of them were destroyed – this was a feat of arms which the oldest, and best-disciplined corps in the world might have in vain hoped to accomplish; yet most successfully and completely was this achieved by the gallant 2nd battalion of the 44th.[13]

This action involved another incident of extraordinary heroism. With the battalion in line, the two colours, positioned in the centre, were especially vulnerable and a party of French lancers made for them, to attempt to capture these most precious symbols of regimental identity. The King's Colour was carried by Ensign Peter Cooke, a 26-year-old from a Tipperary family; he was killed. The regimental colour was borne by Ensign James Christie, who was that rarest of beings, a non-commissioned officer who had been commissioned into his own regiment rather than being transferred to another corps on officially becoming a 'gentleman'. Christie had been the 44th's sergeant major, commissioned on 26 November 1812 and thus the most senior of the battalion's ensigns. A lancer stabbed at him, the lance passing through his left eye, through his tongue and into his lower jaw. Realising that he was desperately wounded,

Christie deliberately fell upon the colour to protect it with his body. All the lancer achieved was to tear off a bit of it, and was bayoneted from his horse before he could ride off with his prize. Christie survived and was promoted to lieutenant, only to be placed on half pay in March 1816. George O'Malley recovered and kept the torn fragment of colour.

In the hiatus between attacks by the French cavalry, the more advanced battalions seem to have withdrawn a short way, although there was clearly some confusion, as observed by James Anton of the 42nd:

> An attempt was now made to form us in line; for we stood mixed in one irregular mass – grenadier, light, and battalion companies – a noisy group; such is the inevitable consequence of a rapid succession of commanders. Our covering sergeants were called out on purpose that each company might form on the right of its sergeant; an excellent plan had it been adopted, but a cry arose that another charge of cavalry was approaching, and this plan was abandoned.[14]

So far, Ney's attempt to drive the allies from the crossroads had failed, although he was making gradual progress in Bossu Wood. The French effort was directed on the right and centre of the allied line; no very serious attempt seems to have been made against the left, and indeed the 79th, still the division's left-hand battalion (excluding the 95th in the woods and buildings further east) was not seriously engaged. The battalion was withdrawn to the road and formed into column (to permit it to move quickly if required), and formed square when the cavalry attacks were mounted elsewhere, but was not threatened. When French troops were not in the way, however, the whole line was pelted with artillery fire, which took a toll. It was recorded that when shells fell among the 92nd – these projectiles sometimes lay and spluttered on the ground before exploding – a rather unedifying scramble occurred as troops sought to distance themselves from the detonation. In one case a Highlander exclaimed to his officer, 'Did you see that, sir?' after a cannon ball clipped off his bonnet, leaving him unharmed but for him having 'a wild look, and the concussion addled his brains for a day or two'.[15] Because a square was especially vulnerable to artillery fire, there was a constant process of change of formation from line to square when cavalry approached, and then back into line again.

Desperate to make an impression as the day wore on, Ney turned to the III Cavalry Corps, commanded by the renowned General François-Étienne Kellermann, comprised of cuirassiers and carabiniers, the heaviest cavalry whose role was almost exclusively as a striking force on the battlefield; but of the four brigades in the corps, only one was present, Guiton's Brigade of L'Heritier's 11th Cavalry Division, comprising the 8me and 11me cuirassiers. Instead of the huge force that might have been employed, the cuirassiers available numbered barely 800; yet Ney ordered them to charge. Their first attack was made against the right of the 5th Division's line, apparently not only against the 42nd and 44th, but the 92nd as well. Wellington was still with the Gordons, which was in line: Lieutenant Robert Winchester recalled: 'Lord Wellington, who was by this time in the rear of the

The pride of Napoleon's army: before the campaign the French cuirassiers were regarded as among the most formidable of the allies' opponents, especially impressive by virtue of their reputation, armour and huge mounts. (*Print by Martinet*)

centre of the Regiment, said, "92nd, don't fire until I tell you", and when they came within twenty or thirty paces of us, his Grace gave the order to fire, which killed and wounded an immense number of men and horses, on which they immediately faced about and galloped off.'[16]

This was the first occasion on which British troops had encountered the armoured cuirassiers, and before the campaign there had been some discussion about how they might be fought, and whether their armoured breastplates really were bulletproof. They were not: initially French cuirasses were supposed to be 'proof' against three musket shots at thirty paces, but when numbers failed this test the standard was reduced to one shot at longer range. When it was realized that the onrushing cavalry were cuirassiers – it was not obvious immediately as some were wearing their cloaks – the order was given to fire at the horses. James Anton described the first charge:

Our last file had got into square, and into its proper place, so far as unequalized companies could form a square, when the cuirassiers dashed full on two of its faces: their heavy horses and steel armour seemed sufficient to bury us under them … General Pack was on the right angle of the front face of the square, and he lifted his hat towards the French officer, as he was wont to do when receiving a salute. I suppose our assailants construed our forbearance as an indication of surrendering; a false idea: not a blow had been struck nor a musket levelled; but when the general raised his hat, it served as a signal, though not a preconcerted one, but entirely accidental; for we were doubtful whether our officer commanding was protracting the order, waiting for the general's command … be that as it may, a most destructive fire was opened; riders, in heavy armour, fell tumbling from their horses; the horses reared, plunged, and fell on the dismounted riders … shrieks and groans of men, the neighing of horses, and the discharge of musketry, rent the air, as men and horses mixed together in one heap of indiscriminate slaughter. Those who were able to fly, fled towards a wood on our right.[17]

Subsequent cavalry attacks seem to have been mounted by cuirassiers and light cavalry in conjunction if contemporary accounts are correct. The next battalion in line from the 42nd was still the 44th, and they also felt the weight of the charge. Having retired from their early advanced position – Lieutenant Alexander Riddock stated the distance to have been 50 or 60 paces – they, like the other battalions in the brigade, had left behind two companies, or as many men as needed to screen the battalion frontage, as skirmishers, and they kept up a constant fire upon the opposing French skirmishers. Riddock, in command of the 44th's advanced party, fired away until his men had exhausted their ammunition, and its resupply was 'intercepted by the frequent and daring charges of the French cavalry round and round, and in the rear of our little Squares'.

With his men falling to the fire of the French skirmishers and unable to reply for want of cartridges, Riddock called his situation to the attention of Pack himself (that indomitable general must have ridden forward in a hiatus in the French cavalry attacks), who told Riddock to rejoin his battalion. He gathered his skirmishers into a body but another cavalry attack swept around them, 'round and round every Square, showing no mercy, dashing at and sticking the helpless wounded Officers and men that unfortunately lay without the protection of our Square. I could compare them to nothing but a swarm of bees.' With his small number of men, Riddock might have sought salvation in a 'rallying square', in which a knot of men gathered closely together and faced outwards, bayonets levelled; but with no ammunition left, a single horseman riding into them could have caused such a formation to collapse; so Riddock chose an audacious manoeuvre:

> I instantly formed four deep and charged bayonets, the rear rank with ported arms, and fought my way through the French Cavalry until I reached the south side of the Square of my Regiment. But so hot and hard pressed was the Regiment on all sides, that I could obtain no admission, and my ammunition being gone … we had no other alternative than lie down close to the Square, and crave their friendly protection.[18]

The 44th was not alone in running out of ammunition. Having driven off the first charge, the 42nd again formed line and inspected their cartridge boxes, and found them almost empty. Their new commanding officer, John Campbell, ordered them to search the cartridge boxes of the dead and wounded, which provided some relief, although as Anton recalled, and notwithstanding the impact of their first volley against the cuirassiers, 'We had wasted a deal of ammunition this day, and surely to very little effect … Our commanding officer cautioned us against this useless expenditure, and we became a little more economical.'[19] The number of young soldiers in the battalion must have been a contributing factor, for it was recognized that such men tended to blaze away with less effect even than the experienced men, whose muskets were inaccurate enough, without firing too high, which was a common failing in the maelstrom of battle.

The division's casualties were mounting to an alarming degree. In total the 42nd lost, in killed and wounded, 18 officers, 16 sergeants and 254 rank and file, not many fewer than the number that would be fit to fight at Waterloo two days later. Alexander Riddock thought that his 44th had lost more than 200 men, although the returns reveal that their casualties in 'other ranks' amounted to 10 dead, 94 wounded and 17 missing. Estimates of casualties often conflict with the perception of those present; many men could be 'missing' and return subsequently so as not to feature in the finalized casualty returns, and some men might slip away for legitimate or other reasons during the fighting, so reducing sometimes quite considerably, the number of stalwarts who continued to stand in the firing line. By the time Riddock rejoined the main body of his battalion the 44th was able only to form four weak companies.

Like the 42nd, the battalion had lost their commanding officer. John Hamerton had been wounded, slightly according to the official returns, but it was sufficiently serious to remove him from the action. Upon his death (as a general) in 1855 his obituary stated that the wounds – in head and thigh – had left him insensible, and that he was only saved by a loyal NCO who conveyed him to medical attention. (The story is perhaps compromised by the fact that the named NCO does not appear to feature in the battalion roll, although two privates of the same name were present.)

Command of the 44th devolved upon George O'Malley, so recently arrived, and he stated that 'the gallantry and coolness of the French Lancers altogether, and the great bravery and steadiness of the soldiers of the 42nd and 44th Regiments, both of which Corps at the time were all strangers to me, made such an impression on my mind as never has, nor never can be, removed.'[20]

It is testimony to the training and resilience of such units, and of the smoothness by which command could pass from one individual to another without much inhibiting efficiency, that even after suffering such losses, especially in officers, battalions could continue to function. The losses were so great, however, that for the remainder of the day the 42nd and 44th acted together as a single entity, under the direct command of Sir Denis Pack himself; perhaps he regarded this as necessary given that one battalion was onto its fourth commanding officer of the day, and the other was led by a stranger.

The next battalion in line, on the extreme left of Pack's Brigade, was the 3/1st Royal Scots, although from the start of the action, almost as soon as it marched into the line, it moved to the left, apparently by order of Picton himself, and acted for the rest of the day not with Pack's Brigade but with Kempt's, under the direction of Kempt and Picton. Sir Thomas seems, at this stage of the day, to have positioned himself at the very centre of the divisional line; as an element of 'command and control' this would have made sense, in the knowledge of the right of the line, the bulk of Pack's Brigade, was under the personal supervision of Wellington.

As with the remainder of the division, the 3/1st suffered a severe trial, as described by one of their officers who had served with them in the Peninsula:

the battalion … never evinced more steadiness and determined bravery … the battalion was taken from its place in the centre of the 5th Division by a movement to its own left, by order of Sir Thomas Picton, and instantly by command of that lamented officer brought into action by a charge upon a column of the Enemy; it succeeded beyond our most sanguine expectations in routing this column, who afterwards formed … and then commenced a most galling fire upon us which we returned with the utmost steadiness and precision. The battalion was brought into action under the most trying circumstances imaginable, and continued so for a long time; but they never for one moment lost sight of that character which upon former occasions they had so well earned and maintained. The ground through which they moved was planted with corn that took the tallest men up to the shoulders; and the Enemy by this, and the advantage of the rising ground, threw in volley after volley of grape and musketry, which did astonishing execution.[21]

No less than eighteen of the battalion's officers became casualties in this furious action, five of whom were killed, and as happened not infrequently in such battles, the regimental colours, the rallying-point of the battalion in time of emergency, became especial targets. Three officers were killed while carrying the colours, including Ensigns Alexander Robertson and James Grant Kennedy, the death of the latter providing one of the most poignant incidents of the campaign. Kennedy, the son of an Inverness physician, was a boy of 16, and bearing his colour in front of the battalion was hit in the arm but continued on until shot dead. He fell, grasping the colour so tightly that when a sergeant – presumably his 'coverer' and in effect bodyguard – tried to raise the flag it could not be prised from his fingers. The sergeant had to lift the body and carry it in order to take the colour to safety, and it was said that the officer commanding the opposing French chivalrously ordered his men not to fire until the boy was back among his comrades. The incident entered regimental folklore to the extent that a representation of it was one of only three illustrations depicting the regiment's history in the regimental handbook of 1960.[22]

Another ensign lost in this action was Charles Graham, also while carrying a colour: he fell as if dead from the concussion of a cannon ball passing his head (a strange injury but one reported on many occasions at the time). He was roused by French soldiers stripping off his clothes – looting the dead was a universal practice – and when he begged for their return they refused, saying he was as good as dead. He was roughly treated while a prisoner, but contrived to escape, almost naked, and was found by some Prussians. He returned to the battalion some four or five days after Waterloo, dressed in Prussian clothing, having been officially listed as dead in the first published list of casualties. So many officers were struck while carrying the colours that at one stage the King's Colour was taken up by the battalion's Sergeant Major Quick; he, too, was killed.

Another officer stated that it was only with difficulty that the battalion was halted after its charge and brought back to its original position, so eager were the men to continue, although the limited nature of a charge was crucial so that the unit could re-form in time to meet any new assault. It was reported that Picton thanked them and said he would bring their conduct to public notice, only for his death to prevent it. This was not an isolated case: he also heartened the 28th by calling, 'Twenty-eighth, if I live to see the Prince Regent, I shall lay before him your bravery this day'[23] and at one critical moment called on them to 'remember Egypt', the scene of their greatest exploits. In the same action Kempt took off his hat and declared that the 28th was still the 28th, and that their conduct would never be forgotten. Knowing the British soldiers' dislike of elaborate oratory this must have been appreciated, for brevity if nothing else, for his remark was answered by a cheer.

The Royal Scots and the 28th suffered such losses in this action that for the rest of the day they were combined to act as a single unit, like the combination of the 42nd and 44th. The Royals lost more than three times the casualties of the 28th – five officers and twenty other ranks killed (plus Graham, captured and believed dead) and twelve officers and 180 other ranks wounded, while the 28th lost eleven dead and sixty-four wounded. Among the 28th's wounded was one of its bravest officers, William Irwin, lieutenant of grenadiers, who was stated to be the strongest man in the regiment (once in the Peninsula he threw onto its back a rampaging bullock that was creating havoc). He had gone out with the battalion's skirmishers and was shot through the thigh, and as the French cavalry charged he managed to crawl back to the battalion and lay beneath the bayonets of the kneeling front rank of the square until the danger had passed.

The next battalion in the line, the 32nd, endured the same trial as the others, described with some sangfroid by Major Felix Calvert:

> [the battalion] formed line awaiting the approach of the Enemy, who were descending in column from the opposite hill. When this attacking force had crossed both hedges lining the meadow in the bottom, and had commenced ascending our position, the 32nd Regiment poured in upon it a heavy fire succeeded by a charge. This the Enemy did not wait to receive, but retired with precipitation, and getting entangled in the hedges on returning to their position must have suffered considerable loss. We halted and re-formed at the first hedge, when Sir Thomas Picton desired the Regiment to retire to its original position. The 79th Regiment on our left, carried on by its ardour, went on much further, crossed the meadow, and even ventured to assail the Enemy's position. They were, however, soon recalled. Attacks similar to the above were received several times during the evening, and always with similar results.[24]

Harry Ross-Lewin described how the 32nd suffered some casualties as they withdrew from their charge, when the French, having struggled back through the hedges, re-formed 'instead of retiring, and commenced from behind it a most destructive fire on our division, which was so much exposed on the side of the hill; in consequence, the regiments were ordered to fall back, and lie down on the reverse slope. My regiment, while retiring thither, suffered severely.'[25]

Among those killed was one of the three Irish captains mentioned previously, Edward Whitty. There are two accounts of his death: Ross-Lewin stated that he was 'remarking what a number of escapes he had had, and showing how his clothes had been shot through, when a musket-ball entered his mouth and killed him on the spot.'[26] Ross-Lewin was presumably with his own company at the time so probably not beside Whitty when he was struck; another officer apparently was, and described the action:

> We fired a volley and charged them down to the ditch, in getting over which they lost numbers. When we got down the bugle sounded for us to

return and form in line upon the colours, which we did, and were pursued by them again; we charged them a second time, and actually the ground was covered with dead and wounded bodies. As our company was next on the left of the colours, we were in the very thick of the fire all the time … In the second charge, a shell burst right on the colours, took away the silk of the regimental colour and the whole of the right section of the fifth company, amongst whom was my lamented friend, Captain W[hitty]; his head was literally blown to atoms. [Ensign James] Mc[Conchy], who held the colour that suffered, was only slightly wounded. This was not a moment for grief or much reflection, as the command of the company devolved on me.[27]

Both the other Irish captains who with Whitty formed a triumvirate of friends were mortally wounded. Ross-Lewin told a poignant story about one of them, who some years before had killed an officer in a duel into which he had been provoked, the circumstances of which 'always affected him most sensibly'. The recollection remained with him to the end: as he was borne away, 'almost the last words that he uttered were in allusion to the fatal termination of his private quarrel. "Whoso sheddeth man's blood," said he, repeating the passage of Scripture, "by man shall his blood be shed."'[28] (Genesis 9, 6). A very great deal more blood was to be shed before the day was out.

For much of the afternoon the bulk of the defence of the position at Quatre Bras had fallen to the 5th Division; their role in holding the crossroads, blocking the route to Brussels and maintaining a west-east communication with the Prussians is difficult to overestimate. A number of episodes could be regarded as crucial to the outcome of the campaign, but the efforts of Picton and his division were more significant than most. Assistance, however, was at last forthcoming.

In the late afternoon reinforcements at last arrived, in two brigades of Sir Charles Alten's 3rd Division, the 5th British Brigade of Major General Sir Colin Halkett, and Count Kielmansegge's 1st Hanoverian Brigade. They had been marching all day – about 27 miles – under a hot sun, with only a brief break at Nivelles to receive rations, but the situation was so critical that they were hurried into action without delay. Kielmansegge's Hanoverians were sent to secure the extreme left of Picton's line, beyond where the 95th were holding on in the woods and buildings. As soon as Halkett arrived he was ordered by

Picton to move through Bossu Wood and if possible to fall upon the French left, in order to secure Picton's precarious right flank. Before Halkett could begin this movement an ADC of Pack's (possibly Edmund L'Estrange) rode up to beg immediate support for Pack's Brigade, which had almost run out of ammunition and without help might have to retire. Immediately Halkett detached one of his battalions – the 2/69th under Lieutenant Colonel Charles Morice – to move to their left and put themselves under Pack's orders. As Halkett began to prepare to obey Picton's instructions he encountered the Brunswick Corps, shaken by the death of their duke, retiring; so he remained there to support them rather than advance on the French left.

A very able and experienced officer, Halkett and an ADC rode forward to reconnoitre in person, and saw large numbers of French cavalry, including cuirassiers, preparing to advance. He sent an ADC to Morice to instruct him to take precautions, and Morice formed his battalion into square. At this moment the 69th was in a small hollow, with standing crops 5 or 6 feet high all round, so that beyond the hollow nothing could be observed. Then a senior officer rode up – Halkett and the 69th's officers were loath to identify him, but it was the Prince of Orange – and asked what Morice was doing. He repeated Halkett's warning, but the prince declared that no cavalry was near and that the 69th should form into line. With their view obscured, the battalion complied with the order just as cuirassiers burst upon them, 'as if by magic ... quite unperceived and [they] rushed out as from an ambuscade on the flank of the line. We were absolutely defenceless: an attempt was made to form square but ... they rode through and over our little Battalion,'[29] according to the 69th's Captain George Barlow. When trying to re-form the square, Major Henry Lindsay had three companies halt their movement and open fire; they were overrun and the square not formed, and to the day of his death Lindsay blamed himself for the slaughter, although the culpability was actually the Prince of Orange's. The battalion lost five officers and 150 other rank casualties, and lost a colour.

The remainder of Halkett's Brigade also suffered; the 30th Foot, apparently the next unit west from the 69th, held firm, but the other two, the 2/73rd and 33rd were forced, under heavy fire, into the cover of Bossu Wood, the 33rd in particular in a state of great disorder and almost losing one of their colours.

This episode deprived Pack of the support he required, so that the 5th Division remained the bulwark against French attacks. Further reinforcement, however, was at hand, in the brigades of Foot Guards under Peregrine Maitland and Sir John Byng, from the 1st Division. They, too, had made a most tiring march – 'The heat was excessive, and the men suffered much from the weight of their packs,' according to Captain Harry Powell of the 1st Foot Guards.[30] As they came up in stages they were directed towards the Bois de Bossu and the region to the west of the Charleroi–Brussels highway; but they arrived in time to open a destructive fire upon the French cavalry rampaging around the 69th. (Morice claimed that but for the arrival of the Guards only he and his adjutant – presumably because they were the only ones mounted – would have escaped; although for Morice himself it was but a temporary salvation, for he was shot four times and killed at Waterloo.)

Along with these newcomers to the battle there came a much-needed reinforcement of artillery, to supplement the outnumbered guns of the 5th Division: the foot companies of Captains William Lloyd of the Royal Artillery and Andrew Cleeves of the King's German Legion, both attached to the 3rd Division, and subsequently the King's German Legion horse artillery troop of Captain Henry Khülmann, attached to the 1st Division. Their arrival was significant, but there still remained a severe trial for the beleaguered 5th Division to withstand.

The first of these was a final great attack by French cavalry, described by Alexander Riddock of the 44th as 'a dreadful contest ... that threatened total destruction'. By this time the infantry they attacked must have been worn down by fatigue as well as casualties, and in the case of the 44th their musketry seems to have become spasmodic. It could be delivered in various ways, from volley firing to 'file firing', in which the men of each file fired in turn, maintaining a continuous discharge along a line but lacking the immediate impact of a controlled volley. This seems to have occurred spontaneously among the 44th, as Riddock recalled:

Sir Denis Pack rode up to the bayonets of the 44th with his hat in his hand waving to cease firing, when Col. O'Malley called out to us, 'You are as brave as lions; attend to my orders, and we shall yet repulse them.' His orders were attended to, and the firing increased with double vigour, with such effect that no penetration could be effected by the French Cavalry on any point of the British Square. The loss of the French Cavalry sustained in this contest was immense; several hundreds of men and horses covered the ground all around us. This was the last charge made by the French Cavalry on the 5th Division for the afternoon, but [it] was succeeded by a hot and destructive fire of musketry and artillery until past eight o'clock p.m.[31]

The supporting fire from the newly arrived artillery companies of Lloyd and Cleeves must have been crucial in repelling this last French cavalry attack, although under fire themselves from French artillery. A section of Cleeves' guns in particular was described as having a devastating effect; Captain Samuel Rudyerd of Lloyd's company recalled how 'two of Major Cleeves' Guns enfiladed the Charleroi road, and had literally macadamized it with the carcasses of the Cuirassiers and their horses, who had made a most desperate charge in great force, but never returned to it.'[32]

Instead, a strong French infantry thrust was renewed in the direction of Quatre Bras village, where the 92nd stood between them and the possibility of breaking the line. The French approached in two columns, one along the highway

The 92nd advance at Quatre Bras. Although there are errors in the uniforms (sporrans were not usually worn on campaign and officers wore trousers), the scene gives an impression of the limited charge that often followed the volley that had initiated the repulse of the enemy. (*Print after Henri Dupray*)

itself and the other in a hollow that ran alongside the eastern edge of the Bossu Wood; they advanced so far as to take possession of the farm and buildings of La Bergerie. As usual, Wellington was present at the point of greatest hazard, and was beside Cameron of Fassiefern as he observed the French attempt to smash through the British line. Cameron, it was said, was chafing at his inactivity and requested permission to lead his battalion in a counter-attack; the duke replied, 'Have patience, and you will have plenty of work by and by.'[33]

Judging the opportune moment, Wellington exclaimed, 'Now, Cameron, is your time – take care of that road'; and, to the battalion, 'Now, 92nd, you must charge these two columns of infantry.'[34] Alongside the duke was the army's adjutant general, Major General Sir Edward Barnes, known as a fire-eater and evidently not satisfied with the administrative position he had been assigned for the campaign: he had had a distinguished career in the Peninsula, where his attitude to the enemy had been described as akin to that of a bulldog, and he knew the 92nd well, the regiment having served there in his brigade of the 2nd Division. The prospect of participating in a charge was too much for him to resist, so calling out 'Come on, my old 92nd!' he joined Fassiefern in leading the attack.

The two-storey farmhouse stood on the eastern side of the highway; on the opposite side of the road was a large garden, surrounded by a thick thorn hedge, with gates giving access. The garden was not occupied by the French, but a large body was gathered to the south of it, with its flank resting upon Bossu Wood. The 92nd's grenadiers and 1st Company went down the highway, led by Cameron and Barnes, while the remainder concentrated on the house. Crossing a ditch, the 92nd advanced against 'one of the heaviest fires of musketry I ever witnessed',[35] according to Lieutenant James Hope. As usual, the colour party attracted the enemy's especial attention: the officer carrying the regimental colour was killed on the spot by a shot through the heart, and the staff of the colour broken into six pieces, while the staff of the King's Colour was also split.

Musketry from the upper floor of the house claimed the British Army's most high-profile casualty of the battle: Cameron of Fassiefern was shot in the groin and lost control of his horse, which bolted towards Quatre Bras, its rider helpless, until they encountered Cameron's groom, with his spare horse, near the village. Perhaps the groom attempted to catch the animal, but it stopped suddenly and pitched off its rider, who fell onto the road.

With Cameron out of the fight, command of the 92nd devolved upon his deputy, Lieutenant Colonel James Mitchell of Auchindaul, but almost immediately he was wounded, and Major Donald Macdonald of Dalchosnie took over. That the battalion continued to act without pause is further testimony of the system of command and control that functioned despite the loss of successive commanding officers. (Macdonald was bruised severely when his horse was killed beneath him, but he continued to lead the battalion, and had another horse wounded at Waterloo.)

Despite the volume of fire that came from the defenders of the house, the Highlanders surrounded and stormed it at the point of the bayonet; as one Gordon described, the French were infesting the place like mice, until 'they were driven oot, and keepit oot'.[36]

The threat still remained from the large column of French troops just beyond the garden hedge. To have advanced down the highway would have exposed the battalion to fire from French artillery and sharpshooters on their left – these were the cause of many of the 92nd's casualties as it was – so it was decided to split the battalion into three columns: one to advance to the right of the garden, one to the left and the third to pass into the garden itself, break down the gate, and advance from there. This central column found no difficulty in traversing the garden and although under fire formed outside its southernmost hedge. The flanking columns joined their line on right and left; all gave three cheers and advanced with the bayonet. James Hope, who had been with the central column, recalled:

> For a few seconds, the enemy appeared rather unwilling to retire; but when they perceived us to be really in earnest, they wheeled to the right–about, and attempted to escape by the hollow up which their left column had advanced. We pursued the fugitives fully half a mile, when the advance of their cavalry rendered it prudent for us to retire to the wood of Bossu. The loss of the enemy in this affair was terrible. At every step, we found a dead or wounded Frenchman.[37]

This was the last French attempt to force their way through to Quatre Bras, although the fighting continued in and around Bossu Wood until after eight in the evening. On Picton's extreme left flank, Bachelu's Division made a prolonged effort to turn the position, and reached the Nivelles–Namur road, but the 1/95th, 2nd Brunswick Light Battalion and Field Battalion Lüneburg from Kielmansegge's Brigade stopped them in their tracks, and, reinforced by another of Kielmansegge's corps, Field Battalion Grubenhagen, drove them back, continued to advance and took more ground.

Finally, in the gathering twilight, when the French attacks had subsided, Wellington advanced to a position in front of his original line, beginning with the troops on both flanks; the 5th Division in the centre was probably too exhausted to move forward as the manoeuvre began. As William Siborne described, 'The loud shouts which proclaimed the triumphant advance of [Wellington's] forces on either flank were enthusiastically caught up and responded to by those who constituted the main central line, and who had so nobly and so resolutely withstood and defied the impetuous battle-shock by which they had been so repeatedly and so pertinaciously assailed.'[38]

As the fighting had progressed, there occurred a feature characteristic of all actions: streams of walking wounded attempting to make their way to the rear to seek medical attention. The regimental dressing stations were often overwhelmed so, with no organized system of casualty evacuation, the wounded were left to their own devices. Their appearance could be dispiriting to troops marching up to join the battle, and those en route to Quatre Bras were left in no doubt that they were needed. Edward Macready of the 30th described some casualties from the 44th, and 'the poor wounded fellows raised themselves up and welcomed us with faint shouts, "Push on, old three tens – pay 'em off for the 44th – you're much wanted, boys – success to you, my darlings",'[39] while Thomas Morris of the 73rd recalled a member of the 92nd, missing an arm, calling 'Go on, 73rd, give them pepper! I've got my Chelsea commission' (i.e. he would receive a pension for the loss of the limb, providing he survived the amputation).

Along with the genuine wounded were those who escaped danger by absenting themselves from the firing line, often on the pretext of helping a wounded comrade, although men who had disappeared and only returned after the fighting usually received the harshest of welcomes from those who had stood their ground. On this occasion, while generally the British stood fast, witnesses reported a torrent of other nationalities mixed with the wounded. Cavalié Mercer was marching with his troop of horse artillery towards the sound of battle and as he got closer he found that:

The road was covered with soldiers, many of them wounded, but also many apparently untouched. The numbers thus leaving the field appeared extraordinary. Many of the wounded had six, eight, ten and even more attendants. When questioned about the battle, and why they had left it, the answer was invariably, '*Monsieur, tout est perdu! les Anglais sont abimés, en déroute, abimés, tous, tous, tous!*' ['All is lost; the English are destroyed, routed …'] and then, nothing abashed, these fellows would resume their hurried route. My countrymen will rejoice to learn that amongst this dastardly crew not one Briton appeared … One red-coat we did meet – not a fugitive though, for he was severely wounded. This man was a private of the 92d [*sic*] (Gordon Highlanders), a short, rough, hardy looking fellow, with the national high cheek-bones, and a complexion that spoke of many a bivouac. He came limping along, evidently with difficulty and suffering. I stopped him to ask news of the battle, telling him what I had heard from the others. 'Na, na, sir, it's aw a damned lee; they were fechtin' yet an I laft 'em; but it's a bludy business, and thar's na saying fat may be the end on't. Oor ragiment was nigh clean swept off, and oor Colonel kilt jist as I awa.' Upon inquiring about his own wound, we found that a musket-ball had lodged in his knee, or near it; accordingly [surgeon Richard] Hitchins, dismounting, seated him on the parapet of a little bridge we happened to be on, extracted the ball in a few minutes, and, binding up the wound, sent him hobbling along towards Nivelle, not having extracted a single exclamation from the poor man, who gratefully thanked us as he resumed his way.[40]

Although most of the seriously wounded had been left to lie where they fell, at the end of the action some efforts would have been made to remove them to the dressing stations, but the relatively small number of surgeons would have been overwhelmed. A yard in Quatre Bras was allocated for the reception of casualties, and it took on the appearance of a shambles. James Hope of the 92nd described it:

The yard, I have been assured by a surgeon, who dressed a number of the wounded, at one time contained upwards of 1,000 soldiers of the 3d [*sic*] and 5th divisions. The ground, inside of the yard, was literally dyed with blood, and the walls very much stained. In short, the interior of that place presented to the eye a scene of unparalleled horror.[41]

The casualty with probably the highest profile among the wounded was Cameron of Fassiefern. In one regard his biography is not altogether reliable – it claims that his horse fell dead under him at La Bergerie, which was not the case – but it states that his foster brother conveyed him to Waterloo, where he was laid in a deserted house. He is stated to have enquired how the battle had been resolved, and that among his last words were 'I die happy, and I trust my dear country will believe that I have served her faithfully'.[42] (Some seventy years after the event, a story was published concerning Cameron's death at Quatre Bras, told by a veteran: that he had been shot by one of his own battalion, a bad lot aggrieved at being flogged at Cameron's behest. He boasted of what he had done, but when the story was published both he and the pensioner who told it were dead, and it was probably just an idle boast.)

At the cessation of fighting, the first task of every battalion was to rally the survivors and collect any men who had become separated, to ensure the safety of their position. In the case of the 92nd, at about 10.00 pm, Pipe Major Alexander Cameron

> took post behind the garden-hedge in front of the village, and, tuning his bag-pipes, attempted to collect the sad remains of his regiment. Long and loud blew Cameron [but] his utmost efforts could not produce above one-half of those whom his music had cheered in the morning, on their march to the field of battle. Alas! many of them had taken a final leave of this bustling world. Numbers of them were lying in the fields, and in the woods …'[43]

Picton apparently had not been on the right wing of his division's position during the day, as testified by accounts of his presence with other units, and thus was unaware of how the 92nd had suffered. When he visited them in the evening such was the state of the battalion that he asked, 'Where is the rest of the regiment?'

When the rolls had been called, the battalion commanders reported their states. Donald Macdonald provided Pack with an account as unemotional as it was succinct:

Colonel Cameron and Lt. Col. Mitchell having both been severely wounded, I have the honour to report, for your information (not having been under your eye during the whole of the day), that the 92nd Regiment repulsed repeated attacks of cavalry, and by a rapid movement charged a column of the enemy, and drove them to the extremity of the wood on our right. Our loss has been severe, as will be seen by the return of killed and wounded.[44]

An assessment of the losses sustained at Quatre Bras in percentage terms is difficult to ascertain. The exact number of men present in an action might be fewer than those listed in the 'morning states', for example if men detached to the rear as guards for the regimental baggage were included in those listed as 'present', even though they were not in the firing line.

Similarly, some men might have been recorded incorrectly in the casualty returns, for example in the case of Ensign Charles Graham of the 3/1st, as already mentioned, who was reported killed but returned some days later. In the 'morning states' subsequent to the battle the figures for the 'absent sick', which might be expected to represent recent casualties, might also include men infirm for other reasons, or who reported themselves as injured after the first collation of returns. There are some anomalies in the first statistics recorded for the 5th Division: for example, the 3/1st reported 180 wounded but subsequently had 253 'absent sick'. Men at first listed as 'missing' might include undiscovered casualties as well as prisoners, although in this particular case this factor was not of much relevance, as the entire division returned only seventeen men missing after Quatre Bras, all from the 44th.

Some participants in such actions subsequently disputed the accuracy of the published statistics, perhaps in part because men who had become separated from their battalions might have rejoined before the statistics were compiled, so that a unit at the conclusion of an action might actually have been weaker than apparent from the figures.[45]

Despite these caveats, it is possible to establish approximate losses in percentage terms for Picton's battalions; actual figures are given in the appendix. These show, for example, that James Hope's estimate that only half his battalion could be gathered on the evening of 16 June is not so wide of the mark when the stragglers who might have returned in subsequent hours are considered.

The published statistics suggest that the 92nd lost about 39 per cent of the rank and file, the third most serious loss percentage-wise in the division. The 42nd appears to have taken the worst hit, with a loss of 46 per cent, and the 79th, 41 per cent. The Royal Scots lost about 32 per cent, the others in the 20s, with the 28th and 1/95th only about 12 per cent.

Casualties among the officers are somewhat easier to ascertain, if only because each man was listed by name in the published account of casualties, although some fatalities may have been returned initially as wounded, and some officers with lighter wounds either admitted their injuries yet remained with their battalion for the next stage of the campaign, or never reported themselves as wounded at all. This seems to have been the case with the 92nd, for example; at Quatre Bras four officers were returned as killed and twenty-one wounded, and twenty-two were present on the morning of Waterloo, suggesting an original total of forty-seven; but even including the surgeons and paymaster, it appears that there were only thirty-eight officers in the campaign in total. Indeed, five of the Quatre Bras wounds were described as 'slight', so it might be expected that these men would certainly not have quitted the ranks. Such undoubtedly was the case of Captain Neil Campbell of the 79th; he was listed as having been slightly wounded at Quatre Bras but clearly refused to leave his battalion, fought at Waterloo and was wounded severely, from which he died. In the 3/1st, Captains Lawrence Arguimbau and Hugh Massey were both slightly wounded at Quatre Bras, and again at Waterloo, Massey's injury being described as severe, and it is recorded that even some of the more seriously hurt hung on as long as they could, until the weakness resulting from their wounds compelled them to leave on the morning of Waterloo. (It was fortunate that the one-armed Arguimbau did remain with the battalion, as he was the senior officer after its commander was hit at Waterloo.)

Some regiments were hit especially hard – in general, officer casualties often exceeded in percentage terms those of the other ranks – with the 42nd and 92nd losing more than half their officers, and the 32nd not far behind. The remainder lost about a third, excepting the 28th, which lost only about 10 per cent (four wounded and no fatalities).

The most serious factor in the loss of officers must have been in the field of command and control, for the ranks of the most influential officers were hit especially hard: at sunset, half the units in the division were no longer under the command of the officers who led them into the battle early that afternoon. The 42nd lost its commanding officer, his second in command and five out of seven captains; the 44th had its commanding officer and four out of five captains wounded; the 79th had its commanding officer, both lieutenant colonels and six out of ten captains wounded, and the adjutant killed; the 92nd lost its commanding officer, his second in command and four out of six captains. That battalions were still able to function without their efficiency being materially affected after such losses is testimony to the resilience of the system by which officers stepped up in the echelon of command according to their seniority, and to the inherent professionalism of the officer corps in general.

Among the officers who declined to report themselves as wounded was Picton himself. The circumstances of his injury are unclear, but it seems likely that he was hit in the body by a grapeshot at the very limit of its range – a so-called 'spent ball' that hit but did not penetrate – but in Picton's case it was enough to cause a fairly severe injury, probably breaking two or three ribs, resulting in heavy bruising and perhaps some internal injury. Certainly it did not penetrate his clothing, and initially he may not have realized how serious an injury it was; and it was perhaps in the knowledge of this escape that led him to remark to Tyler, 'I shall begin to think I cannot be killed after this.' The blow was the cause of such damage and pain that Picton would have been justified in retiring from the field for treatment, but aware of his responsibility and that an even greater battle was likely in the coming hours, he deliberately concealed the injury from all but, presumably, his personal servant and perhaps the faithful Tyler, so that he could continue to lead his division.

(His was not a unique circumstance: Sir John Lambert, commanding the 10th Brigade and, effectively, the 6th Division, was struck similarly by a spent ball at Waterloo, and hid the injury completely. It only came to light when his brigade major, Harry Smith, caught him changing his shirt on the following day: 'I saw he had received a most violent contusion on his right arm. It was fearfully swelled … and as black as ebony from the shoulder to the wrist. "My dear General," I said, "what an arm! I did not know you had been wounded." "No, nor you never would, if accident had not shown you." He made me promise to say nothing.'[46] The responsibility of command weighed heavy in the minds of the best officers.)

In the evening of the 16th the security of the position at Quatre Bras had to be assured by a screen of picquets facing those of the French, who similarly had held their positions. It must have been obvious that the 5th Division was entirely exhausted, so Sir Edward Barnes allocated the picquet duty to Colin Halkett and his brigade, an order that Halkett found flattering, 'although more fatigued than ever I felt.'[47] Escaping this task, the battalions of Picton's Division moved back a little from their battle line, as much to escape the sight of the field as for any tactical reason. An idea of its appearance was given by Lieutenant William Hay of the 12th Light Dragoons, one of the cavalrymen who had been hurried towards the battle but had arrived too late to participate. He was an experienced Peninsular campaigner, but, 'After the many actions and fields covered with dead and dying I had witnessed, it was, I thought, no novel sight to me; but the number of men and horses lying there far exceeded anything I could have formed any conception of … I was rendered speechless with wonder.'[48]

As the collection of wounded continued, a rescue was attempted from under the noses of the French. Before the 1/95th withdrew a short way and settled down to rest – in column of companies, with officers on the flanks, so as to be up and immediately in perfect formation in the event of an alarm – Sir Andrew Barnard called attention to one of his men, lying wounded dangerously near the French position. 'Gentlemen, if one of you would remain here with two or three men, and bring that poor fellow off, it would be a glorious act indeed.'[49] While light remained, George Simmons aligned some sticks to point to the man's position, and as darkness fell crept towards him. The rifleman had both legs broken, so Simmons and one of his men carried him back to receive treatment at Quatre Bras.

The remainder of the survivors settled down to rest and eat. They would still have some of the rations issued early that morning, and more could be acquired from the bodies of the dead; and a novel way of cooking was recorded by a number of witnesses. Scavenging the battlefield and looting the dead was a universal practice, and it was observed that where cuirassiers had fought, piles of cuirasses were always strewn over the field, not necessarily taken from the dead but discarded as encumbrances by dismounted men trying to make their escape. These were appropriated by the British for use in cooking their supper: meat was almost always boiled, using the kettles provided for each section, but the opportunity to use a cuirass as a frying pan must have provided a welcome change in menu. It was observed, though, that some cuirasses were pierced, so that the gravy ran out; the question as to whether they were actually bulletproof had been solved.

The troops held their positions overnight, but despite their tiredness some were disturbed. At one point early in the night great cheering was heard from the French lines – supposed to have been caused by the reception of the news that Napoleon had defeated the Prussians at Ligny – and the French picquets seemed unusually keen on firing at any pretext, to the extent that the light troops of Halkett's Brigade were turned out to support the British picquets.

Probably relatively few of the survivors of the fight had any concept at this stage of the consequences of their successful defence of the crossroads. In retrospect, one officer of the Royal Scots remarked upon how

the poor Fifth Division ... stood its ground manfully. (Some enthusiasts liken it to the defence of Thermopylae by the Spartans against the Persians.)

Little has been said about the operations of the 16th June, notwithstanding the terrible result in killed and wounded; because, as the crowd say, it had

The village of Quatre Bras, looking north, with the Brussels–Charleroi highway. Immediately after the battle, as pictured here, graves were visible everywhere: Charlotte Waldie described the road as 'one long uninterrupted charnel-house'. (*Print published by R. Bowyer, 1816*)

no consequences. The question is, what would have *been* the consequences had not the Fifth Division been thrust in to stop up the gap? The action could never be meant to be decisive; it was useful in a superlative degree in checking the enemy until the great body of the army concentrated. It would have ranked high as an example of the steadiness and determined bravery of British troops, had it not been eclipsed by that of the 18th, and its extraordinary consequences.[50]

This presents perhaps the most realistic assessment of the battle. It was never intended by Napoleon to be a potentially decisive engagement, but merely as a way of occupying Wellington's army while he, Napoleon, dealt with the Prussians at Ligny. Had Ney been successful at Quatre Bras, however, the campaign could have taken a radically different course. A French victory at Quatre Bras would have probably entailed the destruction or scattering of the 5th Division, seriously weakening Wellington's force for the subsequent battle, and would have so destabilized his position that an orderly retreat upon Mont St. Jean would have been made much more difficult if Ney had pursued with the vigour that could have arisen from a victory. Picton's stand at Quatre Bras would prove to have been one of the most significant episodes of the campaign, but his success had been bought at a fearful cost.

'A night of horror which hath no parallel'

(James Hope, 92nd)

Withdrawal

Although the firing between opposing picquets had died away during the night, it broke out again on the early morning of 17 June, as recalled by John Kincaid, adjutant of the 1/95th:

> An hour before daybreak … a rattling fire of musketry along the whole line of piquets [*sic*] made every one spring to his arms; and we remained looking as fierce as possible until daylight, when each side was seen expecting an attack, while the piquets were blazing at one another without any ostensible cause; it gradually ceased, as the day advanced, and appeared to have been occasioned by a patrol of dragoons getting between the piquets by accident; when firing commences in the dark it is not easily stopped.[1]

Among the new arrivals to the field was Cavalié Mercer's troop of horse artillery, which had settled down for the night in the open field. Mercer was awakened as dawn was breaking by the prolonged rattle of musketry between the opposing outposts, but the other infantry, perhaps more experienced than Mercer himself, appeared unconcerned: 'Our infantry were lying about, cleaning their arms, cooking, or amusing themselves, totally regardless of the skirmish.'[2]

Daylight revealed the full horror of the previous day's fighting: 'a savage unsettled appearance; the fields were strewed with the bodies of men, horses, torn clothing, and shattered cuirasses.'³ Daylight also brought the return of Wellington, who had spent the night at Genappe; the morning was cold, threatening rain, and he dismounted and asked, 'Ninety-second, I will be obliged to you for a little fire.'⁴ They gathered kindling and lit it for him; and, having despatched his ADC Lieutenant Colonel Sir Alexander Gordon and a troop of cavalry to ride east to discover exactly what had occurred to the Prussians, the duke lay down, covered his face with a newspaper, and fell asleep.

With little activity visible among the enemy bar a little desultory skirmishing, and certainly no immediate prospect of renewed fighting, the troops had the chance to eat and check their arms and equipment. George Simmons of the 1/95th lit himself a fire and, foraging about in Quatre Bras, bought a ham from a farmer whose house was crammed with more than fifty wounded Frenchmen; Simmons' riflemen took them water as he cooked his ham for breakfast. Most others followed suit: Anton of the 42nd recalled that with the village and farms being so near, every camp kettle contained a fowl and vegetables foraged from the neighbouring gardens.

When reports came in to Wellington that Blücher and the Prussians had received 'a damned good licking' at Ligny, as the duke was reported to have remarked, it was obvious that the position at Quatre Bras could not be held: with the Prussians retiring northwards, Wellington would have to fall back in the direction of Brussels, both to stay in contact with his allies and to prevent his own forces from being exposed and overwhelmed. He retired to a hut to write his orders but came out on hearing loud cheering from the 92nd, heralding the arrival of his deputy, Rowland Hill, commander of II Corps. 'Daddy' Hill was universally popular from the paternalistic attitude that had given rise to his nickname.

[The 92nd] had long been under his command in the Peninsula, and loved him dearly, on account of his kind and fatherly conduct towards us. When he came among us he spoke in a very kindly manner, and inquired concerning our welfare. He also expressed his sorrow that the colonel was wounded; and gave us a high character to the Duke of Wellington, who replied that he knew what we could do, and that by-and-by he would give us something to keep our hands in use.⁵

As Wellington prepared his orders the division continued to collect the wounded and began to bury some of the dead, mainly the officers; it was a matter of honour that they should not be left to putrefy in the open air like the hundreds of 'other ranks'.

Orders were issued for an immediate withdrawal towards Brussels, which had a dampening effect on those who had so resolutely defended their position on the previous day: the news 'acted like a shower-bath on the spirits of the army; all buoyancy and excitement of feeling vanished at once, and faces, radiant with hope and smiles a few minutes before, were at once elongated in a most marvellous manner.'[6]

Among these was Picton himself. Basil Jackson, serving as DAQMG, thought that the first hint that Picton received that the army was to retire was when Wellington told him to evacuate as many of his wounded as he could; when Picton 'growled out, "Very well, sir", in a tone that showed how reluctant he was to relinquish the ground for which his troops had contended so bravely the day before. Most of the wounded were placed on cavalry horses, and thus taken to the rear.'[7] Many could not be moved: especially affecting was the case of a young soldier of the 42nd, mortally wounded in the head and insensible though still breathing. His friends had dug his grave and were seated beside him while he lived, but when they were ordered to march were mortified to leave him 'to the hands of strangers'.[8]

Similar scenes must have occurred all along the line. One melancholy incident occurred further to the rear: having succumbed to his injury, Cameron of Fassiefern was buried quietly by the Ghent road, with only a few in attendance: his faithful foster brother Ewen Macmillan, his close friend, the regimental paymaster James Gordon, and a few 'walking wounded' of his battalion who were too injured to remain with their comrades.

Once begun, the retirement proceeded in an ordered manner. By then most of the British cavalry had come up, and they and the horse artillery remained to hold the position while the infantry got away first. Some at least marched at a leisurely pace, exemplified by the 30th's light company, much exercised on the previous day and during the night, which halted for a nap on a comfortable dunghill as a break on their route.

During a halt near Genappe Picton took the opportunity of holding a court martial on some soldiers for 'wantonly firing away their ammunition. This practice is very common among the foreign troops, and it is but too much so amongst our own. It cannot be too much reprobated, as it is not only highly detrimental to the service, but endangers the life of many a brave soldier,'[9] according to James Hope. The sentence – presumably flogging – was carried out on the spot.

Although not called into the picquet line during the night because of their exhaustion, despite being the most skilled skirmishers in the army, the 1/95th was now called upon to make good their boast of being the last out of action, as Kincaid recalled:

> Sir Andrew Barnard was ordered to remain as long as possible with our battalion, to mask the retreat of the others; and was told, if we were attacked, that the whole of the British cavalry were in readiness to advance to our relief. I had an idea, however, that a single rifle battalion in the midst of ten thousand dragoons, would come but indifferently off in the event of a general crash, and was by no means sorry when, between eleven and twelve o'clock, every regiment had got clear off, and we followed, before the enemy had put anything in motion against us.[10]

The 1/95th had in fact been sent into a relatively exposed position, based on the farm of Gemioncourt, south of Quatre Bras, with an advanced picquet of two officers and twenty men sheltered by a wall and a ditch. They were ordered not to fire, so when the French picquets found that their musketry was not returned, they ceased shooting. The riflemen cooked their breakfast at Gemioncourt and sent rations forward to the men in front. When all were away the riflemen pulled back, but suffered one casualty in the process: Sergeant Robert Fairfoot, a Peninsular veteran and an excellent NCO, was hit in the right arm by a French skirmisher but before he retired took a last shot at the enemy, using his left arm with his officer's shoulder as a rest.

The infantry got away from Quatre Bras with hardly any loss: the total recorded casualties were just five men killed and eight wounded, with nine missing, and the only officer casualty, Lieutenant Joseph Strachan of the 73rd, was killed when the musket of one of his men went off accidentally. There were no casualties recorded for the 5th Division, so perhaps Fairfoot declined to leave at this stage; he was not reported as 'present sick' on the following day but clearly was still around because of the assistance he rendered subsequently to his wounded officer.

The march north was not without incident, for there descended the heaviest and most prolonged rainstorm that anyone present had ever witnessed. The day had become increasingly sultry, and then 'Heaven's artillery opened with a roar so terrible as to shake the very earth beneath us … the rain descended as if the windows of heaven had been opened,'[11] according to Lieutenant Frederick Pattison of the 33rd, and it turned the roads into muddy torrents. As the French finally began to follow, there was a sharp cavalry action at Genappe, just as the 1/95th, the infantry rearguard, was passing through. To escape the worst of the storm the riflemen had taken shelter in buildings in the town, but so near was the French pursuit that they were ordered out and formed up in battle order, although were not called upon to act. After an initial reverse, the cavalry successfully stalled the French pursuit, and the retreat continued.

The position to which the army retired was midway between Genappe and Brussels, on the low ridge of Mont St. Jean, which straddled the main Charleroi–Brussels highway, and to the south of the village of Waterloo. It was a position previously earmarked by Wellington for defence, although it may not have been that actually selected: his military secretary, Fitzroy Somerset, believed that the original position had been along the ridge to the south, that to be occupied by Napoleon on the day of the battle, only for Sir William De Lancey to judge the ridge too extended for defence, so moved the location of the army's intended line of battle to the next ridge to the north.

There was some relatively minor skirmishing as the pursuing French pressed up against Wellington's rearguard, but the 5th Division was not involved beyond two artillery companies temporarily appropriated by Picton. The companies of Lloyd and Cleeves, officially part of the 3rd Division and which had been engaged at Quatre Bras, were ordered by Picton to engage the French at quite long distance, and one of their officers remarked subsequently that the head of the pursuing French column must have suffered quite severely as the press of other units behind them prevented them from retreating quickly out of range. Wellington himself ordered them to cease firing but they retained their position until morning, when they rejoined their own division.

Mercer's troop of the Royal Horse Artillery was also involved in an exchange of long-range artillery fire, though suffered nothing more than a broken handspike. Mercer recalled that

While we were thus engaged, a man of no very prepossessing appearance came rambling amongst our guns, and entered into conversation with me on the occurrences of the day. He was dressed in a shabby old drab greatcoat and a rusty round hat. I took him at the time as some amateur from Brussels (of whom we had heard there were several hovering about), and thinking many of his questions rather impertinent, was somewhat short in answering him, and he soon left us. How great was my astonishment on learning soon after that this was Sir Thomas Picton![12]

On this day Picton lost his unofficial aide. Rees Gronow recalled how Chambers told him that the losses among the Guards had been quite severe and that he had better rejoin his regiment as he really had nothing to do with Picton in an official capacity. Gronow did as he was advised, and once his fellow Guardsmen had recovered from the surprise of seeing him when he was supposed to be in London, he was assigned duties with them; but it was not his last encounter with Picton's staff. In the evening some French prisoners, taken at Quatre Bras, attempted to escape and were fired upon; and a number of staff officers turned out to ascertain the cause of the musketry. Among them was Chambers, who on meeting Gronow invited him to Picton's quarters for a late supper. As they groped their way into the gloom of the house they passed the door to Picton's room and heard him groaning from his wound, but dare not intrude, and continued on towards their cold meat and wine.

Few enjoyed the comfort of a roof during a night of unrelieved downpour that soaked men and horses and turned much of the ground into a morass: William Hay recalled that he rolled himself in his cloak upon the highest ridge he could find, but on waking discovered that he had sunk 6 or 8 inches into the ground. Witnesses described how soldiers spent the most wretched night imaginable, sitting upon their knapsacks and hunched under the rain that made sleep impossible, so soaked that rainwater ran out of the ends of their sleeves. James Hope of the 92nd wrote a graphic account of the night:

> misery, in its most hideous form, stared us in the face. Fancy yourself seated on a few small twigs, or a little straw, in a newly ploughed field, well soaked with six hours heavy ran; your feet six or eight inches deep in mud; a thin blanket your only shelter from the surly attacks of the

midnight hurricane – cold, wet, and hungry, without a fire, without meat, and without drink. Imagine yourself placed in such a situation, and you will have a faint idea of what we suffered on the night of the 17th, and the morning of the memorable 18th of June. A sound sleep was a luxury which none of us could expect to enjoy. The men were seated in pairs, with their backs to the storm, and their blankets between it and them; some of them were recounting their former sufferings in Portugal, Spain, and France; others their deeds of arms in the same countries; and not a few were humming a verse of some warlike song; all were attempting to pass away the dreary hours in the best manner they could, in hopes that the morning would present them with something more comfortable. Though the men bore their sufferings with great patience and fortitude; and, at all times, appeared ready to perform their duty when called upon, yet it would be vain to assert, that the spirits of the army were not greatly depressed … It was a night of horror which hath no parallel. The dreadful tempest continued with unabated violence till eight o'clock in the morning of the 18th.[13]

David Robertson of the same regiment was less sanguine, recalling how some men cut clover and bits of hedges to sit upon. The misery of their situation gave rise to unusually gloomy thoughts:

there was no apparent possibility of escape, if we should be discomfited, as the fields were quite open to cavalry as far as the forest … the ground being soft and heavy, and we were so encumbered and loaded with our wet blankets and clothes, that getting away seemed entirely out of the question. The contemplation of all these gloomy appearances threw a damp over our minds, but we tried to cheer our drooping spirits by the thought that we had never run out of the field.[14]

Nevertheless, some of the old Peninsula hands knew how to exert a degree of comfort in even the worst circumstances, including constructing 'Portuguese tents', blankets thrown over a framework of muskets. George Simmons of the 95th adopted another old campaigning trick: he found a bundle of straw to lie upon and covered himself with a blanket made waterproof by smearing the upper side with thick, clayey mud, and spent a relatively warm and dry night. His companion, Jonathan Leach, recalled that he was so tired after the exertions of the previous two days that he never slept sounder in his life. Rank had its privileges: the commander of the 1/95th, Sir Andrew Barnard, occupied a small cottage near the Namur road, and thus was one of the few who enjoyed a relatively dry night.

The miserable existence of Pack's Brigade was disturbed during the night when an onset of particularly heavy rain caused a commotion nearby, among either Belgians or the enemy across the way; sentries gave the alarm and the brigade stood-to for an hour, sinking ankle-deep in mud, until all became quiet and the men were allowed to return to their sodden bivouacs.

Many of the Peninsular veterans, however, found the downpour oddly reassuring, for a number of Wellington's most significant victories had been preceded by heavy rain, and thoughts that it might be a lucky omen no doubt alleviated some of the gloom.

Undoubtedly many men spent a hungry night. The old hands, aware of how the delivery of supplies could be interrupted on campaign, knew how to eke out

A bivouac. Although not concerning the Waterloo campaign specifically, this scene of a camp in bad weather would have been replicated throughout the army during the wretched night of 17/18 June. (*Engraving after William Heath*)

A cart and team of the Royal Waggon Train. The militarized transport service was quite inadequate in size for the task of moving the army's supplies: immediately prior to the campaign there were just eight troops for the entire army with a total of 1,072 all ranks with 1,000 'spring wagons', twenty-seven forges and ten more for supplies. The forge wagons were attached to cavalry regiments and the remainder distributed among the infantry for the conveyance of casualties, so that the transportation of supplies was left to the commissariat and its hired civilian vehicles and carters. (*Print by I.C. Stadler after Charles Hamilton Smith*)

their rations, but the younger soldiers were not so provident; as one remarked, their tommy (ration bread) seldom saw the sunset of the second day (after issue), leaving the third day rationless until the next issue. The commissariat officers found an enormous problem: with the militarized section of the transport service carrying ammunition, food was generally entrusted to local carters hired for the occasion, and many of these, hearing dire reports of Quatre Bras, had been seized with panic. Assistant Commissary General Tupper Carey discovered chaos on the Brussels highway: 'Never did I witness a scene of such confusion and folly. The peasantry, carrying provisions in country waggons, cut the traces of the harness and ran away with the horses, abandoning the waggons,'[15] so that not only was there no way of moving the wagons, but the roads were choked with vehicles. Carey also observed that although the troops had initially received three days' rations, 'their usual improvidence' meant that little was left. By sheer luck he was able to provide his division (the 2nd) with some barrels of biscuit intended for the Netherlands troops and on the point of being abandoned by the nervy carters until he directed them towards his division; but few were so fortunate.

The 92nd was even without water. A fatigue party was sent to Waterloo with the battalion's canteens to find a well; but those they encountered had neither ropes nor buckets, and even with twenty-three canteen straps buckled together, plus a length of rope, few could be accessed, and those that could were dry. The party returned to the battalion without a drop.

Waterloo

The position upon which the army had drawn up was as suitable as any for the defensive battle that Wellington knew he would have to fight. An action of manoeuvre was out of the question: he realized that, with his army of raw troops interspersed by veterans, he had to hold until Blücher's Prussians could come up from the east and exert pressure on Napoleon's right flank. Without the presence of the Prussians on Wellington's far left, with the expectation that they would assist, the duke would surely never have fought where he did, and indeed advised his civilian friends in Brussels to prepare to flee to Antwerp should circumstances force him to 'uncover' the city. However, if he did intend the fight, the position along the ridge at Mont St. Jean was as good as any.

Wellington's front line was roughly along a road running west to east, between the villages of Brain l'Alleud in the east and Ohain in the west, and sometimes referred to as the Ohain road. It was lined with hedges and in places slightly sunken, although not with the 'ravine' sometimes described. Intersecting this road, and dividing Wellington's position roughly in half, was the Charleroi–Brussels highway, which across the Ohain road ran northwards to Brussels, passing alongside the farm and village of Mont St. Jean and, further north, the village of Waterloo. The Mont St. Jean ridge sloped away to the south, so that attackers would have to climb it, from a depression between it and the parallel ridge further south, that upon which Napoleon was to establish his position.

Wellington and his staff at Waterloo. The duke is shown wearing his cape, and while most of his officers wear the staff uniform, the aide in the shako and the 1812 light dragoon uniform must be intended to represent his ADC, Lord George Lennox, son of the Duke of Richmond, a lieutenant in the 9th Light Dragoons. (*Engraving by S. Mitan after George Jones, published 1817*)

The Mont St. Jean ridge sloped away more gently to the north, providing a 'reverse slope' behind the front line that was a feature of Wellington's preferred tactic, of concealing the bulk of his army from the enemy's view, behind the crest of a ridge, thus protecting his own troops from artillery fire and also making the enemy unsure of his position, and thus difficult to decide when their attacking columns should deploy into line for the close-quarter combat. In this case, the task of the attacking French would be made even more difficult by the tall standing crops on parts of the field, further obscuring their enemy.

Wellington's front line was anchored by three strongpoints. At the extreme left flank were the hamlets of Papelotte, La Haie, Smohain and Frischermont; throughout the day they were held by Netherlands troops, without the involvement of any British units. The extreme right of the line was bolstered by the chateau and walled farm of Hougoumont, which was to form one of the focal points of the battle in blocking a route that Napoleon could have used in attempting to turn Wellington's flank. The chateau and grounds were to be held with the greatest determination and heroism by the 2nd and 3rd Foot Guards from the 1st Division, with some lesser contingents. The third strongpoint was in advance of the centre of the line, the farmhouse and grounds of La Haye Sainte, which abutted the Charleroi–Brussels highway, with an excavation known as the gravel or sandpit on the opposite side of the highway and a short way north, which was level with the road on the west side but banked on the other three sides. This feature was to involve men from the 5th Division in the approaching battle.

To the rear of Wellington's position was the Forêt de Soignes, which extended almost all the way from Waterloo to the outskirts of Brussels. A very short time after the Battle of Waterloo Sir Walter Scott described its appearance, when approaching Wellington's position from Brussels:

> a wood composed of beech-trees growing uncommonly close together [which] is traversed by the road from Brussels, a broad long causeway,

The Forêt de Soignes: the thick woodland in the rear of Wellington's position at Mont St. Jean, which by conventional wisdom could have hindered a withdrawal; but the duke and others believed that if the army had been driven off the ridge, they could have held the woods against all comers. (*Engraving by and after J. Rouse, published 1816*)

which, upon issuing from the wood, reaches the small village of Waterloo. Beyond this point, the wood assumes a more straggling and dispersed appearance, until about a mile further, where at an extended ridge, called the heights of Mount St. John, from a farm-house situated upon the Brussels road, the trees almost entirely disappear.[1]

Conventional military wisdom held that giving battle in front of so thick a wood was courting disaster, as it would greatly hinder a retreat; but this was clearly not in Wellington's mind, as Scott recorded. When the duke was questioned on this point he remarked that if they had been forced to retreat, they would have gone no further than the trees. His questioner asked 'if the wood also was forced?'; 'No, no, they could never have so beaten us, but we could have made good the wood against them,'[2] and the opinion that they could never have been driven from the wood was echoed by other experienced campaigners.

The rain abated by early morning, and the army began to shake itself into fighting order. The line presented what an officer of the Royal Scots described

La Haye Sainte: an early view, evidently drawn by Charlotte Waldie's sister Jane, later Watts, showing the damage of battle. The excavation or 'sandpit' and higher ground at right is that defended by the 1/95th, at the right flank of the 5th Division's position. (*Print published by Booth, 1816*)

as 'dismal to a degree, and men and officers, with their dirty clothes, and chins unshorn, had a rather disconsolate look in the morning; however, the sun broke out, and brightened the scene a little, and we were aware of what was coming, which probably removed any little stiffness left by the wet and cold of the night.'[3] Many must have felt like Robertson of the 92nd: 'We were aroused by daylight, on the morning of the 18th, and ordered to stand to our arms, till the line should be reconstructed. During the time I never felt colder in my life; every one of us was shaking like an aspen leaf ... we seemed as if under a fit of ague ...'[4] (The stand-to at dawn, as at twilight, was a common practice; enemy attacks could come almost unrecognized in the half-light, and it was only safe to relax, to use a nautical expression, when a goose could be seen at a mile.)

The certainty of being 'aware of what was coming' to some only became obvious as the morning wore on. John Kincaid of the 1/95th, even though he was the battalion adjutant, could not be sure that the army was going to stand until an order was received to stack reserve ammunition in a safe place behind the line, and to send to the rear, and thus to a place of relative safety, any baggage and draught animals. This made it certain that Wellington was going to accept a battle on the ground where the army had spent the night. The despatch to the rear of any regimental baggage removed a number of officers, NCOs and men from the firing line, weakening even further the more badly hit battalions, but it was a necessary precaution to prevent the baggage from being plundered while the majority were otherwise engaged. The numbers of men so detached is impossible to ascertain with precision, as some units continued to count them as 'present' while others even denied such individuals the Waterloo Medal when it was issued. There did arrive, however, a welcome reinforcement noticed especially by the 5th Division: the brigade of Sir John Lambert came up after marching determinedly from Brussels, having returned only recently from North America. They received some gentle mockery from the 5th Division on account of their smart, clean uniforms, contrasting with the stained, mud–caked appearance of the 5th. The officer quoted above described how the whole line became active as the sky lightened on Sunday, 18 June:

> a moving mass of human beings – soldiers cleaning their arms and examining the locks, multitudes carrying wood, water, and straw from the village and farm of Mont St. Jean; others making large fires to dry their

clothes, or roasting little pieces of meat upon the end of a stick or ramrod, thrust among the embers; a few bundles of straw had been procured, upon which our officers were seated. Though nearly ankle-deep in mud, they were generally gay, and apparently thinking of everything but the approaching combat, which snapped the thread of existence of so many of them.

He noted that the Peninsular veterans always had a little food remaining in their haversacks, and above all attended to their weapons: 'The sound of preparation of so large a body, about 90,000 men, reminded me forcibly of the distant murmur of the waves of the sea, beating against some iron-bound coast.'

A number of officers who had been wounded quite severely at Quatre Bras had nevertheless marched with their battalions on the previous day, but its exertions made it impossible for them to continue any longer; so with much regret the most fragile among them were persuaded to retire to Brussels if they were so ill as to be unable to perform their duty. To them were entrusted messages from those who remained behind, notably brief wills, 'done without the smallest appearance of despondency; but Kempt's and Pack's brigades had got such a mauling of the 16th, that they thought it well to have all straight. The wounded officers shook hands, and departed for Brussels.'[5]

James Anton of the 42nd described how weapons were put in order: old charges extracted, powder washed from the priming pans, the muskets then dried and the locks oiled. There was accommodation in the cartridge box for spare flints, and it was usual before an action to fix a new, sharp flint into the jaws of the cock to minimize misfires. Amid all this activity, some units at last received rations. James Hope of the 92nd, who had eaten nothing for two days, had roasted a steak on a ramrod over his fire, but noted that after so wretched a night many soldiers seemed to have no appetite; until there was an issue of spirits, 'which tended to keep our drooping spirits from sinking under our accumulated load of misery … we lighted fires, pulled off our jackets, shoes, and stockings, dried them, and endeavoured to make ourselves comfortable.'[6] Some even began to make improvised shelters, and Hope had just fallen asleep in one when roused by bugles sounding the assembly.

The position of the 5th Division, on which they were to fight, was a crucial part of the line, occupying most of the left of Wellington's line; despite the

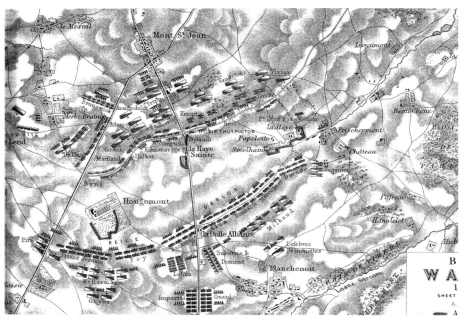

Battle of Waterloo: the opening dispositions, with Picton's Division to the east of the Brussels–Charleroi highway. The cavalry formations behind the infantry line include Ponsonby's Union Brigade and Somerset's Household Brigade.

mauling they had received at Quatre Bras it is likely that it was thought that only the most reliable of troops could be entrusted with such responsibility. The division's position extended from the eastern edge of the Charleroi–Brussels highway, eastwards to the extreme left flank; the only troops initially further to the left were the light cavalry brigades of Sir John Vandeleur and Sir Hussey Vivian, with Prince Bernhard of Saxe-Weimar's Netherlandish troops in advance and to the east of the main line, in the Papelotte/La Haie/Smohain/ Frischermont complex. Kempt's Brigade occupied the right (western edge) of the division's position, with Pack's Brigade further east. Between the two, and originally forward of them, was the Dutch–Belgian brigade of General Major W.F., Count van Bylandt (or Bijlandt; in British service he appeared in the Army List as 'Count William Byland'). Further east from Pack's Brigade was Best's Hanoverian brigade, and as Vincke's Brigade had finally joined the 5th Division, to which it had been allocated, it was posted further east still, so that it was the infantry formation on the extreme left of Wellington's army.

The individual battalions did not remain static throughout the battle, but in general Kempt's Brigade was arrayed with the 1/95th on the extreme right, against the highway, then from west to east the 32nd, 79th, and 28th; then Bylandt's; then Pack's, from west to east the 1st, 42nd, 92nd and 44th. The 1/95th was not initially deployed as a solid body, but as appropriate for the most expert skirmishers in the army, two companies under Major Jonathan Leach were thrown forward to hold the sandpit by the side of La Haye Sainte to support its garrison of King's German Legion 2nd Light Battalion, with Captain William Johnstone's company in support. The remaining three companies of the 1/95th lined the Ohain road east of the Brussels highway. In addition, a party under Lieutenant George Simmons was sent to cut wood to form an abattis (barricade) across the highway, to assist in the defence of the area of the sandpit.

The troops immediately to the west of the highway, thus holding the line on Picton's right flank, were the King's German Legion brigade of Colonel Christian von Ompteda, and to his right the Hanoverians of Count Kielmansegge. To the rear of the 5th Division was positioned Sir William Ponsonby's 2nd Cavalry

Waterloo: French cavalry attacks part of the line held by the 5th Division, with La Haye Sainte at left and the sandpit in mid-ground, centre. (*Print by T. Sutherland after William Heath*)

Brigade, known as the 'Union' Brigade from its composition of English (1st Royal), Scottish (2nd Royal North British) and Irish (6th Inniskilling) Dragoon regiments. In the corresponding place behind Ompteda and Kielmansegge was Lord Edward Somerset's 1st Cavalry or Household Brigade, comprising the 1st and 2nd Life Guards, Royal Horse Guards and 1st (King's) Dragoon Guards.

The only artillery capable of indirect fire – i.e. over the heads of friendly troops – were howitzers, of which each company or horse artillery troop had only one, so that artillery had to be positioned in direct line of sight of the enemy. This meant that the divisional artillery companies had to be positioned among or in front of the infantry, which was the case with the two companies attached to the 5th Division. It was usual for the pieces in the gun line to have sufficient distance between them to permit infantry to advance or retire through the line without becoming disordered, and for only the guns to be in the forward position. Limbers and horse teams would be withdrawn some distance, ideally (and as in the case at Waterloo) in the shelter of ground that fell away in the rear of the gun position, to shield them from enemy fire and yet close enough for the limbers to be advanced to remove the guns or resupply ammunition without difficulty. The company's ammunition wagons would be sited even further back, in a position from which a shuttle service of ammunition could be maintained for the guns, yet out of enemy range for most of the time.

The process of resupply of ammunition to the artillery added to what often resembled chaos behind the firing line, with wounded trying to reach an aid post, shirkers attempting to look busy to keep themselves from danger, and wagons and teams rushing to and fro as often as the rumours that swept the rear areas, as John Kincaid described:

> The rear of a battle is generally a queer place – the day is won and lost there a dozen times, unknown to the actual combatants – fellows who have never seen an enemy in the field, are there to be seen flourishing their drawn swords … while others are flying as if pursued by legions of demons; and, in short, while everything is going on in front with the order and precision of a field–day, in rear everything is confusion worse confounded.[7]

The divisional artillery could be supported by companies or troops from neighbouring formations or from the artillery reserve of batteries not permanently assigned but deployed as needed; but even those that were officially attached to specific divisions could be moved around the field. This was, for example, the case with Rogers's Company of the 5th Division. Initially they were deployed to the left of the Brussels highway, immediately in front of the division, but later in the day, presumably when pressure on the 5th Division had eased, they were limbered-up and transferred to the right of the highway, until, in preparation for the last great French attack, they were moved much further right, to a position on the right of the 1st Division of Foot Guards and on the left of Adam's Brigade, from where it executed its counter-attack at the extreme right of Wellington's position. By this time, however, Rogers's serviceable guns had been reduced from six to three, exemplifying how attrition could reduce the effectiveness of artillery. Early in the battle, when the company's first position appeared in danger of being overrun, an over-zealous NCO had spiked his gun to prevent it being of use to the enemy in case of capture. When the position was stabilized this gun had to be withdrawn from the gun line to a place of safety where the spike could be drilled out – a laborious process. In its second position the company came under heavy fire and two guns lost their horse teams, and were thus immoveable, so that when the company was transferred to its final position it could muster only three pieces of ordnance.

Despite the presence of 'dead ground' behind the front line, so characteristic of Wellington's preferred mode of deployment, some appear to have been extremely nervous about the strength of the position. Among these was Picton himself, for early in the morning of 18 June he appears to have inspected the whole line, not just that occupied by his own division. Colonel John Colborne of the 52nd recalled how

I remember hearing old Picton say just before the battle, 'I never saw a worse position taken up by any army. I have just galloped from left to right.' He went on to talk of the expected *Gazette* in very high spirits, 'Some friends of mine,' he said, 'asked me to write to them, but I said, "Won't the *Gazette* do for you?"' He was killed a few hours after.[8]

Conceivably Picton's optimism may have been dented by the effects of his wound at Quatre Bras, but he was not alone in his concerns. An officer of rank – conceivably Major General Sir Frederick Adam – subsequently confessed to Sir

Walter Scott that he had had 'a momentary sinking of the heart when he looked round him, considered how small was the part of our force properly belonging to Britain, and recollected the disadvantageous and discouraging circumstances under which even our own soldiers laboured'. If this were Adam, he could be excused as he had not served previously under Wellington, his own Peninsular experience being on the east coast of Spain; as in Picton's case, his fears proved groundless. At almost the same time an ADC, equally nervous, spoke to some Foot Guards, urging them to reserve their fire until the enemy was at close range. He was answered by a voice from the ranks: 'Never mind us, sir; we *know our duty.*'[9]

Such concerns must have multiplied as the full extent of Napoleon's forces became evident. The Royal Scots officer quoted previously described how, as the morning wore on, Wellington rode past with his staff (and was greeted with ecstatic cheering: he was never loved by the ordinary soldiers but they had unbounded confidence in him), and then the officer walked forward to the brow of the ridge, where a panorama was stretched before him, of the dip or shallow valley between their own position and the ridge to the south where Napoleon's forces came into view. Cavalry skirmishers were succeeded by light infantry, and then the whole of Napoleon's army appeared:

> dark, deep, and solid masses along the opposite height … Could any one witness the opening scene of this great drama with indifference? Can I ever forget the reflections which filled my mind, to stupefaction almost, at that moment? Napoleon 'le Grand' marshalling the chosen armies of France against those of Britain, almost within gun-shot. Here were, then, those celebrated troops which had held Europe in bonds, and humbled the pride of kings. They looked formidable certainly; and though I had faced them before more than once, they were not then commanded by the Emperor in person.[10]

Sergeant David Robertson of the 92nd felt much the same:

> such numerous columns I had never looked on before, nor do I believe that any man in the British Army had ever seen such a host. I must confess that, for my own part, when I saw them taking up their grounds in such a regular

manner, and every thing appearing so correct about all their movements, I could not help wishing that we had had more troops with which to oppose the thousands that were collecting in our front.[11]

Due to Wellington's practice of concealing much of his army behind a crest, it is unclear how much of his dispositions were visible to the French, although it is said that Napoleon remarked, '*Ou est la division de Picton?*', as if anticipating that it would be one of the hardest parts to crack. His unwilling Belgian guide Jean-Baptiste de Coster related an exchange between Napoleon and his chief of staff, Marshal Jean-de-Dieu Soult, who knew the British Army of old. Surely, Napoleon said, the British troops must give way. Soult disagreed. Why?, asked Napoleon; because, said Soult, they would have to be cut all to pieces before then. His opinion was prophetic.

Each battalion submitted a return of its strength, from which the 'morning state' of the army was prepared; these show just how weak the 5th Division was after the casualties of Quatre Bras. Although the notional establishment of a battalion was about 1,000 rank and file, this was attained only rarely (at Waterloo, excluding the Foot Guards, only the 52nd reached this figure); about 700 was a more common full strength. For Picton's Division on the morning of Waterloo, however, the average battalion strength was about twenty officers and 428 other ranks (full statistics are given in the appendix). The strongest battalion was the 28th, with thirty officers and 522 other ranks; the weakest the 42nd with fourteen officers and 321 other ranks. These figures for officers do not include 'staff' – surgeons, paymasters, quartermasters – who were non-combatants and but for the surgeons generally remained behind in the rear areas with the baggage guard; and these figures may also include some of the less seriously injured who subsequently had to retire to Brussels. These statistics make the efforts of the 5th Division even more remarkable: in terms of rank and file, most battalions were barely at half strength, with the 42nd having hardly enough men to form three companies at the notional establishment, instead of the usual ten. Even the 32nd, the second strongest battalion in the division, had suffered such casualties that, instead of ten companies, had been reorganized into six 'divisions'.

After the dawn stand-to and the attempts to kindle fires and take such refreshment as was available, the army moved into its battle positions. Even when defending a position, the formation and position of infantry units was rarely static: a significant asset was its flexibility of movement, so that it could operate in line when delivering fire, in column when moving or waiting to change formation, in square or oblong when threatened by cavalry; thus during a battle units were often changing their pose according to circumstances. The officer of the Royal Scots attributed some of this flexibility to Picton:

> I had just time, while we awaited the attack, to get a glimpse of Sir Thomas Picton's disposition; it was the most beautiful thing imaginable, and the ground admitted of it being displayed to advantage; all the modern improvements acquired by experience in the Peninsula, in the disposition of both cavalry and infantry, were here brought into play. Some of the regiments deployed and formed line, and were to charge, others followed in their rear, at quarter distance columns, ready to deploy and support the charge, or take the place of those in front, if baulked or defeated, or to throw themselves into squares instantaneously, if threatened by cavalry; and, in short, to conform to the movements of those in front … these armed bodies of infantry of a square form (or columnar) were pliable in every direction; either opening out in line to charge bayonet, or to direct a fire to the front or flanks, and attack or defend in all directions. The only difficulty is, in covering these bodies from the fire of artillery, for which (from their density) they form an excellent mark.[12]

(Despite this witness extolling 'the masterly arrangement of Sir Thomas', it should be noted that such formations, and their flexibility, were part of the operating procedure of the infantry in general; but perhaps Picton made especially good use of the folds in the terrain to maximize their protective nature.)

Before the action commenced the regimental surgeons established their aid posts at the rear of the firing line, in some cases a considerable distance away, but those of the 1/95th chose a position much nearer to the front. Although the hedge lining the Ohain road was fairly sparse at its intersection with the Brussels highway – much thicker to the east – there was a clump of bushes and a tree near the highway. The bushes were those cut down to form the abattis, but the tree was left, and under it the surgeons established their dressing station. It

A French Chasseur à Cheval, the largest proportion of Napoleon's light cavalry regiments, as engaged against the 5th Division. (*Print after Hippolyte Bellangé*)

was so near the front line that one of the first French cannon shots cut it in half, bringing the upper part down upon the heads of the medical officers. Although regimental musicians and drummers were used to remove casualties, most would remain with their units and only visit the aid post when actually helping the wounded reach it. (It is likely that some drummers would remain with their battalion at all times, in case orders had to be transmitted by drum beat; the most distinctive beat, for example, a prolonged and uninterrupted drum roll and thus quite unmistakable, was that used in that most dangerous of situations, to order the forming of a square.)

Napoleon delayed opening the battle for some time, principally to permit the ground to dry out somewhat, but by mid-morning decided to wait no longer. The time at which the battle began is not certain: British witnesses estimated between 11.00 am and 11.50 (watches were not synchronized!), but there appears to have been some preliminary artillery fire before that. Sir James Shaw Kennedy, present at the battle as Captain James Shaw of the 43rd Light Infantry, serving as AQMG with the 3rd Division, estimated that the action began in earnest at 11.30 am, which is probably about right. Napoleon had amassed a formidable force of artillery – 246 guns to Wellington's 156 – the employment of which had been a characteristic of his tactics, and (in the contemporary phrase) 'opened the ball' with a bombardment at relatively long range.

When the 5th Division's battalions had assembled in the morning, they appear to have been withdrawn some distance northwards from the Ohain road, some 50 yards or more, largely to take advantage of the reverse slope of the ridge, and thus with the exception of the deployed light companies would have been to an extent invisible to the enemy. (All the light companies were thrown forward in a skirmish line to blunt the effect of the French skirmishers preceding their

An important early view of the position of the 5th Division at Waterloo. The hedge in mid-ground is that lining the Ohain road, behind which the division was drawn up; this is the view that would have been seen by d'Erlon's corps as it advanced. The Forêt de Soignes is visible on the skyline. The large tree at the right foreground is marked as being near the spot where Picton was killed, and is presumably that under which his body was laid, showing how the division had advanced from its original position behind the hedge. (*Print published by Booth, 1816*)

advance; as an attack drew closer the usual practice was for the light companies to retire through gaps in the main line and re-form in its rear, ready to sally out again as soon as the enemy had begun to retire.)

The first French artillery shots thus made relatively few hits from roundshot, although they might have bounced over the crest of the ridge, but shells from howitzers were also dropped onto the British position. As David Robertson of the 92nd remarked, 'Being placed rather in the rear of the slope, the French canonneers could not hit us with their shot, but they made some shells to bear on us, which made great havoc in our ranks.'[13] The 1/95th, supporting La Haye Sainte with some men on an adjoining knoll, were not quite so protected, for a roundshot 'came from the Lord knows where, for it was not fired at us, and took the head off our right-hand man.'[14]

Compounding the misery of the previous night, the bombardment depressed the morale of the 92nd; James Hope recalled that 'the spirits of the men were very low indeed … there was something wanting to restore their wonted daring.'[15] It came from an unexpected quarter: a visit by Wellington's friend, the Duke of Richmond, who observed the low spirits and announced that Wellington was certain of victory, with the Prussians even as he spoke advancing to their assistance. This news produced a reaction 'truly astonishing' as spirits revived, as did one of the 92nd loudly reciting Robert Burns's *Bruce's Address* suitably altered for the occasion:

> *Now's the day, and now's the hour,*
> *See the front of battle lower,*
> *See approach Napoleon's power,*
> *His chains and slavery!*
> *Lay the proud Usurper low,*
> *Tyrants fall in every foe,*
> *Liberty in every blow,*
> *Let us do or die!*

As the poem suggests elsewhere, some of those who heard it were indeed to find a gory bed.

Richmond was not the only visitor to the 5th Division, for another was the cause of an unusual preoccupation for Lieutenant John Campbell, who commanded the 44th's light company. His father was Lieutenant General Archibald Campbell, a veteran of the American war and of West Indian campaigns, and who was lieutenant governor of Fort Augustus, Inverness. The general turned up to visit the 44th, riding a small grey pony, at the rear of his son's company. Lieutenant John was so nervous for his father's safety as the bullets began to fly that he pleaded with the general to leave, or he would not be able to concentrate upon his duty. Appreciating the situation, Archibald took himself off and joined Wellington's staff instead. Both Campbells came through the battle unscathed.

Some of the early long-range cannonade fell among Rogers's company, by which some horses were lost. It was always galling to suffer casualties without replying, but 'counter-battery fire' – i.e. against the enemy's artillery – was not advocated, as being thought wasteful of shot for little effect, with ammunition being of much greater use against enemy troops. On this occasion, Rogers seems to have considered returning fire, but was restrained by Picton himself.

After the initial cannonade, Napoleon opened the battle in earnest with a furious assault upon Hougoumont, the anchor of Wellington's right flank. Although Picton's Division was posted well to the east, at least some 1,500 yards away, the beginning of the action was clearly visible from the crest of the ridge. A group of officers from the 1/95th gathered in front of their position to observe, when Kempt rode up and declared, 'Now, gentlemen, here you are, as usual, congregated together talking.' 'Scamp' Stilwell, the supposed natural son of the Duke of York, was untroubled by this mild rebuke: 'Oh, yes, Sir James,' he replied, 'we were just observing that there appears to be a slight difference of opinion down yonder,' pointing to the fighting at Hougoumont.[16] It was one of the last quips that the noted wit would make: he did not survive the day.

The troops of the 5th Division were not to remain idle spectators for long, however, for Napoleon's next movement was the launch of a huge infantry attack against Picton's line, intended, even at this early stage of the battle, to be a decisive blow. It involved the whole of the French I Corps of General Jean-Baptiste Drouet, comte d'Erlon, arrayed in four columns in echelon from the left: the divisions of Generals Joachim-Jerome Quiot de Passage, deputising for the official divisional commander, General Jacques-Alexandre Allix de Vaux, who had not joined the army by the time the campaign had begun; François-Xavier Donzelot; Pierre-Louis Binet, baron de Marcognet; and, at the extreme right, Pierre-François, comte Durutte. In total, the eight infantry brigades involved numbered some 686 officers and 16,380 other ranks, thus very greatly outnumbering the 5th Division which, despite the support of non-British elements, would have to bear the force of the attack. Cavalry was present on both of d'Erlon's flanks, and the supporting artillery bombardment intensified. As they advanced on a wide front, d'Erlon's troops would be opposed by Kempt's Brigade on their left flank, and by Pack's on their right-centre.

The advance of d'Erlon's Division was an awesome spectacle, accompanied as usual by a tumult of noise, of which some British observers were traditionally dismissive: 'cheering and beating their drums, as if they had been going to scare crows from a corn-field … Their officers too were in front of their men, waving their swords and swaggering like showmen at a fair,' as a member of the 42nd recalled.[17] Watching from the knoll near La Haye Sainte, John Kincaid observed the French advance and clearly heard them chanting '*Vive l'Empereur!*', 'backed by the thunder of their artillery, and carrying with them the *rubidub* of drums, and the *tantarara* of trumpets, in addition to their increasing shouts, it looked, at first, [as] if they had some hopes of scaring us off the ground; for it was a singular contrast to the stern silence reigning on our side, where nothing, as yet, but the voices of our great guns, told that we had mouths to open when we chose to use them.'[18]

The noise made by the French when advancing to the attack was calculated deliberately to intimidate: the shouts of their men were described by George Gleig of the British 85th, who encountered them in the Peninsula, as a 'discordant yell ... a sort of shout, in which every man halloos for himself, without regard to the tone or time of those about him'.[19] The advance was always accompanied by the relentless hammering of drum beats, not primarily to keep the men in step but again to intimidate; the British described this French *pas de charge* drumming as 'Old Trousers', the name perhaps deriving from 'tow row', the

French infantry advancing to the attack. The traditional French column of advance was very different from the concept of a column of march: a *colonne d'attaque par division* had a frontage of two companies, each arrayed in three ranks (as shown here), so that a battalion advancing in this manner would be nine ranks deep. The companies following were intended to deploy into line, alongside the two leading companies, before exchanging musketry with the enemy, thus maximising their firepower. (*Print after Raffet*)

phonetic expression of a beating drum, as in the chorus of the ancient song *The British Grenadiers.*

Conversely, the complete absence of sound or motion from the British ranks in these circumstances had probably a greater psychological effect on the French than did their own shouting; French witnesses described how unnerving the silent, motionless red wall appeared, almost as if they were automata awaiting activation rather than flesh and blood. Not until they mounted their own counter-charge with the bayonet would the British cheer, and this, too, had the psychological edge: a concerted, ear-splitting roar calculated to strike such terror into an enemy already wavering after receiving a blast of British musketry that almost inevitably they fled before the British got near enough to use their bayonets.

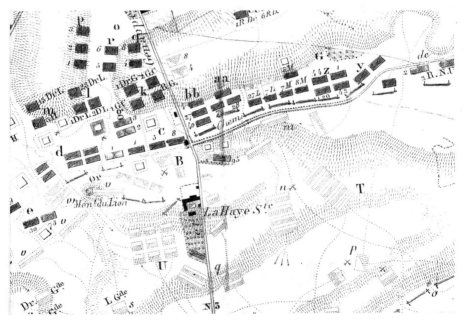

One of the earliest detailed maps showing the position of individual battalions, that of the Belgian engineer W.B. de Craan, produced at the behest of the King of the Netherlands. 'bb' represents Lambert's Brigade (4th, 27th and 40th Regts.), 'aa' Kempt's (with the 32nd mistakenly captioned as '23'), 'Z' Pack's (with the 92nd mistakenly captioned '29'). The five battalions of Bylandt's Brigade are shown holding the line between Kempt and Pack, although by the time Lambert had moved into the line, almost all had retired in disorder.

The French bombardment and the sight of d'Erlon's advance, however, had a dire consequence for Picton's position. There is still doubt over exactly what occurred with Bylandt's Netherlands brigade, still positioned between the brigades of Kempt and Pack. Bylandt's Brigade comprised five battalions, three of untried militia, the 27th (Dutch) Jägers that had suffered severely at Quatre Bras, and the 7th (Belgian) Line. Initially it had been posted on the forward slope of the ridge, in clear view of the enemy, where 'it jutted forward in front of the real line of battle and was directly opposed to the fire of the greatest French battery,'[20] according to Shaw Kennedy. It has been stated that the casualties incurred in this exposed position caused the brigade to break, but actually it appears to have been withdrawn to a safer position at about noon, according to the report of Colonel F.H. van Zuylen van Nyevelt, chief of staff

A classic tactic: a British line, two ranks deep, repels a French attack in column, advancing uphill, as employed by the 5th Division at Quatre Bras and Waterloo. The troops depicted wear the 1812 infantry uniform, with the officer placed correctly at the flank of his company, with his 'covering' colour sergeant behind him. The second rank is at the position of 'make ready', about to add their musketry to that of the front rank. (*Print after Richard Simkin*)

of the Netherlands 2nd Division to which the brigade belonged, 'in order not to hinder the evolutions of the English guns placed in their rear, and also to be less exposed to the fire of the enemy.'[21] They were in this position when d'Erlon attacked, although probably still somewhat in advance of the adjoining British brigades, and it was from this position that they broke.

Shaw Kennedy described how Bylandt's Brigade, 'leaving its position on the first advance of the French attacking columns, retreated through the British lines, and placed itself on the reverse slope of the position, against orders and remonstrances, and took no further part in the action.'[22] Most of the front line of the brigade fell back behind its reserve battalion, the 5th Militia, to the dismay of the adjoining British units, as the officer of the Royal Scots described: 'Presently we perceived the Belgian troops coming towards us in great numbers from the brow, where they had been posted as a kind of first line. It appears that they had "turned tail", and no exertions on the part of the officers could stop them – some of our men wanted to shoot them.'[23] This was no isolated sentiment; Corporal John Dickson of the 2nd Dragoons – Royal Scots Greys – stationed in the rear of the 5th Division, described how 'a great noise of firing and hisses and shouting commenced, and the whole Belgian brigade … came rushing along and across the road in full flight. Our men began to shout and groan at them too. They had bolted almost without firing a shot, and left the brigade of Highlanders to meet the whole French attack,'[24] retreating in what Anton of the 42nd called 'in one promiscuous mass of confusion'.[25] It was even wondered if the troops in question, given their nationality, were sympathetic to Napoleon.

In reality, it appears that the one regular Belgian unit in the division, Colonel van den Sanden's 7th Line, did hold its position and traded musketry with the approaching French; it was presumably that individual that the officer of the Royal Scots recalled: 'It should not be forgotten that a fine old brave Belgian Colonel, having a cocked-hat like the sails of a windmill, followed the movements, with his gallant little band, of our division the whole day – always in the thickest of the fire.'[26] Subsequently the gallant van Zuylen van Nyevelt – who shortly before had been fighting *for* Napoleon as a member of the Lancers of the Imperial Guard, and had survived the Russian campaign – managed to gather about 400 of the fugitives and led them back to support the 7th; but nevertheless the disintegration of Bylandt's Brigade had left a gap in Wellington's line, into which the advancing French began to penetrate.

In his Waterloo despatch Wellington described this moment as 'one of the most serious attacks made by the enemy on our position',[27] and indeed it could have been decisive: at least initially it might not be too much of an exaggeration to state that the fate of the campaign hinged upon the two under-strength brigades commanded by Sir Thomas Picton. On the extreme right of the French advance, Durutte's Division was not heavily involved, but Bourgeois's Brigade of Quiot's Division, and the divisions of Marcognet and Donzelot (in that order from left to right) seem to have gravitated towards the centre and almost became one huge formation, those on the left in part impelled towards their right by the volume of rifle fire being delivered against their left flank by the 1/95th in the sandpit and on the knoll. So overwhelmingly numerous was the French attack, however, that the position of these riflemen soon became untenable, so they fell back upon their other companies lining the Ohain road. Some confusion occurred at this point, due to the incapacitation of both the battalion commander, Sir Andrew Barnard, and his deputy, Lieutenant Colonel Alexander Cameron, wounded at almost the same moment. Next in seniority was Major Jonathan Leach, who had been with the advanced party; he began to make his way to join the main body, and according to John Kincaid thought that he was supposed to retire the whole battalion to a position in line with the remainder of the brigade. Kincaid knew differently: as the battalion adjutant he had earlier spoken to Kempt, who told him that he intended to advance the whole brigade when the time was right, so Kincaid halted the retreat of the 95th about 10 yards behind the hedge that lined the road, and began to fire on the approaching French. He had only three companies with him, for those in advance had, in the usual way, 'doubled' to the rear to re-form under cover of those in the line, but before the riflemen could be overwhelmed Kempt did indeed advance his brigade, not quite in line with Kincaid's men, but began to fire about 20 yards from the hedge. The 32nd was on the right of this advancing formation and partly behind the 95th, so that only about two thirds of the battalion was able to use its musketry.

As usual, both Wellington and Picton were on hand at the most desperate points of the action, giving orders and encouraging the men. Also still present was the Duke of Richmond, accompanied by his son, the 15-year-old William Pitt Lennox, a cornet in the Royal Horse Guards who had been intended to serve as ADC to Peregrine Maitland, commander of the 1st (Foot Guards) Brigade, but who had suffered a terrible fall from his horse at Brussels, breaking his arm and losing the sight of his right eye. Thus denied an active role, the boy accompanied his father to the battlefield. Richmond spoke to Picton just as the French approached, and although advised to retire he and his son stayed on as spectators, the duke remarking to William, 'I'm glad to see you stand fire so well,'[28] although in reality the boy was only worried about trying to control his skittish horse with only one arm.

The 32nd, moving up to the left and partially behind the 1/95th, fired at the advancing French at very close range. They continued to advance, over the Ohain road, and it was apparently in this action that a notable incident occurred around the 32nd's colours. Ensign John Birtwhistle, carrying the regimental colour, went down with a severe wound; the precious flag was taken from him by Lieutenant Robert Belcher, commanding the left-centre 'division'. As they continued to advance the French immediately in their front began to retire; a French officer whose horse had been shot extricated himself from beneath it and grabbed at the colour, and began to draw his sabre. Belcher retained hold of the flag and his comrades rushed to his assistance. Major William Toole, commander of the right-centre division, cried out, 'Save the brave fellow!' – the French officer – but too late. Belcher's covering sergeant, Christopher Switzer, ran his spontoon into the Frenchman's breast and Private William Lacey fired a shot into him; the officer fell dead at Belcher's feet.

Next in line to the east of the 32nd was the 79th, who traded musketry with the head of the French column in their front, but the moment was desperate, as Wellington recalled:

A column of French was firing across the road at one of our regiments. Our people could not get at them to charge them, because they would have been disordered by crossing the road. It was a nervous moment. One of the two forces must go about in a few minutes – it was impossible to say which it might be. I saw about two hundred of the 79th, who seemed to have had more than they liked of it. I formed them myself about twenty yards from the flash of the French column, and ordered them to fire; and, in a few minutes, the French column turned about.[29]

Picton also saw the 79th wavering, and seeing nearby one of the ADCs to the army's cavalry commander, the Earl of Uxbridge, Captain Horace Seymour of the 18th Hussars (Uxbridge himself was with the heavy cavalry to the rear of the position), Picton called on him to rally them. Such was the confusion of the moment – the position would at this time have been wreathed with musket smoke – that Seymour was not certain of the identity of the troops in question, but he named them as Highlanders so they must have been the 79th. At that instant French musketry brought down Seymour's horse and sent a ball through Picton's forehead. Killed on the spot, the general fell from his horse, and by the time Seymour had struggled from under his own mount, he saw a grenadier of the 28th beginning to loot Picton's body, taking his purse and spectacles from his trouser pocket. Seymour recovered the booty and handed it to Tyler, who must just have arrived on the spot.[30]

Rank was no guarantee against the looting of the dead: it was a universal practice, even in the heat of battle, as the officer of the Royal Scots observed:

I saw … a greater number of our soldiers busy in rifling the pockets of the dead, and perhaps the wounded, that I would have wished to have seen; with some exertion we got them in. Those of our own Regiment the

The death of Sir Thomas Picton during the attack of d'Erlon's corps. The scene is not entirely accurate: Picton is shown incorrectly wearing the staff bicorn hat instead of his 'round hat', and apparently there was no ADC immediately beside him when he fell. (*Engraving by S. Mitan after Capt. George Jones, published 1817*)

Colonel beat with the flat of his sword as long as he had breath to do so. The fellows knew they deserved it; but they observed, some one else would soon be doing the same, and why not they as well as others?[31]

Tyler moved his general's body to a position beneath a tree, where it could easily be located, and then went to find Kempt, who had now automatically become commander of the 5th Division, while Sir Philip Belson of the 28th stepped up to lead Kempt's Brigade.

On the left of Kempt's Brigade, the 28th also advanced towards the looming French formation, and on reaching the hedge observed the French attempting to deploy from column into line, to maximize the number of their men who could fire, as described by Lieutenant William Mountsteven of the 28th:

The 28th was lying a short distance behind the hedge when the Enemy's Columns were put in motion. When they had advanced pretty near, we were moved up to the hedge, and on our reaching it found a French Column attempting to deploy at probably thirty or forty yards on the other side … I well recollect looking over the hedge the moment before we charged, and admiring the gallant manner the French Officers led out their Companies in deploying … We then poured in our fire, sprung over the fence, and charged. The Enemy ran before we could close with them, and, of course, in great confusion.[32]

(Both he and another witness who recorded his memories, Private Alexander Cruikshank of the 79th's light company, were adamant that the French never crossed the hedge, and Cruikshank stated that the only French who got near it were some sharpshooters who had become mixed up with the 79th's own retiring skirmishers.)

The 28th split into two 'wings', the left half of the battalion moving some way down the slope after the retiring French, while the right wing halted upon glimpsing a body of troops through the smoke, who they mistook for Belgians. They realized their error when these troops fell back towards the French lines, by which time it was too late for the right wing of the 28th to fire and pursue.

On the other side of the breach in the line caused by the flight of Bylandt's Brigade, Sir Denis Pack put his own brigade into motion, advancing towards the road and hedge. The 44th was held back as a reserve, while the other three battalions advanced in echelon from the left, so that the 92nd came into action first. The battalion had been lying down under cover when Pack ordered them up, and called, '92nd, everything has given way on your right and left and you must charge this column.'[33] The French column had reached the hedge with ordered arms and was in the act of shouldering them when the 92nd, formed four deep, fired into them.

The position at this moment was critical. On the right, Kempt, who at this stage may not have realized that he now commanded the division, galloped along the line of his brigade, urging his men to stand, and, seeing Kincaid of the 95th (who as the battalion's adjutant would have stood out from the rest by virtue of being mounted), called to him by name and begged 'that I would never quit this spot'. Kincaid told him that he could depend upon it, but then almost had to run for it as French cavalry on the flank of d'Erlon's infantry made towards him, and Kincaid realized with horror that the previous night's rain had rusted his sword fast into its scabbard. The intervention of British cavalry, as recounted below, saved him from having to ride for his life.

Pack's Brigade was exchanging musketry with the approaching French and doing them terrible damage, but with their weakened numbers apparently found it impossible to stand. De Lacy Evans of the 5th West India Regiment, serving as ADC to the commander of the Union Brigade, Sir William Ponsonby, was in the immediate rear of Pack's men and thought that the infantry had 'been obliged to yield', but for some 'stragglers of our Infantry who remained behind',[34] and were still doggedly firing into the French formation. Other members of the Union Brigade concurred: Captain Alexander Kennedy Clark of the Royal Dragoons thought that the infantry in his front – Kempt's Brigade – no longer defended the hedge but had been wheeled back so that they were firing into the left flank of the French column, which was advancing rapidly onto the centre of the position. This was either Bourgeois's Brigade of Quiot's Division or Donzelot's Division, and the troops he saw having wheeled back were probably one wing of the 28th, as described above.

So desperate did the moment seem that it was at this point that one of the NCOs commanding one of Rogers's guns drove a spike into its touch hole to prevent the gun from being turned upon the British once it had been captured, thus depriving the company of one sixth of its power for the remainder of the battle. Further east, Lieutenant Charles Wyndham of the Scots Greys seemingly had no doubt about the critical nature of the moment, as he thought that the 92nd appeared to be giving way before the French advance. Then the cavalry intervened.

The Earl of Uxbridge, Wellington's cavalry commander, was present with his two brigades of heavy cavalry in the rear of the 5th Division, and, crucially, Wellington had given him the freedom to act on his own initiative. Uxbridge and his two subordinate brigadiers must have ridden forward to observe the progress of the French advance and realized the critical nature of the moment – and also, probably, that although the infantry was being forced back, they were doing such damage to the advancing French that they were ripe for counter-attack. De Lacy Evans observed of one French column – either Bourgeois or Donzelot, for he was on the right of the Union Brigade's position – that it had suffered so severely, and lost so many officers, that it seemed incapable of deploying, was by this stage firing only spasmodically from the front and flanks, and was already on the point of breaking up. Infantry not in the best of discipline was terribly vulnerable to an attack by cavalry, and so it proved.

The story of the 92nd charging with the Scots Greys was of early origin, though magnified in later years. This version shows the Highlanders seconding the Greys (in the background); the uniforms are portrayed accurately, without sporrans and with the officer in trousers. (*Engraving by S. Mitan after Capt. George Jones, published 1817*)

A charge of the Life Guards at Waterloo: the first charge by the Household and Union brigades helped defeat the great attack against the 5th Division. (*Engraving by William Bromley after Luke Clennell*)

Charge of the Life Guards at Waterloo, engaging the French cuirassiers who advanced on the left flank of d'Erlon's great attack. (*Print after Harry Payne*)

Uxbridge ordered the Household Brigade to advance, almost entirely to the west of the highway against the cavalry on d'ErIon's left flank, and rode with them himself, having also ordered the Union Brigade to move through Picton's Division against d'Erlon's infantry. The charge they executed was different from the full-blown gallop portrayed in later pictures, but actually moved at a trot or even slower. Uxbridge had instructed the Royals and Inniskillings to charge, with the Scots Greys to remain as a reserve, but all three charged, with severe consequences to themselves.

On the left flank of the 5th Division, the Scots Greys passed right through the wavering 92nd, who wheeled into open column to let them pass; Corporal John Dickson distinctly recalled the 92nd's officers calling to their men to wheel back to let the horsemen through. Rough rider James Armour described how

We gave our countrymen in front of us three hearty huzzas, and waving our swords aloft in the air, several swords were struck with balls while so doing; and I must not forget the piper:

The piper loud and louder blew,
The balls of all denominations quick and quicker flew ...

The Highlanders were then ordered to wheel back ... when they had, and were wheeling back imperfectly, we rushed through them: at the same time they huzzaed us, calling out, 'Now my boys – Scotland for ever!' I must own it had a thrilling effect upon me, I am certain numbers of them were knocked over by the horses; in our anxiety we could not help it. Some said, 'I didna think ye wad hae saired me sae' – catching hold of our legs and stirrups, as we passed, to support themselves.[35]

That they were able to pass through the Gordons doing so little damage must in part have been due to the relatively low speed at which they were charging. Indeed, Lieutenant Robert Winchester of the 92nd recalled that they 'literally walked over this [French] Column, and in less than three minutes it was totally destroyed.'[36]

Lieutenant James Hope of the 92nd was a near witness to the effect of the Greys upon the French column, and the same occurred further along the line with the Royals and Inniskilling Dragoons:

For some minutes the carnage was truly dreadful. The French troops, showing an unwillingness to go to the rear … and many of them having refused to move one way or the other, were cut down without ceremony … When the Scots Greys charged past the flanks of the 92d [*sic*], both regiments cheered, and joined in the heart-touching cry of 'Scotland for ever!' These words possessed a charm, which none but those ardently attached to their native country ever rightly understood. The mere sound of them, in the ears of every one who was present, will ever recall to their rembrance one of the most interesting and awfully grand scenes which man ever beheld … I never saw the soldiers of this regiment so very savage as they were on this occasion; they repeatedly cried to the cavalry to spare none of the French – that they did not deserve mercy at their hands.

This most unusual sentiment Hope attributed to reports of the maltreatment of British prisoners taken at Quatre Bras, magnified by rumour, although the very desperate situation, the loss of so many comrades, and the death of their colonel, must all have conspired to create an attitude of relentless hostility to the unfortunate Frenchmen who were going down beneath the sabres and hooves of the cavalry. Hope continued:

The death of their companions, they imagined, called loudly for revenge. Our soldiers no longer looked on those of France as the enemies of their country only, but as a horde of barbarians, let loose upon the inhabitants of every civilized state. I firmly believe, that the soldiers, before the commencement of the battle, had agreed, amongst themselves, to send as many of their enemies into another world as they could. Whatever may have been the cause, I never saw the same kind of feeling pervade these soldiers in any former battle in which I had been engaged. Towards the close of the battle, when the enemy were more to be pitied than feared, they assumed a very different air, and treated those who were made prisoners with the kindness characteristic of the British soldier.[37]

Hope also stated that 'he never saw anything to equal the enthusiasm of both Corps when the Greys passed through the 92nd to charge – that they mutually cheered each other on – that the 92nd seemed half mad, and that it was with the greatest difficulty that the Officers could preserve anything like order in the ranks'.[38]

This action gave rise to one of the most famous incidents in regimental folklore: that the Greys and 92nd charged together, the Highlanders catching hold of the Greys' stirrup leathers and dashing together into the fray. It is a great exaggeration, for although some participants related how the regiments 'charged together' (for example Robert Winchester), probably only a few Highlanders actually went into the fight, and Sergeant Richard Johnston of the Greys stated that although some did join in the advance, he made it clear that they then remained behind to shepherd French prisoners to the rear.[39] Sergeant Major William Crawford of the Greys recalled that 'As we advanced we were met by a number of the 92nd Regiment, who turned and ran into the charge with us,'[40] which suggests a very haphazard affair involving troops who were in the act of retiring before the cavalry charged.

It seems likely that, even if the 'stirrup charge' never occurred in the manner described in legend, the 92nd did follow the Union Brigade some distance, and a few men were involved in the hand-to-hand fighting that destroyed the head of the French column. The fury of the Highlanders was presumably only encouraged by Pipe Major Cameron, who was recognized by Dickson, playing *Hey Johnny Cope* as the Greys charged. A strange story originated from this moment. Aspects of what in modern parlance is termed the paranormal were not unknown in Highland culture, from second sight and premonition to the appearance of spirits, and at this point one of the 92nd's pipers was said to have exclaimed that he saw Fassiefern in front of them, waving his bonnet as of old. Amid the smoke, confusion, excitement and terror probably anything could have been imagined, although doubtless many would have agreed that Fassiefern would have been there, if he could.

On the right of Pack's Brigade the Inniskilling Dragoons passed through gaps in the line of the 3/1st and 42nd, which regiments wheeled back to let them through. The 42nd at least had advanced right up to the hedges lining the Ohain road, but hesitated to go further, as James Anton recalled, due to wearing kilts, because 'our bare thighs had no protection from the piercing thorns', and to go further would have meant 'laceration [and] self-inflicted torture'.[41] They had just begun to break gaps in the hedges when they were ordered to wheel aside to let the cavalry through. There was some confusion: the Inniskillings' commander, Colonel Joseph Muter, stated that 'some, I fancy, got through [the hedges] rather irregularly.'[42] The regiment had approached the crest of the ridge on foot, and mounted only at its top, so they, too, must have hit the French at no more than a trot, but the French were already shaking before contact, and probably unnerved by the Inniskillings' 'Irish howl' that they were said to have bellowed.

To their right, the Royal Dragoons passed through the 28th and fell upon the French infantry in their front. Captain Alexander Kennedy Clark of the Royals wrote a memorandum of the regiment's charge that emphasizes not only the devastating force of the cavalry attack, but also how the French, although on the point of breaking through the line, had been mauled severely by the fire of Kempt's Brigade, and notably by the 28th:

> At this moment many of the Artillery (I believe all) were ordered to leave, or did leave, their Guns, which were stationed behind the hedges, and they passed through the intervals of our Squadrons. The Infantry that, I presume, had previously lined the hedges, were wheeled by Sections to their left, and were firing on the *left flank* of the French Column, the head of which by this time *passed both hedges unchecked*, as far as I could perceive, and were advancing rapidly. From the nature of the ground we did not see each other until we were very close, perhaps eighty or ninety yards. The head of the Column appeared to be seized with a panic, gave us a fire which brought down about twenty men, went instantly about and endeavoured to regain the opposite side of the hedges; but we were upon and amongst them before this could be effected, the whole Column getting into one dense mass, the men between the advancing and retiring parts getting so jammed together that the men could not bring down their arms, or use them effectively, and we had nothing to do but to continue to press them down the slope.

The infantry that Clark recalled firing into the French left flank was obviously the left wing of the 28th, and he emphasized the importance of their presence once the French column had been repelled:

> Our infantry, which we passed at the hedge, now proved of essential service to us. They had formed small bodies or squares following in the rear of

the charge, and not only checked pursuit, but without their support and assistance I am satisfied we should not have got back so well as we did, and certainly we could not have secured one-half of the Prisoners taken in the charge. Many who had surrendered effected their escape, yet above 2,000 were secured and went to the rear.[43]

It was in this action that Clark and Corporal Francis Stiles of the Royals took one of the most famous trophies of the battle, the Eagle of the French 105me Ligne; the other Eagle to be taken was, arguably even more famously, that of the 45me Ligne captured by Sergeant Charles Ewart of the Scots Greys, in the same charge.

Only the left wing of the 28th followed the Royal Dragoons some way down the slope. As they retired they escorted back some hundreds of French prisoners and at the rear of the hedge handed them over to some returned dragoons. (Clark's statement that d'Erlon's infantry had crossed the road was, as noted, refuted by William Mountsteven of the 28th: 'this positively never took place in our part of the position; but, on the contrary, the Enemy was routed on his own side of the hedge.'[44] Due to the confused nature of the fighting it is possible that both were correct, in referring to slightly different sections of the line.)

The 28th's left wing continued to fall back until they rejoined the right wing, which had already re-formed about 80 yards behind the road. The regiment sustained some casualties in this action, including Lieutenants Roger Gilbert (severely wounded) and J.P. Clarke (mortally), and it was probably at this time that they also lost Lieutenant James Deares. He appears to have forgotten his duty and in the enthusiasm of the moment ran along with the cavalry on foot, slashing at every Frenchman he came upon. He cut down two and wounded several more before he was overpowered and taken prisoner, only returning to his regiment on the following day, stripped of almost every piece of clothing. His reappearance, wearing nothing but his shirt, might have been the cause of some facetious remarks from his comrades had he not also been badly wounded.

Beyond probably directing some musketry against the extreme left of d'Erlon's advance, the right part of Kempt's Brigade was apparently not as heavily engaged as Pack's and the 28th, although as some of the cavalry began to shepherd French prisoners back through Wellington's front line, Lieutenant John Molloy of the 1/95th intervened to save a life. Two dragoons had captured a French officer and were considering 'sticking' him rather than escorting him to the rear. On the Frenchman calling for mercy, Molloy protested, and the dragoons said they were only intending to do to the enemy what the French were doing to their own comrades, but Molloy persuaded them to take him to safety at the rear. As they left the Frenchman threw away a bundle of papers; Molloy looked at them and discovered they were love letters from a girl in Paris to her Alphonse.

The charge of the Household and Union brigades stopped d'Erlon's advance dead in its tracks and saved the centre of Wellington's line from being pierced, perhaps fatally so. The charge, however, was exceptionally costly. Instead of rallying as soon as the retreat of the French infantry was assured, many of the cavalry charged on, carried away by the emotion and triumph of the moment, even to the French gun line. Some of their officers attempted to rally them, but without much success; the commander of the Union Brigade, Sir William Ponsonby, was killed, as was Colonel James Inglis Hamilton of the Scots Greys, who seems to have been as caught up in the excitement of the moment as everyone else, apparently exhorting his men to charge instead of behaving with the necessary prudence by ensuring that they remained as a reserve to cover the withdrawal of the other two regiments. Uxbridge, who knew well the importance of holding a reserve and had given clear orders to that effect, subsequently blamed himself for charging with the Household Brigade rather than remaining behind to impose some kind of order, but it was certainly not entirely his fault.

Despite its great success in riding down d'Erlon's men, the Union Brigade was dreadfully mauled; some reached the French guns in a completely disorganized state with horses 'blown', and were counter-attacked by French cavalry. With no available reserve to protect their return to the British lines, relatively few of those who had charged on so far managed to get back. Their actions seemed to exemplify Wellington's not entirely justified and perhaps unduly critical complaint about the lack of order in an earlier British cavalry charge: 'the trick of our officers of cavalry have acquired of galloping at every thing, and their galloping back as fast as they gallop on the enemy. They never consider their situation, and never think of manoeuvring before an enemy ... and when they use their arm as it ought to be used, viz., offensively, they never keep nor provide for a reserve.'[45]

With the heavy cavalry thus out of action, temporarily or worse, the security of the centre of Wellington's line again depended upon the dwindling numbers of the 5th Division, now further mauled and with the tiers of command changing constantly as senior officers were killed or wounded. The battalions appear to have fallen back some distance to their original position, although in accord with usual practice the skirmishers would again have moved forward in 'open order' to provide the screen between the main body and the enemy.

Only the British elements of the 5th Division were fully engaged against d'Erlon. Quite early in the battle, the division effectively 'lost' part of its Hanoverian brigade when Vincke was ordered to march westwards with two of his battalions (Gifhorn and Hameln) to bolster the centre, near the Brussels highway. They ceased to be under the control of the 5th Division but instead came under the command of Major General George Cooke's 1st Division, and remained near the firing line but apparently fired not a shot until the final advance. They did, however, sustain some casualties while standing under fire, and Vincke remained throughout with the Gifhorn, for its commander, Major von Hammerstein, was wounded severely as he scorned to lie down to protect himself, and his deputy, Captain George Leue of the 4th Line Battalion, King's German Legion, acting as major to the Gifhorn, was mortally struck.

When Vincke left, his remaining two battalions, Hildesheim and Peine, were ordered to hold their position, but fell victim to what appears to have been a classic consequence of the difficulties of managing a multi-national army. The two battalions were under the command of Count von Westphalen of the Peine, presumably because Major Rheden of the Hildesheim had been wounded early in the day and his battalion was under the command of a relatively low-ranking officer, Captain George von Ludewig of the 4th Line Battalion, King's German Legion. A British staff officer rode up to Westphalen and spoke to him very hurriedly. Westphalen failed to understand what had been said but thought that he had been ordered to retire. Unable to contact Vincke, he conferred with Ludewig and apparently some sharp words were exchanged when the experienced Ludewig objected to leaving their post, but Westphalen prevailed and the two battalions began to withdraw. They were halted by a note from Sir George Scovell, AQMG, a somewhat scathing message that instructed Westphalen to attempt to undo the damage his action had caused by halting and using his battalions as a block to prevent the flight of stragglers and to re-form them upon his own men. Subsequently Vincke reported that such confusion was not uncommon under the circumstances and dispelled any ideas of base motives by stating that Westphalen had shown great composure under fire. Not until the following morning did Vincke's four battalions unite and rejoin the 5th Division.

Having agreed earlier with Vincke that their brigades should act together, Best, of the 4th Hanoverian Brigade, was on his own after Vincke left. His Verden Battalion, and apparently the skirmishers of the others, was deployed largely in open order; the Lüneburg and Osteröde battalions covered Rettburg's guns, and the Munden Battalion formed the reserve. From their position on the left of the line, the brigade was not engaged heavily, as evident from the officer casualties: only one was killed and seventeen wounded, including Baron Reden, commander of the Osteröde. The experienced Best was critical of some members of his command who had decamped, including officers who claimed illness and almost all the administrative staff and baggage, and most of the medical staff and the musicians who helped them. The same occurred with the medical staff of Vincke's Brigade: apparently believing the tales recounted by stragglers and wounded that the French were coming, they abandoned their aid post and headed for Brussels.

Rettburg's company remained in support of the 5th Division throughout, although it did change its position, and having been unable to replenish the ammunition expended at Quatre Bras, latterly Rettburg was only able to fire slowly to conserve what he had left.

Following the repulse of d'Erlon's attack, there was a lull in that part of the battlefield occupied by the 5th Division while the French reorganized. This would have permitted what remained of the division to steady itself after their desperate fight, and to settle into the new command structure brought about by death and injury. After Picton's fall the division became Kempt's, and while the process of the next in seniority stepping up through the tiers of command was not unusual, it produced at least one awkward moment. Major William Staveley of the Royal Staff Corps, attached to the Quartermaster General's Department, was employed during the battle in carrying messages from Wellington, including one to Picton (of unknown content; perhaps just a query about the state of his division). Staveley galloped up and encountered Kempt, and asked for Picton. Kempt just said, 'What are your orders?' Staveley insisted that his message was for Picton alone. Kempt exclaimed tetchily, 'I command the division, sir!' and, throwing out his arm, 'There is Sir Thomas Picton,' pointing to the general's dead body.[46]

Kempt was himself wounded subsequently, quite severely, 'but … never left the field. Like his old commander, Sir Ralph Abercromby, to whom he had been confidential secretary, he allowed no personal consideration to interfere with his duty; and, although unable to sit on horseback from the severity of the wound, he would not allow himself to be carried away from his soldiers, whose situation, pressed by a brave and powerful enemy, required every assistance from his presence and talents.'[47]

With Kempt stepping up to lead the division, command of his brigade fell to Sir Philip Belson of the 28th, by virtue of his seniority. Sir Andrew Barnard, who had commanded a brigade in the Peninsula, would have made an ideal deputy, but he was junior to Belson in terms of the dates of their brevet colonelcies, and in any case by this time had himself been wounded. These changes of command impacted throughout the division, for by the end of the day only one commanding officer was still unhurt, John Hicks of the 32nd; all the others had been killed, wounded or, in Belson's case, moved upwards. Belson's elevation left his own battalion under the command of a captain, Charles Cadell, who was only the sixth officer present with it in terms of seniority prior to the loss of those above him. Such transfers of command must have been fairly seamless for the division continued to function well.

Some succour was provided to the 5th Division in the presence of the 10th British Brigade of Sir John Lambert, which with Best's Hanoverians constituted the whole of the 6th Division. Harry Smith of the 95th, Lambert's brigade major, was at the forefront of the brigade as it moved up to a position ordered by Wellington before the battle began, to buttress Picton's left, and it appeared to Smith that the line was giving way:

For a few seconds, while every regiment was forming square, and the charge of Ponsonby's Brigade was going on (which the rising ground in our front prevented us seeing), it looked as if the formation was preparatory to a retreat. Many of the rabble of Dutch troops were flying towards us, and, to add to the confusion, soon after came a party of dragoons, bringing with them three eagles [*sic*: actually two] and some prisoners. I said to General

Lambert, 'We shall have a proper brush immediately, for it looks as if our left will be immediately turned, and the brunt of the charge will fall on us.'

Smith believed that part of the reason that the line stabilized was because of the failings of Napoleon's infantry:

His artillery and cavalry behaved most nobly, but I maintain his infantry did not … It is true this column [d'Erlon's] advanced under a galling fire, but it succeeded in reaching the spot where it intended to deploy. Kempt ordered the Battalion immediately opposite the head of the column to charge. It was a poor miserable Battalion compared with some of ours, yet it did dash like British soldiers at the column, which went about. It was then that Ponsonby's Brigade got in among them, and took eagles and prisoners.[48]

For the next period of the battle Wellington's line had to withstand an artillery bombardment of a ferocity never experienced by even the oldest Peninsular War veterans. General Maximilien Foy, whose troops were engaged against Hougoumont, witnessed the stoic immobility of the redcoats under such terrible fire and expressed the ordeal in an admiring way: that death was before them and amid their ranks, disgrace in their rear, but it seemed as if they had taken root in the ground. Inevitably there was some shaking, if only because of the need to close the gaps in the ranks opened by the path of roundshot, and some men were seen to duck. Further to the west along the line, Colonel John Colborne observed this among his own 52nd and called to the men, 'For shame! For shame! That must be the 2nd Battalion, I am sure,' whereupon his men all straightened up, not wishing to be mistaken for recruits.[49] The same would have been experienced by the 5th Division.

It was clear that one of the keys to Wellington's position was La Haye Sainte, and Ney made another attempt upon that part of the line, covered by the massed artillery. Quiot's troops marched against the farmhouse itself, while one of Donzelot's brigades advanced to cover their right flank, preceded by a cloud of skirmishers. The officer of the Royal Scots recalled how Pack, 'whom I always admired as a "soldier brave", stood near me, gazing with intense anxiety, as if he could penetrate the veil of smoke which then shrouded our position. I observed his large cocked hat riddled with musket-balls. He was the greatest fire-eater and keenest soldier I ever knew.'

This attack seems not to have been pressed with the determination of the first:

> This column was suffered to come to the very crest of our position ... composed of fine fresh-looking men, [it] approached us with great steadiness and regularity ... It was evidently the intention, that they should *deploy*, open a fire, get up supports, and so penetrate our line; but, to our amazement, they stood *stock-still*, looking like people bewildered. I imagine their commander must have been killed in coming through the hollow.[50]

As they approached, Pack turned to the new commanding officer of the 3/1st, Major Robert Macdonald (Lieutenant Colonel Colin Campbell and Lawrence Arguimbau had by this time both been wounded), and asked, 'Do you think you can hit those fellows from here?' Macdonald replied, 'No, but more to the right I think they could,'[51] and so the light company was thrown forward, followed by the rest of the battalion, the more effectively to use their muskets.

It worked, and once this second attack had been repelled, a primary consideration must have been to replenish the 5th Division's ammunition. The resupply of cartridges during an action is a factor often overlooked, but was one of crucial significance. Each man was supposed to carry sixty rounds, and while three rounds per minute was an achievable rate of fire, this could never have been long sustained as firing was generally restricted to those moments than an enemy was visible and within range. Nevertheless, in a protracted action it was possible to blaze away and exhaust all the cartridges carried by the individual, even if some had stowed extra rounds in a supplementary magazine or, as apparently was common, in the jacket pockets, making resupply essential. A calculation was made regarding the expenditure of ammunition at Vittoria by Sir Richard Henegan, head of the Ordnance Field Train in the Peninsula. In round numbers, he estimated the British and Portuguese infantry at 50,000 men (the Spanish had their own system of supply), which at sixty rounds apiece amounted to 3,000,000 cartridges. During the battle a further 1,350,000 rounds were distributed, of which Henegan estimated about half were used, so that on average each man would have fired more than seventy rounds each. According to circumstances some would have fired more, some less, but it serves to underline that a ready resupply of ammunition was required in a pitched battle. (It is interesting to note that Henegan calculated that only one shot in 459 took effect, and these figures apparently take no account of the casualties inflicted by artillery; a telling comment upon the accuracy and efficiency of the smoothbore musket and the manner in which it was used.)

The usual practice for resupply was to have carts or tumbrils loaded with casks of ammunition driven to where it was accessible to the formations for which it was intended, and there unload the barrels of cartridges. The best-known incident at Waterloo involving ammunition concerned the resupply of the garrison of Hougoumont by an intrepid member of the Royal Waggon Train who drove his wagon right into the compound despite the extreme danger, to whom it was said that the successful defence of the place was attributed. (His name was unrecorded at the time but almost certainly it was Joseph Brewer.)

Another heroic deed involved the resupply of the 3/1st. As the battle continued into the late afternoon, the battalion ran so low on ammunition that the skirmishers had to be called in, having nothing left to shoot. As they retired the opposing French skirmishers were emboldened and advanced, firing as they approached. In the usual manner an ammunition cart had been driven up as near as possible to the battalion, the horses being removed to prevent them bolting and taking the ammunition with them; but the position was so exposed that the men sent to get it were hit, until one man at last succeeded. According to the battalion's John Douglas, Henry Connor (or O'Connor) had been a sergeant until shortly before the battle but had been temporarily reduced in rank for 'losing' a prisoner, a light-fingered drummer who was due for court martial for theft. Connor ran to the cart and hoisted a cask of cartridges on his shoulder, but was hit on the way back. He had the presence of mind to throw the barrel so that it rolled down a slope and reached the battalion. The skirmishers were immediately resupplied and the French were driven back. Douglas states this to have occurred at Quatre Bras, but the Royal Scots officer who wrote of the division's experiences is clear that 'my hero' Connor performed his feat at Waterloo. (His injury is also disputed: the officer states that it was a ball in the heel, while Douglas claimed it hit his backside, but whatever the case, Connor was restored to his previous rank.)

The next stage in the Battle of Waterloo, although one of the most celebrated, did not much affect the 5th Division: the massed French cavalry attacks upon Wellington's line. Such assaults were most effective when the enemy had been weakened fatally by artillery bombardment, but the advance of Napoleon's main force of cavalry was both premature and ill-coordinated. The reason for the timing of the attack has been much discussed, but it is likely that Ney initiated it after mistaking the withdrawal of elements of Wellington's line into dead ground behind the crest of the ridge as a sign of retreat. French witnesses confirmed that the undulations of the terrain and the smoke of battle made it difficult to gauge the real situation, and furthermore the ground was still saturated from the recent rain and unsuited for cavalry charging uphill. The attacks were also poorly managed, without the close support of horse artillery that could have slaughtered Wellington's infantry at close range, and without the necessary tactical control. Captain Fortuné Brack of the Lancers of Napoleon's Imperial Guard claimed that his brigade was virtually sucked into the assault without specific orders, which may also have been true of other formations, and that the charges continued long after it was clear that Wellington's line was holding. The allied troops were universally admiring of the heroism with which the French cavalry pressed the attack, even when it was obvious that they were doomed to fail, but equally critical of the commanders who sent them to their ruin: 'Stand forth, mighty strategists, enlightened tacticians, and high-minded liberals, and explain to us the military genius evinced in such measures! or tell us, could the humblest sentinel in the French Army show less talent and judgment than was here displayed?'[52]

All along the line infantry battalions formed square to resist the cavalry, and although the attacks were mounted on the right half of Wellington's line, in the space between Hougoumont and La Haye Sainte, the units to the east of the Brussels highway were also in square at times, in case the cavalry mounted a major assault in that region also. By about 5.00 pm it is estimated that some 10,000 cavalrymen were committed to the attack, as wave after wave was beaten off. The unimaginative nature of Napoleon's tactics even disappointed Wellington, who earlier had remarked to Sir Andrew Barnard, 'Damn the fellow, he is a mere pounder after all.'[53]

Although the 5th Division was not threatened as seriously as elsewhere on the line of battle, an officer who took refuge in a square observed how the

Highlanders almost welcomed the approach of French cavalry as it provided a respite from the artillery bombardment, and were heard to joke and chat as they loaded and fired, comparing the cuirassiers' armour to that of crabs, and quipped about 'cracking the partan's shell' ('partan' being Scottish dialect for crab).

Otherwise the artillery fire continued unabated, while French skirmishers still exchanged shots with the division's light companies, which at times turned into more regular musketry. The experience of the 3/1st was probably typical; for some time after the repulse of d'Erlon's second attack they had been ordered to lie down, to avoid the worst effects of the incoming shot, and to amuse themselves some of the battalion searched French knapsacks abandoned by those sent to the rear as prisoners, reading letters they found within. The officer who left his account remarked how literate and proper the letters were, thinking that they showed an unexpectedly 'advanced state of morality and education'. They also passed some time chatting to wounded Frenchmen who had not been sent to the rear. All the while the battalion's skirmishers exchanged fire with their French counterparts, and it seems as if they and their officers were relieved periodically by others from the battalion, taking casualties all the while.

He also observed how soldiers with bad muskets 'might be seen creeping about to get hold of the firelocks of the killed and wounded, to try if the locks were better than theirs, and dashing the worst on the ground as if in a rage with it'; which, he remarked, had been quite common during the Peninsular War.

As Kempt's Brigade – now under Belson – continued to dwindle under the relentless fire, the line edged in towards the centre to reduce the gaps,

sometimes moving to the rear, or to a flank in quarter distance column, sometimes in line; and then wheeling backwards into open column to avoid the enemy's shot and shells as much as possible, as they were still pouring them into our position. This was the most unpleasant service of the whole day, as we stood a mark for their grape and shell without the power of ourselves giving a musket shot in reply. Our frequent change of position … was our only relief, as it gave us hopes of employment and occupied the mind, [although, he added, they still] had ample time to think of the imprudence of former days, and vow to amend our ways.[54]

Standing impotent under such heavy fire led the troops to become restive, but not with a desire for flight. The same officer reported that 'I could hear the soldiers say, "Take us out of this – are we to be massacred? Let us go and fight them."' The same was evidently expressed elsewhere along the line, and even in Wellington's hearing: 'Are we to be massacred here? Let us go at them, let us give them Brummagum!' (i.e. Birmingham, where the steel of the bayonets was manufactured). 'Wait a little longer, my lads, you shall have at them presently,' the duke supposedly replied.[55] If officers had difficulty in controlling their men under such a trial, Piper Kenneth Mackay of the 79th calmed and heartened his comrades by walking up and down in front of them, playing *Cogadh no Sith* (*Peace or War*) on his pipes.

In contrast to the many reports of foreign troops deserting under the pretext of helping the wounded, the reverse seems to have been the case with the British, as the Royal Scots officer recalled the steady trickle of wounded men

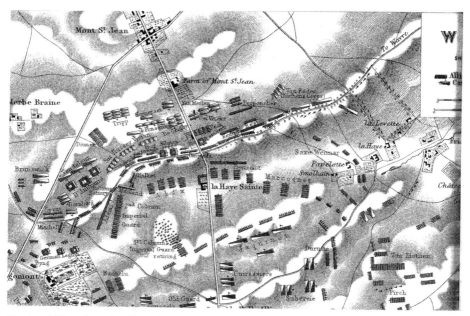

Battle of Waterloo: the dispositions at the time of the last French attack, with Napoleon's Imperial Guard being repelled on the French left flank. At this stage of the battle, Lambert's brigade has been pushed into the line alongside the Brussels–Charleroi highway, and Pack's brigade has been positioned in support. Prussian forces are arriving on Napoleon's right flank.

rejoining the battalion with wounds patched up, returning from the dressing stations bandaged, some with arms in slings, evidently determined to stand with their comrades to the end, including a field officer 'as grim as death', with his head swathed in a white napkin under his cap.

Only after the destruction of much of his cavalry did Napoleon finally authorize the concerted attack by all arms that should have been mounted much earlier. It was made in the knowledge that at last the Prussians were coming up on Napoleon's right, forcing him to divert resources to hold them in check, and although the battle was slipping from his grasp he knew that he could yet win if he breached Wellington's line. Enough cavalry remained operational to hover around the flanks of his infantry, forcing Wellington's troops to remain in square when threatened, in which formation they were terribly vulnerable to the artillery that accompanied and supported the assault. Harry Smith made a succinct comparison: that the battle was like a prize fight in which the protagonists would 'mill away' until one was beaten down.

The renewed French assault finally took the strongpoint in the very centre of Wellington's line: La Haye Sainte. Its German Legion defenders ran out of

A square under attack. Although not a contemporary image, this presents an impression of the desperate nature of resistance against French cavalry. (*Print after P. Jazet*)

ammunition and defended the post with bayonets and rifle butts until overpowered by weight of numbers. This permitted the French to advance from the farm and shelter behind some rising ground. Jonathan Leach, by that time commanding the 1/95th, observed that from this position only their heads could be seen and that the musketry directed against his battalion was the heaviest ever experienced. The members of the 1/95th who had been supporting the garrison of the farm were compelled to fall back towards the main position, from where they continued a fire fight. It was seemingly from this position that Lieutenant Allen Stewart of the battalion, 'a chivalrous and daring Highlander', engaged in a single combat against a French officer. Stewart was stabbed through the left arm and his sword broke off at the hilt, whereupon he closed with the Frenchman, whom 'he finished in an instant', perhaps by battering him with the hilt.[56]

Immediately to the right of Kempt's Brigade in the line of battle, on the western side of the highway, was the 3rd Division of Charles, Count Alten, from left to right the 2nd King's German Legion Brigade of Colonel Christian, Baron Ompteda, then Count Kielmansegge's 1st Hanoverian Brigade, and further west the 5th British Brigade of Sir Colin Halkett. In an attempt to deal with the French skirmishers edging north from La Haye Sainte, Alten ordered Ompteda to advance against them. Ompteda's Brigade was already weakened – it was one of his battalions that had been effectively extinguished at La Haye Sainte – and he protested against the order on the grounds that French cavalry was hovering. The Prince of Orange – Alten's superior – was present, and he insisted that he try. Ompteda led forward his own 5th Line Battalion of the King's German Legion, and the disaster he feared did occur: they were overrun by cavalry almost immediately, Ompteda was killed and hardly any escaped.

This posed a terrible threat to the 5th Division, as there opened a gap that could have been so exploited that it could have split Wellington's position in half, and potentially could have rolled up Kempt's right flank. Evidently there was no general officer in the immediate vicinity, Kempt now supervising the entire division, and the battalion commanders would have been concerned primarily with the situation of their own units. By great good fortune there was one officer present who realized the precarious nature of the situation: Captain James Shaw of the 43rd, AQMG of the 3rd Division, an experienced, heroic and level-headed officer. He left a graphic account of what then occurred, which not only saved Kempt's flank but possibly the entire position:

Ompteda's Brigade was nearly annihilated, and Kielmansegge's so thinned, that those two brigades could not hold their position. That part of the field of battle, therefore, which was between Halkett's left and Kempt's right, was unprotected; and being the very centre of the Duke's line of battle, was consequently that point, above all others, which the enemy wished to gain. The danger was imminent; and at no other period of the action was the result so precarious as at this moment ...

The Duke of Wellington stood at this moment on the right of the Nivelles road, behind the left of Maitland's brigade of Guards. The Prince of Orange, Count Alten, and so many officers of the 3rd division had, before this event happened, been killed, or wounded and obliged to leave the field, that I did not then know, nor do I now know, who was, at the moment I allude to, senior officer of the division on the field; I therefore, as the staff-officer present, galloped direct to the Duke, and informed him that his line was open for the whole space between Halkett's and Kempt's brigades. This very startling information he received with a degree of coolness, and replied to in an instant with such precision and energy, as to prove the most complete self-possession; and left on my mind the impression that his Grace's mind remained perfectly calm during every phase, however serious, of the action; that he felt confident of his own powers of being able to guide the storm which raged around him; and from the determined manner in which he then spoke, it was evident that he had resolved to defend to the last extremity every inch of the position which he then held. His Grace's answer to my representation was in the following words, or very nearly so: 'I shall order the Brunswick troops to the spot, and other troops besides; go you and get all the German troops of the division to the spot that you can, and all the guns that you can find.'

Of such gravity did Wellington consider this great gap in the very centre of his line of battle, that he not only ordered the Brunswick troops there, but put himself at their head; and it was even then with the greatest difficulty that the ground could be held; but Count Kielmansegge soon led back his gallant Germans to the spot; [and] the Brunswickers held their ground supported by part of the Nassau force ...

In no other part of the action was the Duke of Wellington exposed to so much personal risk as on this occasion, as he was necessarily under a close and most destructive infantry fire at a very short distance: at no other period of the day were his great qualities as a commander so strongly brought out, for it was the moment of his greatest peril as to the result of the action.[57]

Wellington's personal intervention had not only prevented an assault on Kempt's flank, but had saved the day.

Although disaster had been averted once more, there was little respite to the troops still clinging to the ridge, as they continued to suffer from incessant fire. Lambert's Brigade was moved up initially in support, and then into the line, to the extreme right of Kempt's position, while Pack's Brigade was formed as a reserve to them both. One of Lambert's battalions, the 27th (Inniskilling) Regiment, was pushed forward to the junction of the highway and the Ohain road, initially in column of companies and subsequently in square. Here it was not sheltered by folds in the terrain but was in full view of the French; the battalion was cut down where it stood, losing about 64 per cent of its strength, with only two or three officers remaining unscathed. Although Pack's Brigade was serving as a reserve, the 3/1st remained in the front line and was extremely exposed, and the 1/95th became somewhat separated from Kempt's Brigade, remaining to the immediate north of La Haye Sainte. Harry Smith recalled that when Lambert advanced into the line, Picton's Division 'had been already severely handled, and we took their position, my old Battalion of Riflemen remaining with us.'[58] It is not certain whether this indicates that the Rifles temporarily came officially under Lambert's control, but the situation was so desperate that under the circumstances such niceties would have been irrelevant.

Such were the losses that along the line requests were made for temporary relief; Colin Halkett asked Wellington in person but was told it was impossible. Robert Macdonald, commanding the 3/1st, made a similar request to Pack; the general did not answer, and Macdonald was himself wounded shortly after. A message was conveyed to the 5th Division by Sir Guy Campbell, AAG, to the effect that even if they were reduced to only 500 men, they *must* hold their ground. Even so, the most stalwart hearts were preparing for the worst: the 3/1st was reorganized into four small divisions to facilitate a possible retreat upon the Forêt de Soignes, 'out of which neither French nor devil could have driven us.'[59]

John Douglas of the 3/1st recounted a story that seems to illustrate the confusion of the moment: he claimed that the quartermaster, Thomas Griffith, came up from the rear when he heard of the battalion's losses and was ordered by Macdonald, upon being wounded, to take command of the battalion. Griffith declared that a relatively short time before he had been a private, and was now in command (he was commissioned as quartermaster in August 1814; prior to that it was stated that he had been temporarily reduced to the ranks for a misdemeanour). The story may not be accurate, as it is likely that Macdonald knew that other officers were still on their feet, including a captain, but it still reflects the terrible level of casualties, particularly among the officers. (Douglas also told how Macdonald had declined to dismount from his horse despite presenting a larger target, saying that he could be killed as easily on foot as on horseback.)

The battalion's plight was not exceptional. George O'Malley, the Irish officer who had tried so hard to get into action against France, and who took command of the 2/44th after Hamerton's injury at Quatre Bras, was twice wounded at Waterloo and had two horses shot from under him, but declined to leave the field or turn over command despite his injuries; fortunately so, for every captain had been hit and the senior unwounded officer was only a lieutenant.

John Kincaid of the 1/95th described how

For the two or three succeeding hours there was no variety with us, but one continued blaze of musketry. The smoke hung so thick about, that, although not more than eighty yards asunder, we could only distinguish each other by the flash of our pieces. A good many of our guns had been disabled, and a great many more were rendered unserviceable in consequence of the unprecedented close fighting ... I shall never forget the scene which the field of battle presented about seven in the evening. I felt weary and worn out, less from fatigue than anxiety. Our division, which had stood upwards of five thousand men at the commencement of the battle, had gradually dwindled down to a solitary line of skirmishers. The twenty-seventh regiment were lying literally dead, in square, a few yards behind us ... The smoke still hung so thick about us that we could see nothing. I walked a little way to each flank, to endeavour to get a glimpse of what was going on; but nothing met my eye except the mangled remains of men and horses, and I was obliged to return to my post as wise as I went.

I had never yet heard of a battle in which everybody was killed; but this seemed likely to be the exception, as we were all going by turns. We got excessively impatient under the tame similitude of the latter part of the process, and burned with desire to have a last thrust at our respective *vis-a-vis*; for, however desperate our affairs were, we had still the satisfaction of seeing that theirs were worse. Sir John Lambert continued to stand as our support, at the head of three good old regiments, one dead (the twenty-seventh) and two living ones; and we took the liberty of soliciting him to aid our views; but the Duke's orders on that head were so very particular that the gallant general had no choice.[60]

The exhaustion, and the decimation of the command element, was universal right along Wellington's line. Westwards from the 3rd Division Major Dawson Kelly of the 73rd, serving as AQMG, was sent by Wellington to get a status report; he rode up to his old battalion and was approached by some sergeants who begged him to take command as they had no officers left (something of an exaggeration; in the whole battalion three lieutenants and two ensigns appear not to have been hit, out of twenty-seven). The 92nd by this time were not in a much better state: they still had a major in command but otherwise were so short of officers that Sergeant David Robertson – clearly a most able NCO – was given command of what remained of two companies, was handed a telescope and told to report anything he saw of importance.

From his position, Robertson must have been one of the first in the army to witness what many would regard as its salvation: the arrival on its left flank of the Prussians, who had been marching all day from the position to which they had withdrawn after Ligny. The pressure they exerted upon Napoleon's right flank, drawing in troops that otherwise could have been hurled upon Wellington's line, finally tipped the scales in favour of the allies.

One of the 92nd's skirmishers ran back to the main position, and informed Robertson (evidently commanding the battalion's left) that 'something extraordinary was going on'. Robertson looked and saw what appeared to be troops in the same uniforms fighting each other; he called the adjutant, Lieutenant Claude Alexander, who wondered if part of Napoleon's army had mutinied. Through the smoke and at a distance the difference between French and Prussian uniforms was impossible to discern, but their puzzlement was almost immediately resolved when an officer came galloping down the line crying, 'The day is our own – the Prussians have arrived!' Robertson's comment that 'Never was reprieve more welcome to a death-doomed criminal'[61] must have been entirely heartfelt.

What was effectively Napoleon's final act was played out to the west of the 5th Division; realizing that the Prussian pressure on his right was swinging the balance, Napoleon made a final, desperate attack with elements of the Imperial Guard against Wellington's right-centre. It was a hopeless endeavour, and its defeat signalled the effective collapse of the French army.

The attack by the Imperial Guard had been seconded along the line by the French units that had been engaged all day, and the repulse of the Guard led to their retreat as well. This movement was hastened, and turned into a torrent of flight, when Wellington ordered a general advance of his entire line, as much as it was able, including his exhausted infantry and, significantly, the light cavalry, which, although engaged throughout, was in a much better state than

Wellington orders the advance towards the end of the battle: the regiment shown is the 52nd Light Infantry of Adam's Brigade in Clinton's 2nd Division, and at right an officer and rifleman of the 95th, of which elements of the 2nd and 3rd battalions were in the brigade. (*Engraving by S. Mitan after Capt. George Jones, published 1817*)

the shattered heavies. Such was the smoke that hung over the centre of the line, however, that like John Kincaid, few had any real conception of what was occurring. Harry Smith, Lambert's brigade major, recalled that the slackening of the firing suggested that one side or the other was beaten, but he was unsure which; 'This was the most anxious moment of my life.' Then the smoke cleared sufficiently for Smith to see 'the redcoats in the centre, as stiff as rocks, and the French columns retiring rapidly, and there was such a British shout as rent the air. We all felt then to whom the day belonged.'

Any doubt was dispelled a moment later:

I saw the Duke, with only one Staff officer remaining, galloping furiously to the left. I rode on to meet him. 'Who commands here?'; 'Generals Kempt and Lambert, my lord.' 'Desire them to get into a column of companies of Battalions, and move on immediately.' I said, 'In which direction, my lord?'; 'Right ahead, to be sure.' I never saw his Grace so animated.[62]

In his ride to urge his troops to advance, Wellington had passed the 1/95th, still in a fog of hanging smoke so that they only knew of his success by the British cheer, which, as Kincaid described,

made every one prick up his ears … it gradually approached, growing louder as it grew near; we took it up by instinct, charged through the hedge down upon the old knoll, sending our adversaries flying at the point of the bayonet. Lord Wellington galloped up to us at the instant, and our men began to cheer him; but he called out, 'No cheering, my lads, but forward, and complete your victory! '

This movement had carried us clear of the smoke; and, to people who had been for so many hours enveloped in darkness, in the midst of destruction, and naturally anxious about the result of the day, the scene which now met the eye conveyed a feeling of more exquisite gratification than can be conceived. It was a fine summer's evening, just before sunset. The French were flying in one confused mass. The British lines were seen in close pursuit, and in admirable order, as far as the eye could reach to the right, while the plain to the left was filled with Prussians. The enemy made one last attempt at a stand on the rising ground to the right of La

Belle Alliance; but a charge from General Adam's Brigade again threw them into a state of confusion, which was now inextricable, and their ruin was complete. Artillery, baggage, and everything belonging to them fell into our hands. After pursuing them until dark, we halted about two miles beyond the field of battle, leaving the Prussians to follow up the victory.[63]

The Prussians had to be left to the pursuit; Wellington's army was just too exhausted.

David Robertson, commanding his two companies, had difficulty restraining his men: 'it was only by force that the non-commissioned officers could keep them from dashing into the French lines. No language can express how the British army felt at this time; their joy was truly ecstatic.'

Once discipline had been restored, the brigade advanced:

we leapt over the hedge ... and in a few minutes we were among the French lines. Nothing was used now but the bayonet; for, after the volley we gave them, we set off at full speed, and did not take time to load. All was now destruction and confusion. The French at length ran off, throwing away knapsacks, firelocks, and every thing that was cumbersome, or that could impede their flight ... One division ... made an attempt to stand ... we rushed upon it like a legion of demons. Such was our excited and infuriated state of mind at the time, and being flushed with the thought of victory, we speedily put an end to their resistance.[64]

So heavy was the smoke hanging over the position of the 5th Division that the last French attack was described by the officer of the Royal Scots as resembling a scene from a camera obscura, with figures flitting back and forth like shadows. All was uncertainty until the British cheers heralded victory, and he described how his regiment shook hands and were 'mad with joy'. As the smoke cleared the retiring French could be seen, withdrawing at that stage still in some order, and he was struck by the way they kept turning around to stare their victors in the face as if unable to accept their defeat. Most firing ceased, with only random shots flashing in the gathering twilight.

Most witnesses commented on the British cheer that always accompanied a bayonet charge; it was a psychological weapon that never failed to damage the enemy's morale, and as such it was usually calculated as carefully as gauging the optimum moment for advancing. On this particular occasion the cheer was probably also as much in relief after hours of trial, and one officer of the 32nd described it in particularly colourful terms:

> When the French came within about forty paces, we set up a death-howl and rushed at them. They fled immediately, not in a regular manner as before, but in the greatest confusion. Their animal spirits were exhausted, the panic spread, and in five minutes the army was in complete disorder … no mob was ever a greater scene of confusion … arms, knapsacks, everything, was thrown away; and *sauve qui peut* seemed indeed to be the universal feeling.[65]

Even in the moment of victory tragedy overtook the 5th Division's remaining staff. Towards the end of the action Newton Chambers led a column to recapture La Haye Sainte, but as he was accepting the surrender of a French officer he was shot through the body and killed on the spot. He was greatly lamented, even the Duke of York declaring that his death had deprived the army of one of its most promising talents. All of Picton's staff suffered in one way or another: Tyler, who following Picton's death had acted as ADC to Kempt, had his horse shot from beneath him and was bruised by a spent ball that hit him as he fell; Langton was reported as slightly wounded at Quatre Bras; and although not listed in the first casualty returns, Barrington Price was evidently injured so seriously that he died in January 1816.

The pursuit by Wellington's army was limited, for reasons of sheer exhaustion, and it was the arriving Prussians that completed the rout of Napoleon's army. The emotions recorded by the 32nd officer must have been very common: 'At eleven o'clock, when we halted … I sank down almost insensible from fatigue; my spirits and strength were completely exhausted. I was so weak, and the wound in my thigh so painful, from want of attention and in consequence of severe exercise, that after I got to Nivelles, and secured quarters, I did not awake regularly for 36 hours.'[66]

Exhaustion was mental as well as physical, as the Royal Scot recalled. His battalion advanced into what had been the heart of Napoleon's position, and bivouacked amid heaps of French bodies. Passing beyond most of the wounded who lay where they fell, the heart-rending cries of 'water' were replaced by what seemed a deep silence, at least when contrasted with the recent roar of battle. This contrast produced unease, and as to what followed, 'It could not be called *rest* – there is nothing I could liken it to but itself. The day looked like a waking dream! Good Heaven! was it real? Had we defeated Napoleon? What will they think of us at home? and such like reflections passed through our minds … a deep and intense feeling of wonder at the magnitude of our victory possessed our faculties.'[67]

With the fighting subsided, consideration was given to the wounded and dead. There being no official system of casualty evacuation, the injured still had either to shift for themselves or rely upon their comrades for assistance, but at least with the battle over there was more chance that men would be permitted to leave the ranks to aid the casualties. There was also no further chance that the injured would be hit again, always a danger while fighting continued. Earlier

Casualty evacuation: the wounded conveyed from the battlefield on carts passing La Haye Sainte, while local people scavenge from and bury the dead. Charlotte Waldie, even some weeks after the battle, found the smell pervading the entire field 'extremely offensive, and in some places scarcely bearable. Deep stagnant pools of red putrid water, mingled with mortal remains, betrayed the spot where the bodies of men and horses had mingled together in death.' (*Engraving by and after J. Rouse, published 1816*)

in the day a sad fate had overtaken Lieutenant Elliott Johnston of the 1/95th, the son of a general in the East India Company. After he was wounded he was conveyed to Mont St. Jean, where some riflemen scouted up a horse to take him to Brussels; they had just got him into the saddle when a roundshot killed him on the spot.

Of those who described medical treatment before and after the battle, some from the 5th Division will serve to exemplify the experiences of the many. Initially the relatively small number of medical officers were overwhelmed: James Hope of the 92nd, returning to Brussels with a shot in the groin, described how 'Waterloo was literally filled with the wounded of the allied army – their cries were piercing … Without legs, without arms, soldiers were seen lying in every direction … many were lying horribly disfigured with numerous wounds, and faintly crying Water, water, water!'

For those who made their own way to Brussels, or were carried thence by the carts allocated to transport the wounded, the first succour they encountered was provided not by the army authorities but instead:

> Nothing could exceed the kindness and attention of the inhabitants to our wounded, on their arrival in the city. All ranks vied with each other in their personal acts of kindness. Many of the most respectable ladies in Brussels stood all the day at the gate by which the wounded entered, and to each soldier, as they arrived, distributed wine, tea, coffee, soup, bread, and cordials of various kinds; others remained at their houses, and ministered to the wants of those wounded who wandered through the streets.[68]

Countless of these Samaritans provided wounded soldiers with a bed in which to recover. Survivors were effusive in their praise for the citizens of the city, although there were occasional disappointments: Hope himself went to an hotel he had frequented before the battle but was turned away, on the excuse that when the French entered the city there would be reprisals against those harbouring a wounded Briton. Instead, he was taken in by a genteel family whose two daughters spent the next days visiting the wounded in their various billets and providing what comforts they could.

The fortitude displayed by the wounded who reached Brussels on their own was a source of wonder to those unused to the resilience of Wellington's soldiers.

One lady – presumably one of those who 'stood all the day at the gate' that Hope described – stated that the injured Scots who hobbled into the city seemed to be made of iron, and cited one, dragging himself along, that she tried to assist. The Highlander drew himself up to his full height, thanked her but declined any help, saying, 'I was born in Lochaber, and I do not care for a wound,' but then rather spoiled the effect by collapsing on the pavement at her feet.[69]

For many of the wounded, the quest to find treatment was slow and painful. With his trigger finger shot off at Quatre Bras, Edward Costello began his march to Brussels on 17 June, having rested for the night in a farmhouse near Quatre Bras. On the way he encountered a little child crying besides its dead mother who had been shot through the head; he rescued the infant and handed it over to a soldier's wife at Genappe, who recognized him as the child of a member of the Royal Scots. Costello spent the next night at Waterloo, then trudged on to Brussels, which he found thronging with Belgian soldiers who 'appeared quite free from wounds', with hundreds of wounded lying on straw in the streets. There was a moment of panic when it was reported that French troops were approaching; some Belgian troops began to load their muskets and Costello, despite his injury, picked up an abandoned rifle and fell in with the British battalion garrisoning the city, the 81st Foot. The alarm passed quickly when it was realized that the approaching column of Frenchmen were prisoners of war under escort.

The flow of wounded entering the city became a torrent on the following morning until the streets were packed with casualties, most temporarily having to lie untreated on the ground until relief arrived as described before:

My pen cannot describe the humane and indefatigable exertions of those praiseworthy ladies of Brussels; their magnanimity surpasses all comments; without exception, all were busily employed, some strapping and bandaging wounds, others serving out tea, coffee, soups, and all other soothing nourishment, others employed in stripping the poor sufferers of their gory and saturated garments, and dressing them in clean shirts and other habiliments. Such acts must ever draw forth the admiration of man towards those fair Belgian surgeons and nurses, who despising all false delicacy, soothed and alleviated the pangs of the dying soldier, and staunched his bleeding wounds; the delicate hands of spinster and matron were busily employed loosening the helpless warrior's accoutrements and dress, to discover and bind up his scars; never will be erazed [*sic*] from my memory the sympathetic feeling of those lovely women.[70]

Costello himself, however, was not regarded as wounded sufficiently seriously to warrant immediate treatment; instead he was sent to Antwerp by canal and only there was what remained of his finger amputated at the joint.

Among the more grievously wounded was Lieutenant George Simmons of the 95th, who received timely assistance from his devoted sergeant, Robert Fairfoot, who was himself seriously injured. After he was hit, Simmons was taken to the battalion aid post, just behind the firing line, where

A good surgeon, a friend of mine, instantly came up to examine my wound. My breast was dreadfully swelled. He made a deep cut under the right pap, and dislodged from the breast-bone a musket-ball. I was suffocating with the injury my lungs had sustained, He took a quart of blood from my arm … Sergeant Fairfoot … got me everything he could, and said he would go and knock some French prisoner off his horse for me in order to get me off … He got me a horse. They tried to lift me upon it, but I fainted; some other officer took it. In consequence of a movement the French made … our people were obliged to retire. If I stayed I must be a prisoner, and being a prisoner was the the same as being lost. Poor Fairfoot was in great agitation. He came with another horse. I remember some Life Guardsmen helped me on. Oh what I suffered! I had to ride twelve miles … the ball went through my ribs and … the motion of the horse made the blood pump out, and the bones cut the flesh to a jelly.

Simmons returned to his recent billet in Brussels, where he received the best of attention from the owner and his family, a Protestant named Overman. Their ministrations helped save his life, for he lay in a desperate state for some time, during which 'my dear little nurse has never been ten minutes from me since I came to the house … For ten nights together she never went to bed, but laid her head on my pillow … I am with the best people in the world.'[71]

Simmons was well enough to return to England in late October 1815 and rejoined his regiment in the following year, albeit 'with his riddled body held together with a pair of stays ... les the burst of a sigh should snap it asunder.'[72] He retired as a major in 1845 and died at the age of 72 in 1858, his survival testimony to the care he received after the battle. His sentiments on that subject would have been echoed by the many who had experienced the humanity of the people of Brussels.

Although many of the wounded would have died before they could receive medical assistance, from shock or loss of blood, those who survived long enough to find a surgeon had a surprisingly good chance of recovery, despite the ghastly conditions endured when the medical establishment was initially overwhelmed by the numbers of wounded. William Hay of the 12th Light Dragoons visited Brussels two days after the battle and found a hospital established in a convent. Even its corridors were choked with wounded, and in one room he found a large table on which lay twenty or thirty men, all awaiting amputation in their turn: 'my feelings were put to a more severe test than any express of mine can give an adequate description of ... Seeing suffering on a field of battle, where all alike are exposed and actively engaged, is nothing compared with this, which made me feel quite sick ... the sights I had already seen made me quite overcome and unequal to further duty that night.' His one consolation was to find that 'almost every private house had been turned into a receptacle for the wounded ... the ladies of the houses attending and dressing their wounds, and nursing them like their own children.'[73]

It is difficult to be precise about the rates of recovery of those who survived to reach hospital. Sir Charles Bell recorded that of 147 primary amputations performed at Brussels, only forty patients died, although the survival rate was much less for secondary amputations. According to statistics compiled by the Adjutant General in April 1816, of 7,687 British soldiers recorded as having been wounded, some 5,086 had returned to their regiments, 167 had been passed fit for service in veteran or garrison battalions, 854 were still in hospital and only 856 had died, a mortality rate of 11.1 per cent, which by the standards of the time must be a testimony to the skill and perseverance of the surgeons, both military and the civilians who travelled to Brussels to lend their medical expertise.

Some bizarre incidents were recorded in the continuing treatment of the wounded, like that concerning a member of the 92nd who had an injury that refused to heal. When it was probed anew, five-franc and one-franc coins were extracted, having been driven into the wound from his pocket, so that ultimately he recovered not only his health but his money as well.

In addition to the wounded, other members of the 5th Division whose experiences are often overlooked were the wives of the soldiers. They had been sent away from the line of battle and retired to the rear, amid the confusion of the wounded and fugitives. James Anton of the 42nd – doubtless more alive to their predicament than many because his own wife had followed him on his campaigning – described that even in the hour of victory 'the poor distressed women' could not celebrate as they

> knew not their husbands' fate. To advance through the forest by night, and on a road … marked with confusion, blocked with overturned baggage, helpless wounded soldiers, and, worst of all, by prowling stragglers, would have been madness. There was no resource but to seek shelter under some hospitable roof; and what city could boast of more hospitality than Brussels? … Each door was opened, and each matron, to whom application was made, gave a British soldier's wife a ready welcome.[74]

Subsequently many of these women made their way to the battlefield to seek the fate of their loved ones, and encountered scenes of unimaginable horror. Even the most hardened campaigners were appalled by the sights that greeted them as the dawn broke on the morning of 19 June. Harry Smith:

> I had been over many a field of battle, but with the exception of one spot at New Orleans, and the breach of Badajos [*sic*], I had never seen anything to be compared with what I saw. At Waterloo the *whole* field from right to left was a mass of dead bodies. In one spot, to the right of La Haye Sainte, the French Cuirassiers were literally piled on each other; many soldiers not wounded lying under their horses; others, fearfully wounded, occasionally with their horses struggling upon their wounded bodies. The sight was sickening, and I had no means or power to assist them … All over the field you saw officers, and as many soldiers as were permitted to leave the ranks, leaning and weeping over some dead or dying brother or comrade.[75]

Two members of the 92nd described similar sights, and similar emotions. James Hope, before he was wounded, noted that 'The field of battle now assumed a horrid aspect. The slope in front of our position was so completely covered with

La Haye Sainte, with the Brussels–Charleroi highway, looking north, the farmhouse and walls showing evidence of heavy damage. The sandpit defended by the 1/95th is on the right side of the road, marking the right flank of the 5th Division's position. Local people are burying the dead. (*Engraving by and after J. Rouse, published 1816*)

the mangled corpses of the enemy, that it was scarcely possible for either man or beast to walk without treading on them.'[76] And on the following morning, David Robertson: 'I confess my feelings overcame me; I wept bitterly, and wished I had not been a witness of such a scene … We moved on as silent as the dead that lay so thickly around us. No one could speak, so awestruck were we with the horrid spectacle.'[77]

At least his battalion had the slight consolation of being thanked by Wellington in person for their conduct on the previous day; but even that was qualified when, characteristically, the duke then scolded them for being too eager to advance, and urged them to pay more attention to their orders in future!

Exhaustion had overtaken many; while his men replenished their ammunition, Cavalié Mercer wandered around the field and 'stumbled on a whole regiment of British infantry fast asleep, in columns of divisions, wrapped in their blankets, with their knapsacks for pillows. Not a man was awake. There they lay in regular ranks, with the officers and sergeants in their places, just as they would stand when awake.'[78]

La Haye Sainte and the Brussels–Charleroi highway, looking north. At right is the hillock and sandpit defended by the 1/95th, the position of the abattis a short distance north of the farm. Hastily constructed graves are at right; Charlotte Waldie noted that 'The effluvia which arose from them, even beneath the open canopy of heaven, was horrible; and the pure west wind of summer, as it passed us, seemed pestiferous'; and so hasty was the interment that she saw a face visible, and 'turned away from the spot in indescribable horror, and with a sensation of deadly faintness.' (*Print published by R. Bowyer, 1816*)

The repose of not a few may have been disturbed by reflections on their narrow escapes. A number of witnesses commented on how Wellington had seemed to have had a charmed life, suffering not a scratch while all around him others were hit, but he was not exceptional. In the 5th Division's upper tier of command, for example, the 32nd's commanding officer, John Hicks, had a horse hit twice at Quatre Bras and three times at Waterloo, had several balls pass through his coat and one graze his forehead, but suffered no other injury. Sir Philip Belson was another, losing two horses killed beneath him and two more wounded, but escaped all injury. A degree of psychological trauma seems to have prevented some from sleeping, as in the case of the Royal Scots. Many were awake in the night before their rations were delivered, so set to cooking them, using discarded cuirasses as frying pans. And among the officers:

> about four o'clock we sat up and conversed. We talked of the battle, our minds more and more filled with what they would say about us at home, than anything else. There was no exultation! None! We had, many of us,

when in the Peninsula, tried the mettle of French soldiers – we concluded the campaign *just begun*, and looked forward to have another desperate fight in a day or two; therefore we determined not to holloa till we had got out of the wood.[79]

As soon as he awoke on the morning of the 19th, Harry Ross-Lewin of the 32nd made his way to an artillery camp where captured horses were being collected, to choose a new mount, having given one of his to one of the battalion's field officers who had lost his own. He picked a mount from the Imperial Guard, slightly wounded but quite fit, and upon it rode over the field, when 'it was difficult to suppress those conflicting sensations of pride, exultation, and grief' at the sight of the wreckage of humanity, and his thoughts represented a universal truth: 'How many an affectionate heart was soon to become the abode of sorrow, when the tidings of the fatal yesterday should reach the ears of bereaved friends and relatives!'

Yet the elation of victory, and possibly that of personal survival, tended to ameliorate the dismal: while reflections on the dead and bereaved 'are mournful, and will often suggest themselves ... there are others which diminish their effect.'[80]

For many, the first task on waking was to scour the battlefield for their friends or for casualties from their own battalion. A fatigue party of the Royal Scots found one of their comrades, already stripped by the scavengers – presumably an officer as there would have been too many 'other ranks' to deal with – and buried him, whereupon one of the Scots in the party pulled out a prayer book and the funeral service was read, 'and during the whole process our wounded soldiers sat up and listened with the most reverend attention. The French raised themselves on their elbows, and gazed at us with astonishment ... "In the midst of life we are in death." Was it ever brought home so forcibly to living men before? They had only to look round them.' The officer superintending the party then gathered up some canteens and filled them at Mont St. Jean before distributing them among the wounded. He then walked over part of the field and was particularly appalled, as had been John Kincaid, by the sight of the 27th lying dead in their square:

There is something peculiarly touching about lowly men sacrificing their lives for their country's glory – thus ennobling themselves ... I had seen everything that morning nearly unmoved – but here I paused. At the sight of these poor fellows, of the humblest classes of society, who had opposed their bodies as a living rampart to the obstinate advance of the enemy – all now lying dead – I am not ashamed to say that a tear fell.

Passing on to the French position, he was again horrified by the evidence of the artillery fire, with bodies torn to pieces; and at Rossomme he found the farm and outhouses crammed with wounded Frenchmen, 'some ... patiently waiting their doom, apparently at hand, and some earnestly begging for water ... One glimpse of this charnel-house was enough, and I returned to our bivouac.'[81]

Another urgent task was to reorganize the battalions and to calculate their casualties, which in some units were catastrophic: Ross-Lewin, for example, found that his company had only eleven men left, forty-nine having fallen. Having already suffered so severely at Quatre Bras, some elements of the 5th Division must have been devastated, in some cases notably in the loss of officers. Although some appear to have continued their duties despite injury, the 3/1st

The field after the battle. John Kincaid recalled that it 'presented a frightful scene of carnage; it seemed as if the world had tumbled to pieces, and three-fourths of everything destroyed in the wreck ... so thickly strewed with fallen men and horses that it was difficult to step clear of their bodies.' (*Print after J.H. Clarke*)

appear to have had only six officers unscathed (out of thirty-six, not including 'staff'); the 42nd had only three out of the nineteen most senior unhurt; in the 44th only O'Malley was uninjured above the rank of lieutenant, two in the 28th; seven out of nine captains in the 32nd were down, ten unhurt out of forty-one in the 79th including only one of the twenty-one most senior, thirteen unhurt out of thirty-seven in the 92nd and eight out of twenty-seven in the 1/95th. Only the 32nd had the same officer in command and unhurt as had begun the campaign, although Campbell of the 3/1st appears to have retained his command despite injury, and Belson of the 28th had stepped up to lead the brigade. The 28th had only one officer fatality on the battlefield: Major William Meacham, killed on the spot by a shot through the heart. In this he was perhaps more fortunate than two of his regiment's wounded officers. Lieutenant George Ingram had a leg shattered by a roundshot; part of it was amputated on the field and more in another operation at Brussels. After this second ordeal he appeared to be doing well, but the dressing on the stump ruptured during the night and he bled to death before anyone realized his plight. The second was Lieutenant J.P. Clarke, who was catastrophically wounded in the abdomen by a shell splinter. He was taken to Brussels and lingered for a couple of days, 'perfectly conscious of his dreadful situation; but with manliness and resignation submitted to his fate, in the same serenity of temper which had always endeared him to his brother officers, until mortification coming on, put an end to his sufferings. He died in the arms of his messmates, Lieutenants [Roger] Gilbert and [J. William] Shelton,'[82] both of whom had been wounded severely, the latter four times.

Among the wounded of the 32nd was the Irish-born Lieutenant Samuel Hill Lawrence. He survived to go on to half-pay as a captain in 1825, but is perhaps more remarkable for the fact that his son, also named Samuel Hill Lawrence, born at Cork in 1831, became an officer in the same regiment and won the Victoria Cross at Lucknow in 1857, another of the regiment's most notable engagements. Perhaps heroism was a family trait, for his cousin, Thomas Cadell, also won the Victoria Cross in the Indian Mutiny when a lieutenant in the 2nd Bengal European Fusiliers, for twice rescuing wounded men under fire at Delhi.

Many witnesses reported the stoicism of the wounded, some of whom lay for days on the field until they were finally removed for treatment, or until their wounds brought their sufferings to an end. Cavalié Mercer encountered an exception:

in a little hollow beneath a white thorn, lay two Irish light- infantrymen sending forth such howlings and wailings, and oaths and execrations, as were shocking to hear. One of them had his leg shot off, the other a thigh smashed by a cannon-shot. They were certainly pitiable objects, but their vehement exclamations, &c, were so strongly contrasted with the quiet resolute bearing of hundreds, both French and English, around them, that it blunted one's feelings considerably,[83]

and he left them cursing him when they realized that he was unable to help them.

The 5th Division's casualty statistics collated after the battle are given in the appendix.

Even before the army moved off, there were sightseers and scavengers roaming the field; Mercer met a tourist 'holding a delicately white perfumed handkerchief to his nose; stepping carefully to avoid the bodies, at which he cast fearful glances *en passant*, to avoid polluting the glossy silken hose that clothed his lower limbs … With a world of bows my man took leave, and proceeded, picking his steps with the same care as he followed the route of his companions in the direction of Hougoumont.'[84]

More obvious than such ghouls were the looters; countless soldiers strayed from their units during the night of the battle in search of booty, and in the morning a horde of civilians descended to pick through the debris and help bury the bodies, a task that began on the day following the battle. Some soldiers were ordered to this unpopular task but much of the work was done by local peasants who flung bodies into mass graves, looting as they went, even before the wounded had been removed. British witnesses were especially appalled when they found peasants abusing and maltreating the helpless French wounded.

One sightseer, initially horrified, was so overwhelmed by the numbers of casualties that

the more I saw the less I felt; so true it is, that habit reconciles everything … thousands of wounded, who could not help themselves, were in want of everything; their features, swollen by the sun, looked livid and bloated … The anxiety for water was indeed most distressing … hundreds must have perished from thirst alone …

[The] general burying was truly horrible; large square holes were dug about six feet deep, and thirty or forty-five young fellows stripped to their skins, were thrown into each, pell mell, and then covered over in so slovenly a manner, that sometimes a hand or foot peeped through the earth.

If the sights were not distressing enough, the sounds compounded the horror: countless wounded calling for water, shots as wounded horses were dispatched and the bang of farriers' hammers as they salvaged horseshoes, and an especial monstrosity: 'some Russian Jews were assisting in the spoliation of the dead by chiselling out their teeth, an operation which they performed with the most brutal indifference. The clinking hammers of these wretched jarred horribly upon my ears.'[85]

It must have been with great relief that the majority of the army, including the 5th Division, reorganized and resupplied, marched off in pursuit of Napoleon's broken army. The Royal Scots officer was among them, but as they moved off, one final horror: he encountered a dead French drummer, sitting bolt upright, who seemed to fix him with his unseeing stare: 'I felt a creeping under my hair ... his fixed, serpent-like gaze at me set my heart a-beating ... the whole

The Brussels-Charleroi highway looking south towards La Belle Alliance, with wounded still being discovered and aided. (*Engraving by and after J. Rouse, published 1816*)

incident discomposed me more than the fighting we had been engaged in the day before. It was the weakness which usually follows excitement. I bade *adieu* to the field, and I have never seen it since.'[86]

In Brussels and elsewhere there had been fear and despondency about the likely success of the French, increased by the sight of the numbers of wounded who poured in during the fighting. The reaction to the news of victory was thus all the more ecstatic, as Charlotte Waldie recorded of its reception in Antwerp where she, like many British tourists, had been evacuated for safety. Many wounded were also sent there for treatment to relieve the pressure on the medical facilities in Brussels. Her account clearly involved 'walking wounded' from the 5th Division: 'To the last hour of my life, never shall I forget the sensations of that moment ... the overpowering emotions which filled my heart were too powerful for expression ... The sudden transition from the depth of despair to joy unutterable, were almost too great to be borne'.

Wounded Highlanders were equally moved and 'kept throwing up their Highland bonnets into the air, and continually vociferating, "Boney's beat! Boney's beat! hurrah! hurrah!"' When an old Flemish woman, not understanding the Scottish dialect, seemed not to comprehend that 'Boney was beat, and rinning away till his ain country as fast as he could gang', the Highlander roared at her, 'Hout, ye auld gowk, dinna ye ken that Boney's beat – what, are ye deef ... I say Boney's beat, woman!'; then, 'When the news was explained to the old women they were in an ecstasy almost as great as that of the Highlanders themselves.'[87] It was remarkable, though, that the Scots 'seemed not to have the smallest pride in what they had done; but to consider it quite as a matter of course; they ... made light of their sufferings, and there was nothing in their words or manner that looked as if they were sensible of having done anything in the least extraordinary.'[88]

As the circumstances of the battle became known, it was realized that their efforts *were* extraordinary. A writer in 1834 encapsulated the conduct of the infantry who stood firm along the ridge in phrases particularly apposite given the national origin of many of the members of the 5th Division: 'Confusion was behind the army, and death raged along its front; but the soldiers engaged stood firm amid the fight, as stand the rocks of the north against the fiercest chafing of the ocean's waves.'[89]

'Impossible for Troops to behave more nobly'

(Kempt on the 32nd)

Reputations

Some participants in the battle seem to have regarded everything that followed as an anti-climax, to what had been, for many, the single most memorable, albeit traumatic, moment in their entire life. The 1815 campaign was not entirely concluded by the Battle of Waterloo; there were further minor actions, including assaults on Cambrai and Peronne, but these were small affairs against unenthusiastic defenders, and neither involved the 5th Division. In reality, Napoleon's power had been smashed forever along the ridge of Mont St. Jean.

The 5th Division participated in the advance into France, with its command echelon altered radically because of casualties. Kempt remained in command but because of his wound only exercised that function when the division was encamped; on the march Pack led it. Philip Belson of the 28th continued to lead Kempt's Brigade, with Captain Charles Cadell, the senior unwounded officer, commanding the 28th. During the advance, two days after the battle, the regiment encamped on the field of Malplaquet, conscious that their regimental forebears had fought in that encounter some 116 years earlier, doubtless providing cause for reflection.

Reorganization in the 5th Division occurred within a relatively short period after the battle. On 3 July the 32nd was transferred out, into the 6th Division, and a month after the battle Major General Sir John Keane (who had served in America with Lambert) was appointed to command what had been Kempt's

Brigade, with Sir Philip Belson being moved to the staff of the 3rd Division. When Belson took his leave of the 28th, which he had commanded for a decade, he departed, he said, with 'the deepest regret; and begs [they] will accept his warmest thanks for the zeal and alacrity with which they have invariably seconded his affairs in the performance of his duty upon so many trying and distinguished occasions … it will ever be with feelings of the utmost pride and pleasure that he looks back to the period of his life when he had the happiness of having them under his command.'[1]

Upon arrival at Paris the division held its first divine service since the battle, at Kempt's headquarters, with a sermon preached by 'the fighting parson', the esteemed Reverend Charles Frith:

The Waterloo Medal: the first British campaign medal awarded to all ranks of the British Army present in an action. Designed by T. Wyon, this includes the original steel clip and ring suspension, which not infrequently was replaced by more elaborate silversmithing by recipients. The reverse was unusual in bearing the name of the commanding general, Wellington.

The Waterloo Medal awarded to members of the Hanoverian army, instituted considerably later than the British medal, in December 1817. Designed by W. Wyon, the inscriptions were in German: on the obverse, 'Georg Prinz Regent', and on the reverse, 'Hannoverscher Tapferkeit', with the date and 'Waterloo'.

The beautiful manner in which he dwelt on the battle, and the sad and sudden loss of friends and comrades, drew tears from many; and when he wound up with the sad pangs it would cause at home, to the widows and orphans, the parents and friends of those that had fallen, concluding with the text, 'Go to your tents and rejoice, and return thanks to the Lord for the mercies he has granted you', there was hardly a dry eye in the whole division, and it had an excellent effect on the men.[2]

When the consequences of victory became known, ending what for Britain had been twenty-two years of almost continuous warfare, and the ordeal that had been endured in order to achieve the victory, the surviving participants were lauded to a degree rarely seen before, as exemplified by the issue of the Waterloo Medal, the first to be awarded to all those who had fought, regardless of rank. In the first flush of exultation, troops returning home were regarded and welcomed as heroes, as when the 42nd marched into Edinburgh among a tumultuous throng, arousing both pride and pity for the

worn-out, travel-stained men [whose] once bright scarlet uniforms exhibited all the shades of depression which that colour is capable of assuming; while very few retained any remnant even of the plume which distinguishes the Highland soldier's head-dress ... No one who has not actually witnessed a similar exhibition of the sad and desolating effects of war can fully conceive what our feelings were on the first appearance of our poor countrymen.[3]

Concern for the soldiers tended to decline subsequently, although when in 1816 the 92nd marched from Hull to Edinburgh on their way home, they were greeted by pealing bells as they passed, and were mobbed when they reached their destination. A member of the 42nd, which regiment had preceded them, remarked that the crowds had been even greater for them, so that 'we could hardly get through them at all!' The reply from a Gordon exemplified the regimental rivalry: 'You should have sent for us to clear the way for you, as we often did in Spain!'[4]

The mass discharge of soldiers following the conclusion of the Napoleonic Wars, coinciding with a depression in many industries, led to widespread poverty and hardship, in which many of Picton's heroes were caught up. Those blinded or having lost a limb received a pension for life, but little enough to compensate for their disability: 1*s*. 6*d*. per diem for sergeants, 1*s*. 2*d*. for corporals, and 1*s*. for privates. Out-pensioners of Chelsea Hospital, who were examined to determine the level of their pension, received £18 5*s*. per year for a first class pension, down to £7 12*s*. for a third class, though by no means all were granted such a boon.

The reputation of some of the officers was cemented by the campaign, notably that of the divisional commander. Although Picton may have thought himself insufficiently rewarded for his service in the Peninsula, he received many

Sir Thomas Picton: a print published shortly after his death exemplifying his fame if not accuracy. (*Print published by Thomas Kelly, 1817*)

posthumous tributes, beginning with that from the Duke of Wellington. In the list of those killed, injured and deserving of especial praise in Wellington's Waterloo despatch, written on the night of the battle, his was the first name mentioned:

> In Lieutenant General Sir Thomas Picton, His Majesty has sustained the loss of an Officer who has frequently distinguished himself in the service, and he fell, gloriously leading his division to a charge with bayonets, by which one of the most serious attacks made by the enemy on our position, was defeated.[5]

Although almost all the dead were buried on or near to the field of battle, generally without a marker or inscription, Picton was not among them. Learning that the general's body was to be returned to England, Wellington provided a guard of honour to escort it to Ostend, and when his coffin was landed at Deal, the fleet in the Downs was firing minute guns. Another escort was formed to convey it to Canterbury, where it was lodged in the same room in the Fountain Inn that Picton had occupied only days before en route to Belgium. From there it was taken to his London house at 21 Portman Square. A tribute was paid to him in the House of Commons by a friend, Lieutenant General Isaac Gascoyne, a well-respected MP who in his parliamentary career had been much concerned with military affairs and who had lobbied successfully for an increase in junior officers' pay and for widows' pensions. In the House Gascoyne declared that

> From the moment General Picton had left this country until he joined the army, he had never entered any bed – he had scarcely given himself time to take any refreshment, so eager was he in the performance of his duty. After the severe wound he had received, he would have been justified in not engaging in the action of the 18th. His body was not only blackened, but even swelled to a considerable degree: those who had seen it wondered that he could take part in the duties of the field. He had fallen gloriously at the head of his division, maintaining a position which, if it had not been kept, would have altered the fate of the day.[6]

Gascoyne and others proposed that Picton should be buried in St. Paul's Cathedral, but instead on 3 July he was interred at St. George's, Hanover Square, although subsequently he was commemorated in St. Paul's. In 1823 a monument was erected in Carmarthen by public subscription, for which King George IV contributed 100 guineas, and it was inaugurated with a ceremony fitting for one of the greatest of Welsh soldiers. Towns named after Picton exist in New South Wales, Ontario, and South Island, New Zealand, and he was the subject of a number of portraits, engravings and busts by the sculptor Lawrence Gahagany, who executed his memorial in St. Paul's. A marble statue by Thomas Crook was placed in Cardiff City Hall in 1918.

Sir Thomas Picton: a portrait medal by E.W. Wyon, engraved by A.R. Freeman.

The shadow of Trinidad may in life have contributed to Picton not receiving a peerage, and arose again more than two centuries after the event, when suggestions were reported that it was inappropriate for his portrait (by Sir Martin Archer Shee), installed in the court house at Carmarthen in 1829, to remain there, given the old stain upon his reputation.

Picton was not the only fallen soldier to be brought home. In April 1816, guided by Ewen Macmillan, Fassiefern's youngest brother found his grave and had the body disinterred, taken to Scotland and laid to rest in the old churchyard at Kilmallie in Lochaber, among his kinsmen; some 3,000 mourning Highlanders attended, and an obelisk was raised subsequently. Sir Walter Scott wrote his epitaph, which closed, 'Reader, call not his fate untimely,

The Picton monument at Carmarthen, unveiled with great ceremony in 1823.

who, thus honoured and lamented, closed a life of fame by a death of glory.'[7]

Although deprived of the decoration he thought he was due in life, John Cameron might have taken some slight comfort from one bestowed after his death: his father was created a baronet in 1816. Following Fassiefern's death, there was no reason for Macmillan to remain in the regiment, so he took up the tenancy of a farm on the Cameron estate; but he 'became rather addicted to a "veteran's failing",'[8] presumably alcohol, and lost his livelihood; but the Cameron family provided him with a comfortable home on the estate, where he died in 1840, and was buried at Kilmallie.

Of Picton's two brigadiers, Sir Denis Pack's active career did not extend beyond the Waterloo campaign. In 1819 he was appointed lieutenant governor of Plymouth, and held the colonelcies of the York Chasseurs (from 1816) and, from September 1822, the 84th Foot. In 1816 he married Elizabeth, daughter of the 1st Marquess of Waterford, half-sister of Marshal William Beresford, and their second son became Beresford's heir and inherited his name. Their eldest son, Arthur John Pack, seems to have inherited both Denis Pack's

The monument to Lieutenant Colonel John Cameron of Fassiefern, at Kilmallie, its inscription by Sir Walter Scott.

temper and his military inclination, for he gained a commission at age 16 and as a lieutenant colonel served with the 7th Royal Fusiliers in the Crimea, receiving a severe wound at the attack on the Redan at Sebastopol. (He was also known as Reynell Pack, having taken the name of his mother's second husband, Sir Thomas Reynell, who had commanded the 71st Light Infantry at Waterloo, the regiment with which Denis Pack was most associated.) Sir Denis died at Beresford's house in London on 24 July 1823, and his widow erected a monument to him in Kilkenny Cathedral, where his father had been dean.

Sir James Kempt enjoyed a much longer career, with a succession of regimental colonelcies. He had been colonel of the 8th Battalion of the 60th (Royal American) Regiment, but that was disbanded in 1816. In 1818 he became colonel of the 3rd West India Regiment, and when that was disbanded in the following year he was removed to the colonelcy of the 81st Foot, moving again in 1829 to the 40th, in 1834 to the 2nd, and in 1846 to the 1st Royal Scots, perhaps appropriately as that regiment had come under his command when he succeeded Picton in leading the 5th Division at Waterloo. Kempt served as Governor General of Canada 1828–30 and as Master General of the Ordnance 1830–34, and died in London on 20 December 1854.

Another of Picton's senior officers achieved fame on another battlefield, and became perhaps the most high profile casualty of all those who had survived Waterloo. Robert Henry Dick, who had taken command of the 42nd after Macara's death at Quatre Bras, was appointed as ADC to King George IV and received the colonelcy of the 73rd Foot in 1845. As a major general he was killed at the moment of victory at Sobraon in the campaign against the Sikhs in February 1846.

Field Marshal Sir William Maynard
Gomm in old age, wearing the star of
the GCB, the Army Gold Cross and the
Waterloo Medal.

Edward Costello of the 1/95th, a
corporal at Waterloo, shown here in
later life after service with the British
Legion in Spain. His British decorations
comprised the Waterloo Medal and the
Military General Service Medal with no
less than eleven clasps.

Picton's faithful ADC John Tyler rose to the rank of lieutenant colonel and
in 1834 was appointed as deputy quartermaster general in the Windward and
Leeward Islands. He died in June 1841 and was buried at Bridgetown, Barbados.

Sir Andrew Barnard, the much esteemed commander of the 1/95th, rose to
the rank of general, held the colonelcy of his old battalion from 1827 (having
been colonel of the regiment's 2nd Battalion from 1822), and was appointed
lieutenant governor of Chelsea Hospital. Prior to his funeral in January 1855 the
pensioners who had served under him were permitted to pay their respects to
his remains, and when they had left it was found that his coffin was covered with
laurel leaves, each man having brought one as a touching and well-deserved
tribute to their old commander.

Of all the members of the 5th Division, perhaps the individual who had the
most distinguished subsequent career was Sir William Gomm, the assistant
adjutant general; he became a field marshal and served as commander-in- chief

in India 1850–56. Perhaps even more remarkably, his horse George, which he rode at Waterloo, lived until 1841 – one of the longest surviving equine veterans of the battle.

No single formation turned the course of the Waterloo campaign against Napoleon; all allied contingents played a role, but few could argue that the contribution of the British infantry was not crucial. Even after the scale of the victory was apparent, Wellington seems privately to have remained unimpressed by much of his army, writing to Earl Bathurst that

> I hope we are going on well, and that what we are doing will bring matters to the earliest and best conclusion, as we are in a very bad way. We have not one quarter of the ammunition which we ought to have, on account of the deficiency of our drivers and carriages; and I really believe that, with the exception of my old Spanish infantry, I have got not only the worst troops, but the worst equipped army, with the worst staff, that was ever brought together.[9]

However much of this was an exaggeration, it is significant that he excepted his 'old Spanish infantry' from criticism: the British infantry that had followed him throughout the Peninsular War and who had played a decisive role in his success. He repeated his admiration for them in a succinct summary of the battle written to his old deputy William Beresford a fortnight after Waterloo:

> Never did I see such a pounding match. Both were what the boxers call gluttons. Napoleon did not manoeuvre at all. He just moved forward in the old style, in columns, and was driven off in the old style. The only difference was, that he mixed cavalry with his infantry, and supported both with an enormous quantity of artillery. I had the infantry for some time in squares, and we had the French cavalry walking about us as if they had been our own. I never saw the British infantry behave so well.[10]

Small wonder that ten days after the battle, writing to the Duke of York, Wellington had endorsed the plan 'of giving to the non-commissioned officers and soldiers engaged in the Battle of Waterloo a medal. I am convinced it would have the best effect in the army; and, if that battle should settle our concerns, they will well deserve it.'[11]

The conduct of the infantry in holding firm against the sternest trial that any of them had ever experienced came to be recognized universally, with the poet Robert Southey even comparing their stand on the ridge at Mont St. Jean to that of Leonidas and his Spartans at Thermopylae:

> *as in that Grecian strait*
> *The funeral stone might say – Go traveller, tell*
> *Scotland, that in our duty here we fell'.*

In the two tumultuous days of battle the part played by the 5th Division was crucial. If at Waterloo they had not attracted the same fame and admiration as the defenders of Hougoumont, the battalions most prominent in resisting the French cavalry charges, or those who defeated the last charge of the Imperial Guard, the division's stand at Quatre Bras probably saved the campaign, even though it may have been overshadowed by the even greater battle two days later.

Two days after the 32nd received its orders to transfer from the 5th to the 6th Division, Sir James Kempt issued a divisional order expressing his gratitude for the way that the regiment had conducted itself in the campaign:

> he cannot part with this regiment without again expressing the very high sense he entertains of its distinguished conduct in the battles of the 16th and 18th of June; it was quite impossible for troops to behave more nobly than the 32d [*sic*] regt. did on these glorious occasions; and he begs that Lt. Col. Hicks, the officers, and men, will accept of his best thanks for their distinguished service while under his command.[12]

While written to one particular battalion, the comment that it could not have behaved more nobly could surely have been applied to the whole of Picton's Division. Its members were not alone in their exertions, but had helped to change the course of European history.

Notes

The following abbreviations are used:

USJ: *United Service Journal*

WD: *Dispatches of Field Marshal the Duke of Wellington*, ed. J. Gurwood, London 1834–38.

The 1815 Campaign

1. The news of Napoleon's escape from Elba was communicated thus by a stagecoach guard to William Hay of the 12th Light Dragoons: Hay, W., *Reminiscences Under Wellington 1808–1815*, ed. Mrs. S.C.I. Wood, London 1901, p. 158.
2. Brussels, 8 May 1815; WD Vol. XII, p. 358.

The Divisional System

1. *British Military Library or Journal*, London 1798, Vol. II, p. 477.
2. Smith, Sir Harry, *The Autobiography of Sir Harry Smith*, ed. G.C. Moore Smith, London 1910, p. 45.
3. Ibid., p. 135.
4. *General Regulations and Orders for the Army*, London 1811, p. 123.
5. Donaldson, J., *Recollections of the Eventful Life of a Soldier*, Edinburgh 1854, pp. 221–2.
6. Schaumann, A.L.F., *On the Road with Wellington: the Diary of a War Commissary*, ed. A.M. Ludovici, London 1924, p. 38.
7. Brussels, 8 May 1815; WD Vol. XII, pp. 357–8.
8. In British service German officers were commonly referred to by an Anglicization of their German first names.
9. Hope, J., *Letters from Portugal, Spain and France … and from Belgium and France, in the year 1815* (published anonymously: 'by a British Officer'), Edinburgh 1819, p. 218.
10. Wellington, Duke of, *Supplementary Despatches and Memoranda of Field Marshal the Duke of Wellington*, ed. 2nd Duke of Wellington, London 1858–72, Vol. X, p. 219.

Sir Thomas Picton

1. Description of Sir Thomas Picton from Anon., *The Military Sketch-Book*, quoted in *The Naval & Military Magazine*, London 1827, Vol. I, p. 493.
2. *Gentleman's Magazine*, November 1811, p. 488.

3. This 75th Regiment had no connection to the next and more famous 75th, formed in 1787 and subsequently the 1st Battalion Gordon Highlanders (from 1881).

4. Stanhope, Philip, 5th Earl, *Notes on Conversations with the Duke of Wellington*, London 1888, pp. 68–9.

5. Smith, p. 176.

6. Oman, C.W.C., *History of the Peninsular War*, Oxford 1902–30, Vol. VII, p. 527.

7. Grattan, W., *Adventures with the Connaught Rangers 1809–14*, London 1847, r/p, ed. Sir Charles Oman, London 1902, p. 200.

8. Kincaid, Sir John, *Adventures in the Rifle Brigade*, London 1830, and *Random Shots from a Rifleman*, London 1835; combined edn. London 1908, pp. 58, 108.

9. George Westcott was at that time brigade major, and subsequently in Picton's own 77th Foot; Sir Galbraith Lowry Cole was commander of the 4th Division. Smyth, B., *History of the XX Regiment 1688–1888*, London & Manchester 1889, p. 395.

10. Grattan pp. 15–16.

11. Ibid., p. 17.

12. Hamilton, H.B., *Historical Record of the 14th (King's) Hussars from AD 1715 to AD 1900*, London 1901, p. 166.

13. USJ 1836, Vol. II, p. 494.

14. Grattan, pp. 147–8.

15. Ibid., p. 166.

16. Ibid., p. 200.

17. Craufurd, Rev. A.H., *General Craufurd and his Light Division*, London n.d., p. 121.

18. Napier, W.F.P., *History of the War in the Peninsula and in the South of France from the Year 1807 to the Year 1814*, London 1828–40, Vol. V, pp. vi–vii. (Robinson's biography of Picton denies that the meeting ever happened, but Napier provides evidence it did.)

19. Ibid., Vol. Ill, pp. 294–5.

20. Smith, pp. 47, 163.

21. 10 September 1813; WD Vol. XI, pp. 97–8.

22. Napier, Vol. V, p. xxiii; see also USJ 1827, Vol. II pp. 493–4 where the story appears.

23. Stanhope pp. 322–3.

24. Ross-Lewin, H., *With The Thirty-Second in the Peninsular and other Campaigns*, ed. J. Wardell, Dublin & London 1904, p. 286.

25. Stanhope, p. 69.

26. Whittingham, S.F., *Memoir of the Services of Lieutenant General Sir Samuel Ford Whittingham*, ed. Maj.Gen. F. Whittingham, London 1868, p. 497.

27. See Ward, S.G.P., 'Three Watercolour Portraits' in *Journal of the Society for Army Historical Research* Vol. LXVI (1988), pp. 63–71.

28. *General Regulations & Orders for the Army*, London 1811, p. 96.

The British Infantry

1. Creevey, T., *The Creevey Papers*, ed. J. Gore, London 1934, p. 404.

2. USJ 1839, Vol. II, p. 204.

3. See Holme, N., & Kirby, Maj. E.L., *Medal Rolls: 23rd Foot – Royal Welch Fusiliers*, Napoleonic Period, Caernarvon & London, 1978.

4. Scott, Sir Walter, *Paul's Letters to his Kinsfolk*, Edinburgh 1816 (published anonymously), p. 21.

5. Hope, p. 207.
6. Cadell, Lt.Col. C., *Narrative of the Campaigns of the 28th Regiment since their Return from Egypt in 1802*, London 1835, p. 96.
7. Blakeney, R., *A Boy in the Peninsular War*, ed. J. Sturgis, London 1899, p. 144.
8. *Colburn's United Service Magazine* 1847, Vol. Ill, p. 4.
9. Leach, J., *Rough Sketches of the Life of an Old Soldier*, London 1831, p. 262.
10. Simmons, G., *A British Rifle Man*, ed. W. Verner, London 1899, p. 322.
11. Kincaid, p. 112.
12. *Royal Military Calendar, or Army Service and Commission Book*, London 1820, Vol. Ill, p. 274.
13. Anon., *The Personal Narrative of a Private Soldier, who served in the Forty-Second Highlanders, for Twelve Years during the Late War*, London 1821, pp. 200–201.
14. Oatts, L.B., *Proud Heritage: The Story of the Highland Light Infantry*, London 1952, Vol. I, p. 172.
15. Anton, J., *Retrospect of a Military Life*, Edinburgh 1841, pp. 108–109.
16. The regimental history calls his 'Arquimbau', but 'Arguimbau' is the contemporary spelling.
17. Stewart of Garth used the spellings 'Freicudan Du' and 'Seidaran Dearag'.
18. Stewart of Garth, Col. D., *Sketches of the Character, Manners and Present State of the Highlanders of Scotland*, Edinburgh 1822, Vol. I, pp. 591, 595.
19. Anton, pp. 190–1.
20. Carter, T., *Historical Record of the Forty-Fourth or the Essex Regiment*, Chatham 1887, p. 75.
21. Clerk, Rev. A., *Memoir of Colonel John Cameron, Fassiefern*, Glasgow 1858, pp. 2–3.
22. Gardyne, Col. C. Greenhill, *The Life of a Regiment: The History of the Gordon Highlanders*, London 1929 (orig. pub. 1901), Vol. I, pp. 358–9, 428.
23. Clerk, p. 69.
24. Ibid., p. 29.

In Brussels

1. Ross–Lewin, p. 249.
2. Scott, p. 388.
3. Frye, W.E., *After Waterloo: Reminiscences of European Travel 1815–1819*, ed. S. Reinach, London 1908, pp. 8–9.
4. Scott, p. 97.
5. Kelly, C., *The Memorable Battle of Waterloo*, London 1817, p. 90.
6. USJ 1831, Vol. II, p. 204.
7. Anton, p. 185.
8. Frye, p. 12.
9. Hope, p. 218.
10. Brussels, 13 June 1815; WD Vol. XII, p. 462.
11. Waterloo, 19 June 1815; WD Vol. XII, p. 478.
12. Siborne, W., *History of the War in France and Belgium in 1815*, London 1844, Vol. I, pp. 76–7; 3rd edn., London 1848, p. 36.
13. Maxwell, Sir Herbert, *The Life of Wellington*, London 1899, Vol. II, p. 13.
14. Gardyne, Vol. I, p. 349.

15. Du Cane, E., 'The Peninsula and Waterloo: Memories of an Old Rifleman', *Cornhill Magazine*, December 1897, p. 757 (John Molloy, 1/95th).
16. Ross–Lewin, p. 253.
17. Hope, p. 220.

The Assembly
 1. Scott, pp. 97–8.
 2. USJ 1840, Vol. I, p. 361.
 3. Hope, p. 222.
 4. Eaton, C.A., *Waterloo Days: The Narrative of an Englishwoman Resident at Brussels in June, 1815*, ed. E. Bell, London 1888 (orig. pub. anonymously: the author was Charlotte Waldie prior to her marriage).
 5. Maxwell, Vol. II, p. 13.
 6. Eaton, pp. 22–3.
 7. Anton, p. 188.
 8. Stewart of Garth, Vol. II, p. 237.
 9. De Lancey, Lady M., *A Week at Waterloo in 1815: Lady De Lancey's Narrative*, ed. B.R. Ward, London 1906, pp. 45, 107.
10. Eaton, pp. 24–5.
11. USJ 1840, Vol. I, p. 361.
12. Anton, pp. 188–9.
13. USJ 1840, Vol. I, p. 361.

Quatre Bras
 1. Anton, p. 191.
 2. Ibid., p. 190.
 3. Fitzmaurice, G., *Biographical Sketch of Major General John Fitzmaurice, KH*, Anghiari 1908, p. 50.
 4. USJ 1840, Vol. I, pp. 362–3.
 5. Spelling as in the official casualty return: otherwise he is listed as 'Jenisch'.
 6. Ross–Lewin, p. 260.
 7. Siborne, Maj.Gen. H.T., (ed), *The Waterloo Letters*, London 1891, p. 348.
 8. Daniel, J.E., *Journal of an Officer of the Commissariat Department*, London 1820, p. 425.
 9. Scott, p. 105.
10. Anton, p. 193.
11. Kelly, p. 92.
12. Lagden, A., & Sly, J., *The 2/73rd at Waterloo*, Brightlingsea 1998, pp. 205–11 (rev. edn., orig. pub. 1988).
13. W. Siborne, Vol. I, pp. 120–1.
14. Anton, pp. 193–4.
15. Gardyne, Vol. I, p. 352.
16. Lieutenant Robert Winchester, 92nd; H.T. Siborne, p. 386.
17. Anton, pp. 194–5.
18. H.T. Siborne, p. 381.
19. Anton, p. 196.
20. H.T. Siborne, p. 379.

21. Anon., *The Battle of Waterloo ... forming an Historical Record of the Operations in the Campaign of the Netherlands, 1815 ... by a Near Observer*, London & Edinburgh 1816, pp. lxvii-lxviii; the same text with slight differences also appears in Leask, J.C., & McCance, H.M., *The Regimental Records of The Royal Scots (The First or Royal Regiment of Foot)*, Dublin 1915, p. 334.

22. Anon., *The Royal Scots: The First and Royal Regiment of Foot: Handbook of the Regiment*, Glasgow, n.d. [1960], p. 46.

23. Cadell, p. 239.

24. H.T. Siborne, pp. 353–4.

25. Ross-Lewin, p. 257.

26. Ibid., p. 261.

27. Swiney, Col. G.C., *Historical Records of the 32nd (Cornwall) Light Infantry*, London & Devonport 1893, p. 116. The writer is not identified but is most likely to have been Lieutenant Michael Meighan.

28. Ross-Lewin, p. 261.

29. Owen, E. (ed.), *The Waterloo Papers*, Tavistock 1997, p. 39.

30. H.T. Siborne, p. 250.

31. Ibid., p. 382.

32. Ibid., p. 231.

33. Clerk, p. 79.

34. H.T. Siborne, p. 387.

35. Hope, p. 230.

36. Gardyne, Vol. I, p. 355.

37. Hope, p. 232.

38. W. Siborne 1844, Vol. I, p. 158.

39. Macready, E.N., 'On a Part of Captain Siborne's History of the Waterloo Campaign', *Colburn's United Service Magazine* 1845, Vol. I, p. 389.

40. Mercer, A.C., *Journal of the Waterloo Campaign*, Edinburgh & London 1870, Vol. I, pp. 250–1.

41. Hope, pp. 235–6.

42. Clerk, p. 80.

43. Hope, p. 235.

44. Gardyne, Vol. I, pp. 357–8.

45. See, for example, the opinion of Edward Macready of the 30th in *Colburn's United Service Magazine* 1845, Vol. I, p. 403; and also USJ 1834, Vol. II, p. 477.

46. Smith, pp. 279–80.

47. H.T. Siborne, p. 323.

48. Hay, p. 165.

49. Cope, Sir William, Bt., *The History of the Rifle Brigade (The Prince Consort's Own, formerly the 95th)*, London 1877, p. 199.

50. USJ 1841, Vol. II, pp. 174–5.

Withdrawal

1. Kincaid, p. 160.

2. Mercer, Vol. I, p. 259.

3. Kincaid, p. 160.

4. Hope, p. 236.
5. Robertson, D., *Journal of Sergeant D. Robertson, late 92nd Foot*, Perth 1842, pp. 149–50.
6. USJ 1834, Vol. II, p. 449.
7. *Colburn's United Service Magazine* 1844, Vol. II, p. 163.
8. Anton, p. 205.
9. Hope, p. 240.
10. Kincaid, p. 161.
11. Pattison, F.H., *Personal Reminiscences of the Waterloo Campaign*, Glasgow 1873, p. 14.
12. Mercer, Vol. I, p. 284.
13. Hope, pp. 241–2.
14. Robertson, p. 152.
15. Carey, T., 'Reminiscences of a Commissariat Officer', *Cornhill Magazine* Vol. VI (1899).

Waterloo

1. Scott, p. 138.
2. Ibid., p. 176.
3. USJ 1841, Vol. II, p. 175.
4. Robertson, p. 153.
5. USJ 1841, Vol. II, pp. 175–6.
6. Hope, p. 243.
7. Kincaid, p. 257.
8. Moore Smith, G.C., *The Life of John Colborne, Field Marshal Lord Seaton*, London 1903, p. 216.
9. Scott, pp. 146–7.
10. USJ 1841, Vol. II, pp. 176–7.
11. Robertson, p. 151.
12. USJ 1841, Vol. II, p.178.
13. Robertson, p. 153.
14. Kincaid, p. 164.
15. Hope, p. 248.
16. Du Cane, p. 757.
17. Anon, *Personal Narrative … Forty-Second Highlanders*, pp. 245–6.
18. Kincaid, pp. 165–6.
19. Gleig, Rev. G.R., *The Subaltern*, Edinburgh 1872, p. 100.
20. Shaw Kennedy, Maj.Gen. Sir James, *Notes on the Battle of Waterloo*, London 1865, p. 61.
21. Boulger, D., *The Belgians at Waterloo*, London 1901, p. 60.
22. Shaw Kennedy, pp. 111–12.
23. USJ 1841, Vol. II, pp. 177–8.
24. MacBride, McK. (ed.), *With Napoleon at Waterloo*, London 1911, p. 141.
25. Anton, p. 210.
26. USJ 1841, Vol. II, p. 177.
27. WD Vol. XII, p. 483.
28. H.T. Siborne, p. 36.
29. Maxwell, Vol. II, p. 70.
30. H.T. Siborne, p. 21. (Writing in 1842 Seymour thought the ADC was named Tucker, but he also identified him as 'the stoutest of the ADCs', so it clearly was Tyler.)

31. USJ 1841, Vol. II, p. 11.
32. H.T. Siborne, pp. 350–2.
33. Ibid., p. 383.
34. Ibid., p. 61.
35. In Alison, Sir Archibald, Bt., *History of Europe from the Commencement of the French Revolution to the Restoration of the Bourbons*, Edinburgh & London 1860, Vol. XIV, p. 308.
36. H.T. Siborne, p. 383.
37. Hope, pp. 254–6.
38. H.T. Siborne, p. 77.
39. His account is in 'A Waterloo Journal', ed. C.T. Atkinson, *Journal of the Society for Army Historical Research*, Vol. XXXVIII (1960).
40. H.T. Siborne, p. 82.
41. Anton, p. 210.
42. H.T. Siborne, p. 84.
43. Ibid., pp. 70–1. Alexander Kennedy Clark subsequently changed his surname to Clark Kennedy.
44. Ibid., pp. 351–2.
45. Salamanca, 18 June 1812; WD Vol. IX, p. 240.
46. Jackson, Maj.Gen. Sir Louis, 'One of Wellington's Staff Officers: Lieutenant General William Staveley, CB, *Journal of the Society for Army Historical Research*, Vol. XIV (1935), p. 161.
47. Stewart of Garth, Vol. II, p. 214.
48. Smith, pp. 270, 277.
49. USJ 1834, Vol. II, p. 459.
50. USJ 1841, Vol. II, p. 181.
51. H.T. Siborne, pp. 374–5.
52. USJ 1834, Vol. II, p.459.
53. Ellesmere, Francis, 1st Earl of, *Personal Reminiscences of the Duke of Wellington*, London 1904, p. 179.
54. USJ 1841, Vol. II, pp. 183–4.
55. Cotton, E., *A Voice from Waterloo*, 9th enlarged edn., Brussels 1900, p. 108.
56. Cope, p. 211.
57. Shaw Kennedy, pp. 127–9.
58. Smith, pp. 270–1.
59. USJ 1841, Vol. II, p. 184.
60. Kincaid, p. 170.
61. Robertson, p. 159.
62. Smith, p. 272.
63. Kincaid, pp. 170–1.
64. Robertson, p. 159.
65. Swiney, p. 127.
66. Ibid.
67. USJ 1841, Vol. II, p. 188.
68. Hope, pp. 268–9.
69. Gardyne, Vol. I, p. 380.

70. USJ 1840, Vol. I, pp. 363–4.
71. Simmons pp. 367–8, 371.
72. Kincaid, p. 285.
73. Hay, pp. 208–209.
74. Anton, p. 217.
75. Smith, p. 275.
76. Hope, p. 258.
77. Robertson, p. 161.
78. Mercer, Vol. I, p. 341.
79. USJ 1841, Vol. II, p. 189.
80. Ross-Lewin, pp. 283–4.
81. USJ 1841, Vol. II, pp. 190–2.
82. Cadell, pp. 235–6.
83. Mercer, Vol. I, p. 341.
84. Ibid., p. 246.
85. Anon., 'Waterloo, the Day after the Battle', in Miles, A.H., *With Fife and Drum*, London, n.d., pp. 14–15.
86. USJ 1841, Vol. II, p. 193.
87. Eaton, pp. 72–3.
88. Ibid., pp. 78–9.
89. USJ 1834, Vol. II, p. 468.

Reptuations

 1. Cadell, p. 240.
 2. Ibid., p. 238.
 3. *Chambers' Edinburgh Journal*, 3 May 1851, p. 288.
 4. Gardyne, Vol. I, p. 392.
 5. *London Gazette* 22 June 1815; also WD Vol. XII, pp. 482–3.
 6. Shand, A.I., *Wellington's Lieutenants*, London 1902, p. 234.
 7. Clerk, p. 91.
 8. Ibid., p. 83
 9. Joncourt, 25 June 1815; WD Vol. XII, p. 509.
10. Gonesse, 2 July 1815; WD Vol. XII, p. 529.
11. Orville, 28 June 1815; WD Vol. XII, p. 520.
12. Divisional Order, Arnouville, 5 July 1815.

Appendices

Order of Battle, 5th Division
Commander: Lieutenant General Sir Thomas Picton, GCB
ADCs: Captain Algernon Langton, 61st Foot
   Captain John Tyler, 93rd Foot
   Captain Newton Chambers, 1st Foot Guards
   Captain Barrington Price, half-pay (Extra ADC)
   Lieutenant Rees Howell Gronow, 1st Foot Guards (unofficial)
Asst. QMG: Lieutenant Colonel Sir William Maynard Gomm, KCB, 2nd Foot Guards

8th (British) Brigade
Commander: Major General Sir James Kempt, KCB
ADC: Captain Hon. Charles Stephen Gore, 85th Light Infantry
Major of Brigade: Captain Charles Eeles, 95th Rifles
1st Battalion, 28th (North Gloucestershire) Regiment: Colonel Sir Charles Philip Belson, KCB
32nd (Cornwall) Regiment: Lieutenant Colonel John Hicks
79th Regiment (Cameron Highlanders): Lieutenant Colonel Neil Douglas
1st Battalion, 95th Regiment (Rifles): Lieutenant Colonel Sir Andrew Francis Barnard, KCB

9th (British) Brigade
Commander: Major General Sir Denis Pack, KCB
ADC: Major Edmund L'Estrange, 71st Light Infantry
Major of Brigade: Major Charles Smyth, 95th Rifles
3rd Battalion, 1st Regiment (Royal Scots): Lieutenant Colin Campbell
42nd (Royal Highland) Regiment: Lieutenant Colonel Sir Robert Macara, KCB
2nd Battalion, 44th (East Essex) Regiment: Lieutenant Colonel John M. Hamerton
92nd (Highland) Regiment (Gordon Highlanders): Colonel John Cameron of Fassiefern

5th Hanoverian Brigade
Commander: Colonel E.von Vincke
Landwehr Battalion Hameln: Lieutenant Colonel Klenke
Landwehr Battalion Hildesheim: Major Rheden
Landwehr Battalion Peine: Major Count von Westphalen
Landwehr Battalion Gifhorn: Major Hammerstein

4th Hanoverian Brigade (6th Division but attached to the 5th)
Commander: Colonel Charles Best
Landwehr Battalion Lüneburg: Lieutenant Colonel de Ramdohr
Landwehr Battalion Verden: Major Decken
Landwehr Battalion Osteröde: Major Baron Reden
Landwehr Battalion Münden: Major De Schmidt

Artillery
Divisional artillery commander: Major Lewis Heise
Rogers's Company, Royal Foot Artillery: Major Thomas Rogers
Braun's Company, Hanoverian Foot Artillery: Captain William Braun (allocated to the 5th Division but actually served with the 6th)
Rettburg's Company, Hanoverian Foot Artillery: Captain Charles von Rettburg (allocated to the 4th Division but actually served with the 5th)

Strength 18 June (from Lt.Col. John Waters's 'morning state'; WD Vol. XII, pp. 486–7)

1/28th: 2 field officers, 8 captains, 20 subalterns, 5 staff officers, 36 sergeants, 1 present sick, 2 absent sick, 1 on command; 27 drummers, 1 absent sick; 458 rank and file, 88 absent sick, 9 on command, 2 missing

32nd: 2 field officers, 4 captains, 14 subalterns, 6 staff officers, 36 sergeants, 6 absent sick, 2 on command; 14 drummers, 1 absent sick; 427 rank and file, 218 absent sick, 17 on command

79th: 4 captains, 17 subalterns, 5 staff officers, 30 sergeants, 12 absent sick, 3 on command; 10 drummers, 2 absent sick, 1 on command; 374 rank and file, 5 present sick, 290 absent sick, 34 on command

1/95th: 1 field officer, 3 captains, 7 subalterns, 6 staff officers, 27 sergeants, 11 absent sick; 10 drummers, 2 absent sick; 364 rank and file, 185 absent sick

3/1st: 1 field officer, 5 captains, 23 subalterns, 7 staff officers, 34 sergeants, 14 absent sick; 17 drummers, 3 absent sick; 366 rank and file, 236 absent sick, 2 on command

42nd: 1 captain, 13 subalterns, 3 staff officers, 25 sergeants, 12 absent sick, 1 on command; 15 drummers, 1 absent sick; 272 rank and file, 9 present sick, 220 absent sick, 25 on command

2/44th: 2 field officers, 4 captains, 18 subalterns, 6 staff officers, 39 sergeants, 2 present sick, 2 absent sick, 3 on command; 15 drummers, 1 absent sick; 396 rank and file, 12 present sick, 39 absent sick, 15 on command

92nd: 1 field officer, 2 captains, 15 subalterns, 4 staff officers, 27 sergeants, 16 absent sick, 1 on command; 12 drummers, 3 absent sick, 1 on command; 361 rank and file, 217 absent sick, 10 on command

The statistics do not accord with those published by William Siborne (*History of the War in France and Belgium*, 1st edn, Vol. I, pp. 423–6); the latter are clearly derived from Waters's morning state but list only rank and file and do not deduct those absent sick and on command. For example, Siborne gives the strength of the 92nd as 588 'men', whereas Waters shows that only 361 rank and file were present on 18 June, with a total of 427 of all ranks.

5th Hanoverian Brigade (rank and file only):
    Battn. Hameln: 669
    Battn. Hildesheim: 617
    Battn. Peine: 611
    Battn. Gifhorn: 617

4th Hanoverian Brigade (rank and file only):
    Battn. Lüneburg: 624
    Battn. Verden: 621
    Battn. Osteröde: 677
    Battn. Münden: 660

Casualties
The following are the first casualty statistics to be published (*London Gazette*, 1 and 6 July 1815), including the names of officer casualties; officers were listed according to their regimental ranks, not brevet ranks, and slight corrections to the spellings of names have been included below.

Quatre Bras, 16 June 1815

8th Brigade
Staff: Wounded: Captain Algernon Langton (slightly).
1/28th: Killed: 11 rank and file.
              Wounded: Captains William Irving, John Bowles (severely); Lieutenant William Irwin (severely), Lieutenant John Coen (slightly); 4 sergeants; 56 rank and file.

32nd: Killed: Captain Edward Whitty; 21 rank and file.
              Wounded: Captain Jacques Boyse (severely, since dead); Captains Thomas Cassan, John Crowe (severely [Cassan died]); Captains William H. Toole, Charles Wallet (slightly); Lieutenants George Barr, John Boase, James Robinson, James Fitzgerald, Henry Quill, Edward Stephens (severely); Lieutenants Henry W. Brookes, Michael W. Meighan, Samuel H. Lawrence, Henry Butterworth, Thomas J. Horan, David Davies (adjutant) (slightly); Ensigns Charles R.K. Dallas, Alexander Stewart (severely); Ensigns Henry Metcalfe, John Birtwhistle (slightly); 4 sergeants; 1 drummer; 48 rank and file.

79th: Killed: Lieutenant John Kynock (adjutant); 28 rank and file.
              Wounded: Lieutenant Colonel Neil Douglas (severely); Majors Andrew Brown, Duncan Cameron (severely); Captain John Sinclair (severely, since dead); Captains Thomas Mylne, William Marshall, Malcolm Fraser, William Bruce, Neil Campbell (severely); Lieutenants Thomas Brown, William Maddocks, William Leaper, James Fraser, William A. Riach (severely); Lieutenant Donald McPhee (slightly); Ensign James Robertson (severely); 10 sergeants; 248 rank and file.
              Missing: Captain Robert Mackay (severely wounded [he died]).

1/95th: Killed: 2 sergeants, 6 rank and file [also 1st Lieutenant William Lister, mistakenly included under 92nd].
Wounded: First Lieutenants J.P. Gardiner, John G. Fitzmaurice. (severely); First Lieutenant Orlando Felix (slightly); Second Lieutenant William Shenley (severely); 3 sergeants; 48 rank and file.

9th Brigade
Staff: Wounded: Captain Charles Smyth (since dead).
3/1st: Killed: Captain William Buckley; Lieutenants John Armstrong, John E. O'Neil; Ensigns James G. Kennedy, Charles Graham [he survived], Alexander Robertson; 2 sergeants; 18 rank and file.
Wounded: Captain Robert Dudgeon (severely); Captains Lawrence Arguimbau, Hugh Massey (slightly); Lieutenants William J. Rea, John N. Ingram, William Clarke, James Mann, Allen Cameron (adjutant) (severely); Lieutenants Robert H. Scott, Joseph Symes, George Stewart, James Alstone (slightly); 13 sergeants; 167 rank and file.

42nd: Killed: Lieutenant Colonel Sir Robert Macara; Lieutenant Robert Gordon; Ensign William Gerard; 2 sergeants; 40 rank and file.
Wounded: Major Robert H. Dick (severely); Captains Archibald Menzies, George Davidson, Donald McDonald, Daniel Mcintosh, Robert Boyle (severely); Lieutenants Duncan Stewart, John Malcolm, Alexander Dunbar (severely); Lieutenants Donald McKenzie, Hugh A. Fraser, James Young (adjutant) (slightly); Ensigns William Fraser, A.L. Fraser (slightly); 14 sergeants; 1 drummer; 213 rank and file.

2/44th: Killed: Lieutenant William Tomkins; Ensign Peter Cooke; 1 drummer; 9 rank and file.
Wounded: Lieutenant Colonel John M. Hamerton (slightly); Captains Adam Brugh, David Power, William Burney, Mildmay Fane (severely); Lieutenants Robert Russell, Robert Grier, W.B. Strong, W.M. Hern (severely); Lieutenants Alexander Campbell, James Burke (slightly); Ensigns James Christie, Benjamin Whitney, James C. Webster, Alexander Wilson (severely); 12 sergeants; 82 rank and file.
Missing: 1 sergeant; 2 drummers; 14 rank and file.

92nd: Killed: Captain William Little; Lieutenant James J. Chisholm; Ensigns Abel Becher, John M.R. McPherson; 2 sergeants; 35 rank and file. (First Lieutenant William Lister, 1/95th, as mentioned above, was mistakenly included in the 92nd's list of casualties).
Wounded: Lieutenant Colonel John Cameron (severely, since dead); Major John Mitchell (severely); Captain George W. Holmes, Dugald Campbell, William C. Grant (severely); Lieutenants Thomas Hobbs, Thomas Mackintosh, Ronald Macdonald, George Logan, John M'Kinlay, George Mackie, Alexander McPherson, Ewen Ross (severely); Lieutenants Robert Winchester, James Kerr Ross, Hector Innes (slightly); Ensigns John Bramwell ('right leg amputated'), Angus McDonald,

Robert Hewett (severely); Ensign Robert Logan (slightly); Assistant Surgeon John Stewart (slightly); 13 sergeants; 1 drummer; 212 rank and file.

Waterloo, 18 June 1815
Staff: Killed: Lieutenant General Sir Thomas Picton. [Captain Newton Chambers was killed but not recorded in the original list.]

8th Brigade
Staff: Major General Sir James Kempt (slightly).
1/28th: Killed: Captain William P. Meacham; 1 sergeant; 17 rank and file.
Wounded: Major Robert Nixon (severely); Captains Richard Llewellyn, Thomas English (severely); Captain Richard Kelly (slightly); Lieutenants John F. Wilkinson, Roger P. Gilbert, Henry Hilliard, Charles B. Carruthers, John P. Clarke (severely); Lieutenant George Ingram (severely, since dead); Lieutenants John W. Shelton, James Deares, Thomas Bridgeland (adjutant) (slightly); Ensign William Mountsteven (slightly); 6 sergeants; 1 drummer; 136 rank and file.
[Some officers' ranks are incorrectly stated in the original list; the above are correct ranks.]

32nd: Killed: 28 rank and file.
Wounded: Captain Hugh Harrison (severely); Lieutenants Thomas J. Horan, Jonathan Jagoe, David Davies (adjutant) (severely); Lieutenants Thomas Ross-Lewin, James R. Colthurst (slightly); Ensign James McConchy, John Birtwhistle, William Bennet (severely); 11 sergeants; 126 rank and file.

79th: Killed: Lieutenants Donald McPherson, Ewen Kennedy; 2 sergeants; 27 rank and file.
Wounded: Captain John Cameron (severely, since dead); Captains James Campbell, Neil Campbell (severely); Lieutenants John Powling, Donald Cameron [he died], Ewen Cameron (severely); Lieutenants Alexander Cameron, Charles McArthur, Alexander Forbes (slightly); Ensigns John Nash, Alexander S. Crawford (slightly); 7 sergeants; 4 drummers; 121 rank and file.
Missing: 1 rank and file.

1/95th: Killed: First Lieutenant Edward D. Johnston; 4 sergeants; 16 rank and file.
Wounded: Lieutenant Colonel Sir Alexander F. Barnard (slightly); Major Alexander Cameron (severely); Captains Edward Chawner, William Johnstone (severely); Lieutenant John Stilwell (severely, since dead); 1st Lieutenants John Molloy, John Gardiner, George Simmons (severely); 2nd Lieutenants Allen Stewart, William Wright, James Church (severely); 7 sergeants; 1 drummer; 116 rank and file.

9th Brigade
Staff: Wounded: Major General Sir Denis Pack (slightly); Major Edmund L'Estrange (severely, since dead).

3/1st: Killed: Lieutenant William Young; Ensign William Anderson; 1 sergeant; 12 rank and file.
Wounded: Major Colin Campbell (severely); Captains Robert Macdonald, Hugh Massey (severely); Captain Lawrence Arguimbau (slightly); Lieutenants Archibald Morrison, George Lane, John F. Miller, William Dobbs (severely); Lieutenants Robert H. Scott, J.L. Black (slightly); Ensign Leonard M. Cooper (severely); Ensigns Thomas Stevens, Joseph M'Kay (slightly); Quartermaster Thomas Griffith (slightly); 4 sergeants; 111 rank and file.

42nd: Killed: 5 rank and file.
Wounded: Captain Mungo Macpherson (slightly); Lieutenants John Orr, George G. Munro (severely); Lieutenants Hugh A. Fraser, James Brander (slightly); Quartermaster Donald Mcintosh (slightly); 6 sergeants; 33 rank and file.

2/44th: Killed: 4 rank and file.
Wounded: Major George O'Malley (slightly); Lieutenant James Burke (severely); Ensign Thomas McCann (adjutant) (severely); 3 sergeants; 54 rank and file.

92nd: Killed: 1 sergeant, 13 rank and file.
Wounded: Captains Peter Wilkie, Archibald Ferrier (slightly); Lieutenants Robert Winchester, Donald Macdonald (severely); Lieutenant James Hope (severely); Lieutenant James Kerr Ross (slightly); 3 sergeants; 93 rank and file.

5th Hanoverian Brigade (losses 16–18 June)
Battn. Hameln:
    Killed: 9 privates.
    Wounded: 4 officers; 3 NCOs; 57 privates.
    Missing: 7 privates.
    Officer casualties, 18 June:
    Wounded: Major Strube (slightly); Captain Blankhart (slightly); Lieutenant Kohle (severely); Lieutenant Kistner (slightly).

Battn. Hildesheim:
    Killed: 3 privates.
    Wounded: 1 officer; 1 NCO; 2 drummers; 17 privates.
    Officer casualties, 18 June:
    Wounded: Major Rheden (severely).

Battn. Peine:
    Killed: 8 privates.
    Wounded: 2 officers; 1 NCO; 1 drummer; 38 privates.
    Missing: 1 drummer; 5 privates.
    Officer casualties 18 June:
    Wounded: Captain Bertram (severely); Ensign Kohler (slightly); (Lieutenant Helmrick, 7th Line Batt, KGL attached also severely wounded).

Battn. Gifhorn:
>   Killed: 2 officers; 13 privates.
>   Wounded: 3 officers, 4 NCOs, 65 privates.
>   Officer casualties 18 June:
>   Only one fatality listed by name: Major Leue, 4th Line Battn. KGL attached.
>   Wounded: Major Hammerstein; Captain Wredenfeld (slightly); Lieutenant Schmidt (severely).

4th Hanoverian Brigade
Battn. Lüneburg:
>   Killed: 10 privates.
>   Wounded: 5 officers; 1 NCO; 36 privates.
>   Officer casualties 16 June:
>   Wounded: Captain Reicke; Lieutenant Dapue.
>   Officer casualties, 18 June:
>   Wounded: Captain Kampf; Ensigns Dornauer and Meyer.

Battn. Verden:
>   Killed: 2 officers; 10 privates.
>   Wounded: 4 officers; 1 NCO; 96 privates.
>   Missing: 3 officers; 1 NCO; 42 privates.
>   Officer casualties 16 June:
>   Killed: Lieutenant Wegener.
>   Wounded: Captain Witzendorf, Lieutenant Hinuber.
>   Missing: Ensigns State, Hotzebue.
>   Officer casualties, 18 June:
>   Wounded: Lieutenants Hartzig, Wiencoken; Ensign Ziegener. (Other casualties are not listed by name.)

Battn. Osteröde:
>   Killed: 2 officers, 12 privates.
>   Wounded: 5 officers; 2 NCOs; 91 privates.
>   Missing: 14 privates.
>   Officer casualties 16 June:
>   Killed: Lieutenant Janish.
>   Officer casualties, 18 June:
>   Killed: Ensign Schautz.
>   Wounded: Major Reden; Captains Paper, Ingersleben; Lieutenants Groebe, Sambrecht.

Battn. Münden:
>   Killed; 1 NCO; 11 privates.
>   Wounded: 6 officers; 4 NCOs; 1 drummer; 92 privates.
>   Missing: 1 drummer; 16 privates.
>   Officer casualties 18 June:
>   Wounded: Captain Harstein; Lieutenants Brisberg, Brenning, Schwencke; Ensigns Murray, Oppermann.

Bibliography

Included in the select bibliography are titles with particular relevance to the 5th Division and its members. In the case of personal accounts, the identity of the author's regiment is given in parentheses if not obvious from the title.

Adkin, M., *The Waterloo Companion*, London 2001.

Anon., 'The Campaign of Waterloo, Strategically Examined', *United Service Journal* 1834, Vol. II, pp. 444–78.

Anon., *Historical Records of the Queen's Own Cameron Highlanders*, Edinburgh 1909.

Anon., 'Operations of the Fifth or Picton's Division in the Campaign of Waterloo', *United Service Journal* 1841, Vol. II, pp. 170–203. (The author is stated to be 'An Officer of the Division', the account written in 1835 from memoranda made shortly after the battle. From clues within the text he was clearly a member of the 3/1st and identifies himself as a subaltern commanding a company. The senior unwounded officer, Captain William Gordon, died in 1834; only two lieutenants were unwounded, Thomas Gordon and James Mann, Gordon the senior.)

Anon., *The Personal Narrative of a Private Soldier, who served in the Forty-Second Highlanders, for Twelve Years during the Late War*, London 1821.

Anon., *The Royal Military Calendar, or Army Service and Commission Book*, London 1820.

Anton, J., *Retrospect of a Military Life*, Edinburgh 1841 (42nd Highlanders).

Barbero, A., *The Battle: A New History of Waterloo*, trans. J. Cullen, London 2005.

Barnard, Sir Andrew, *The Barnard Letters 1778–1824*, ed. A. Powell, London 1928 (1/95th Rifles).

Beamish, N.L., *History of the King's German Legion*, London 1837.

Cadell, Lt.Col. Charles, *Narrative of the Campaigns of the 28th Regiment Since their Return from Egypt in 1802*, London 1835.

Caldwell, G.J., & Cooper, R.B.E., *Rifle Green at Waterloo: An Account of the 95th Foot in the Netherlands Campaign of 1813–14, at Quatre Bras and Waterloo*, Loughborough 1990.

Carter, F., *Historical Record of the Forty-Fourth, or The East Essex Regiment of Foot*, Chatham 1887 (orig. pub. 1864).

Clerk, Rev. A., *Memoir of Colonel John Cameron, Fassiefern*, Glasgow 1858 (92nd).

Cope, Sir William, Bt., *The History of the Rifle Brigade (The Prince Consort's Own, formerly the 95th)*, London 1877.

Costello, E., *Memoirs of Edward Costello*, London 1857; r/p as *The Peninsular and Waterloo Campaigns*: Edward Costello, ed. A. Brett-James, London 1967. Quotations used in the present work are taken from the original publication in *United Service Journal*, 1840 (1/95th Rifles).

Cotton, E., *A Voice from Waterloo*, 5th enlarged edn., Brussels 1900.

Dalton, C, *The Waterloo Roll Call*, London 1904 (rev. edn.; orig. pub. 1890).

Daniell, D.S., *Cap of Honour: The Story of the Gloucestershire Regiment (The 28th/61st Foot) 1694–1950*, London 1951.

De Lancey, Lady M., *A Week at Waterloo in 1815*, ed. B.R. Ward, London 1906.

Douglas, J., *Douglas's Tale of the Peninsula and Waterloo*, ed. S. Monick, London 1997 (3/1st Royal Scots).

Du Cane, E., 'The Peninsula and Waterloo Memories of an Old Rifleman', *Cornhill Magazine*, December 1897, pp. 750–8 (1st Lieutenant John Molloy, 1/95th).

Eaton, C.A., *Waterloo Days: The Narrative of an Englishwoman Resident at Brussels in June, 1815*, ed. E. Bell, London 1888 (orig. pub. anonymously; in 1815 the author was Charlotte Waldie, prior to her marriage).

Ellesmere, Francis, 1st Earl of, *Personal Reminiscences of the Duke of Wellington*, London 1904.

Fitzmaurice, G., *Biographical Sketch of Major General John Fitzmaurice*, Anghiari 1908 (1/95th Rifles).

Fortescue, Hon. Sir John, *History of the British Army*, Vol.X, London 1920, r/p as *The Campaign of Waterloo*, Elstree 1987.

Foulkes, N., *Dancing into Battle: A Social History of the Battle of Waterloo*, London 2006.

Frye, W.E., *After Waterloo; Reminiscences of European Travel 1815–1819*, ed. S. Reinach, London 1908.

Gardyne, C. Greenhill, *The Life of a Regiment; The History of the Gordon. Highlanders from its Formation in 1794 to 1816*, London 1929 (orig. pub. 1901).

Glover, G., *Letters from the Battle of Waterloo; The Unpublished Correspondence by Allied Officers from the Siborne Papers*, London 2004.

Glover, G., *The Waterloo Archive*, London from 2009.

Gomm, Sir William, *Letters and Journals of Field-Marshal Sir William Maynard Gomm ... from 1799 to Waterloo 1815*, ed. F.C. Carr-Gomm, London 1881.

Grattan, W., *Adventures with the Connaught Rangers 1809–1814*, ed. Sir Charles Oman, London 1902.

Gronow, R.H., *The Reminiscences and Recollections of Captain Gronow*, London 1892 (orig. pub. 1862–6; new edn. under same title, ed. J. Raymond, London 1964).

Harvard, R.G., *Wellington's Welsh General; A Life of Sir Thomas Picton*, London 1996.

Haythornthwaite, P.J., *The Armies of Wellington*, London 1994.

Haythornthwaite, P.J., *Redcoats: The British Soldier of the Napoleonic Wars*, Barnsley 2012.

Haythornthwaite, P.J., *The Waterloo Armies: Men, Organization and Tactics*, Barnsley 2007.

Haythornthwaite, P.J.: *Waterloo Men: The Experience of Battle 16–18 June 1815*, Marlborough 1999.

Hofschröer, P., *The Hanoverian Army of the Napoleonic Wars*, London 1989.

Hope, J., *Letters, from Portugal, Spain, and France ...*, Edinburgh 1819 (pub. anonymously: 'by a British Officer') (92nd Highlanders).

Hope J., *The Military Memoirs of an Infantry Officer 1809–1816*, Edinburgh 1833 (pub. anonymously) (92nd Highlanders).

Jackson, B., *Notes and Reminiscences of a Staff Officer*, ed. R.C. Seaton, London 1903 (orig. pub. 1877).

Johnston, Col. W., *Roll of Commissioned Officers in the Medical Service of the British Army ... 1727 to 1898*, Aberdeen 1917.

Kelly, C., *A Full and Circumstantial Account of the Battle of Waterloo* (or *The Memorable Battle of Waterloo*), London 1817.

Kennedy, General Sir James Shaw, *Notes on the Battle of Waterloo*, London 1865.

Kincaid, Sir John, *Adventures in the Rifle Brigade*, London 1830, and *Random Shots from a Rifleman*, London 1835; combined edn. London 1908 (1/95th Rifles).

Leach, J., *Rough Sketches in the Life of an Old Soldier*, London 1831 (1/95th Rifles).

Leask, J.C, & McCance, H.M., *The Regimental Records of the Royal Scots*, (*The First or Royal Regiment of Foot*), Dublin 1915.

Low, E.B., *With Napoleon at Waterloo*, ed. McK. MacBride, London 1911.

Mackenzie, T.A., Ewart, J.D., & Findlay, C., *Historical Records of the 79th Queen's Own Cameron Highlanders*, London & Devonport 1887.

Maxwell, Sir Herbert, *The Life of Wellington*, London 1899.

Mercer, A.C., *Journal of the Waterloo Campaign*, Edinburgh & London 1870.

Meulenaere, P. de, *Bibliographie Analytique des Témoignages Oculaires de la Campagne de Waterloo*, Paris 2004.

Miller, D., *The Duchess of Richmond's Ball*, 15 June 1815, Staplehurst 2005.

Myatt, F., *Peninsular General: Sir Thomas Picton 1758–1815*, Newton Abbot 1980.

'Near Observer', *The Battle of Waterloo ... forming an Historical Record of the Campaigns in the Campaign of the Netherlands, 1815 ... by a Near Observer*, London & Edinburgh 1816.

Pack-Beresford, D.R., *A Memoir of Major-General Sir Denis Pack*, Dublin 1908.

Robertson, D., *The Journal of Sergeant D. Robertson, late 92d [sic] Foot*, Perth 1842.

Robinson, H.B., *Memoirs of Lieutenant-General Sir Thomas Picton*, London 1835.

Ross-Lewin, H., *With the 'Thirty-Second' in the Peninsular and Other Campaigns*, ed. J. Wardell, Dublin & London 1904.

Scott, Sir Walter, *Paul's Letters to his Kinsfolk*, Edinburgh 1816 (pub. anonymously).

Shand, A.I., *Wellington's Lieutenants*, London 1902.

Siborne, Maj.Gen. H.T. (ed.), *The Waterloo Letters*, London 1891.

Siborne, W., *History of the War in France and Belgium in 1815*, London 1844; 3rd rev. edn. London 1848; often styled (as in 1990 r/p) *History of the Waterloo Campaign*.

Simmons, G., *A British Rifle Man*, ed. W. Verner, London 1899 (1/95th Rifles).

Smith, Sir Harry, *The Autobiography of Sir Harry Smith*, ed. G.C. Moore Smith, London 1910.

Stanhope, Philip, 1st Earl, *Notes on Conversations with the Duke of Wellington, 1831–51*, London 1888.

Stewart of Garth, Col. D., *Sketches of the Character, Manners and Present State of the Highlanders of Scotland ...*, Edinburgh 1822.

Swiney, Col. G.C., *Historical Records of the 32nd (Cornwall) Light Infantry, now the 1st Battalion Duke of Cornwall's L.I.*, London & Devonport 1893.

Ward, S.G.P., *Wellington's Headquarters: A Study of the Administrative Problems in the Peninsula 1809–1814*, Oxford 1957.

Wellington, 1st Duke of, *Dispatches of Field Marshal the Duke of Wellington*, ed. J. Gurwood, London 1834–38.

Wellington, 1st Duke of, *Supplementary Despatches and Memoranda of Field-Marshal the Duke of Wellington*, ed. 2nd Duke of Wellington, London 1858–72.

Index

Note: ranks given are generally those held at the time of the Waterloo campaign. The locations of illustrations are indicated by numerals in **bold** type.